MANAGING UNDER AUSTERITY, DELIVERING UNDER PRESSURE

Performance and Productivity in Public Service

MANAGING UNDER AUSTERITY, DELIVERING UNDER PRESSURE

Performance and Productivity in Public Service

Edited by John Wanna, Hsu-Ann Lee and Sophie Yates

Australian
National
University

PRESS

ANU
PRESS

the Australia and New Zealand
School of Government

Published by ANU Press
The Australian National University
Acton ACT 2601, Australia
Email: anupress@anu.edu.au
This title is also available online at press.anu.edu.au

National Library of Australia Cataloguing-in-Publication entry

Title: Managing under austerity, delivering under pressure :
                  performance and productivity in public
                  service / editors John Wanna, Hsu-Ann
                  Lee, Sophie Yates.

ISBN: 9781925022667 (paperback) 9781925022674 (ebook)

Subjects: Public administration--Australia.
                  Public administration--New Zealand.
                  Finance, Public--Australia.
                  Finance, Public--New Zealand.
                  Civil service--Labor productivity--Australia.
                  Civil service--Labor productivity--New Zealand.
                  Australia--Appropriations and expenditures.
                  New Zealand--Appropriations and expenditures.

Other Creators/Contributors:
                  Wanna, John, editor.
                  Lee, Hsu-Ann, editor.
                  Yates, Sophie, editor.

Dewey Number: 351.994

Cover design and layout by ANU Press

CONTENTS

PART ONE: THE IMPERATIVE TO IMPROVE PRODUCTIVITY AND PERFORMANCE

PART TWO: THE NEED FOR GOVERNMENTS TO INNOVATE

PART THREE: COLLABORATION WITH THE PRIVATE AND THIRD SECTORS

LIST OF FIGURES AND TABLES

FOREWORD

This volume had its genesis in an Australia and New Zealand School of Government (ANZSOG) conference titled 'Delivering under Pressure'. And that is certainly what many public sector managers feel they are doing these days. In a short space of time, many have gone from one extreme to another: from having to expend vast sums quickly on infrastructural and other programs to stem contagion from the Global Financial Crisis—and, in Australia, devising large-scale social expenditure programs leveraged by the Mining Boom—to having to do their bit to reduce resulting deficits and debt. In Australia at least, this ongoing challenge appears to have been made harder politically by public attitudes and expectations conditioned by the earlier largesse.

While only recently embraced, it would seem that public sector 'austerity' is here to stay. The term has been used by some to denote overreaction to budgetary pressure. But spending remains historically high, and in Australia (New Zealand has done much better) the fiscal problems are big and will not be resolved quickly. It is also clear that the magnitude of the necessary correction needs something better than mere trimming of budgets and time-honoured, across-the-board efficiency dividends. There is a growing recognition that governments must think more strategically about their roles in society and, in particular, how much they should be doing and funding at taxpayers' expense—on the 'what' question as well as the 'how'. Doing more with less, and doing only what the public sector can do best, have become dual imperatives—though arguably they should have been so all along.

'Productivity' as an operational concept is most commonly associated with the private sector, although it is just as relevant to the public sector. But the conduits for productivity gains—innovation within organisations, and the ascendancy of more productive or valued activities over others—do not come easily within the public sector, not least because of the more muted incentive systems that are obtained there. Moreover, measuring any gains is inherently problematic for services that are delivered in non-market settings and motivated by 'public value'.

How do we best foster public sector innovation in the absence of competitive pressure? How do we decide which activities are most valuable, or which are better performed by or through other agents? And how do we know if we are performing well according to the public value test? These are all important questions for which there is no settled 'theory' and for which answers are still emerging through observed practice.

The issues raised and the experiences related in this volume provide useful guidance. If I were to summarise the key insights for me, they would be:

- Churchill's maxim, 'never waste a good crisis', with the current need to spend less being seized as an opportunity to actually serve the public better.
- 'Frugal innovation'—changes in programs and processes that pay as much attention to the costs to the taxpayer-cum-citizen as to the benefits.
- The value of experimentation, of 'having a go' and, even more importantly, learning from the experience.
- Harnessing the advantages of the private and, especially, 'third' sectors, in pursuing public purposes.
- The importance of measurement to the pursuit of cost-effective management of scarce public resources.
- Promoting public understanding of both the 'why?' as well as the 'what?' questions in order to successfully implement reform initiatives.

ANZSOG is committed to assisting governments in all these areas. Its programs of teaching, research and discussion for executives combine the best of academia with the in-depth experience of top practitioners. For, in the end, how successfully the public sector 'delivers under pressure' depends on the capability and motivation of its leadership.

Professor Gary Banks AO
Chief Executive and Dean, ANZSOG
29 June 2015

CONTRIBUTORS

Peter Achterstraat was appointed the Auditor-General of New South Wales in 2006. Before that, he was the Chief Commissioner of State Revenue for New South Wales from July 1999. Achterstraat spent 20 years in the Australian Tax Office where he had a variety of roles, and was appointed Deputy Commissioner of Taxation with the Australian Taxation Office in 1987. He is a Barrister of the Supreme Court of New South Wales and is a Fellow of the Institute of Chartered Accountants in Australia, a Fellow of CPA Australia, a Fellow of Chartered Secretaries Australia and a Fellow of the Institute of Public Administration Australia.

Deborah Blackman is Professor in Public Sector Management Strategy at the School of Business, University of New South Wales, Canberra. Her academic background is in human resource management and development as well as management of change and organisational behaviour. She researches knowledge transfer in a range of applied, real-world contexts. The common theme of her work is developing effective knowledge acquisition and transfer in order to improve organisational effectiveness. Deborah Blackman has published extensively in a range of international journals and is a member of the Editorial Board for Management Learning.

Fiona Buick is Assistant Professor in Management at the University of Canberra and the Research Project Manager for the 'Strengthening the Performance Framework' project—a project that is implementing Recommendation 7.4 of the Australian Public Service (APS) Blueprint for Reform. She previously worked on an Australian Research Council grant research project on Whole of Government on an Australian Postgraduate Award Industry scholarship. She has also been a HR practitioner in various APS agencies and the Commonwealth Scientific and Industrial Research Organisation (CSIRO). These roles covered generalist HR, strategic HR and learning and development responsibilities.

Patrick Dunleavy is Chair of the London School of Economics Public Policy Group, an applied research and consultancy organisation at the London School of Economics, which brings together a wide range of academics to focus on public policy topics. He also works with overseas governments and agencies, major consultancy firms, think tanks and foundations on policy evaluation and trends analysis issues. The Group has additional expertise in electoral systems design, democratisation and citizenship issues. Professor Dunleavy has authored and edited numerous books on political science theory, British politics and urban politics, as well as more than 50 articles in professional journals.

Rory Gallagher is Senior Policy Advisor, UK Behavioural Insights Team Cabinet Office, but is currently on secondment to the Department of Premier and Cabinet in New South Wales. He led the Behavioural Insights Team's work on job centres, consumer empowerment, and fraud, error and debt, which identified savings of over GBP300 million and received a Civil Service Award for innovation. Prior to joining the Behavioural Insights Team, he worked for the UK Prime Minister's Strategy Unit and the Department for Education and before that completed a PhD at the University of Cambridge.

Andrew Greaves became the 22nd Auditor-General of Queensland in December 2011. Prior to his appointment he had been an Assistant Auditor-General at the Victorian Auditor-General's Office (VAGO) since 2006 and headed both the Financial Audit Group and the Performance Audit Group at VAGO. Andrew has nearly 30 years' experience in public sector external and internal audit, at the Commonwealth, state and local government levels.

David Halpern is a fellow at the Institute for Government, currently on secondment to both No. 10 Downing Street and the UK Cabinet Office to head the Behavioural Insights Team, and support on the Big Society and well-being agendas. He previously worked as Chief Analyst in the UK Prime Minister's Strategy Unit (2001–07). Before entering government, he held tenure at the Faculty of Social and Political Sciences, Cambridge University, where he still remains an Affiliated Lecturer. He has also held posts at Nuffield College, Oxford; the Policy Studies Institute, London; and as a Visiting Professor at the Centre for European Studies, Harvard.

Jean Hartley is Professor of Public Leadership in the Department of Public Leadership and Social Enterprise at the UK's Open University Business School. She is also a Visiting Professor at the Australian and New Zealand School of Government, a Fellow of the British Academy of Management and a Fellow of the British Psychological Society. Her research has shaped some of the thinking and ideas in the field, for example, the value and use of political astuteness skills among public servants, the interplay between political and managerial leadership, and innovation in governance and public services.

Les Hems is a Director within the Climate Change and Sustainability Services team of Ernst & Young. He recently transferred from the Net Balance Research Institute, where he was the inaugural Director of Research and Development. His academic and applied research interests include the roles for mutuals, cooperatives and hybrid organisational forms in delivering public services; the development and implementation of new mechanisms for delivering and funding social programs including payment by results mechanisms and social impact bonds; impact investing; and the applicability and effectiveness of collective impact and other related approaches to address 'wicked' societal problems.

Steven J. Kelman is Professor of Public Management at Harvard's John F. Kennedy School of Government. He is the author of many books and articles on policymaking process and improving the management of government organisations. From 1993 through to 1997, he served as Administrator of the Office of Federal Procurement Policy in the Office of Management and Budget. During his tenure as Administrator he played a lead role in the Administration's reinventing government effort.

Paul McClintock is Chairman of Myer Holdings Limited, Thales Australia, I-MED Network, NSW Ports, a director of St Vincent's Health Australia Limited and a member of the New South Wales Public Service Commission Advisory Board. He was formerly Chairman of the Council of Australian Governments (COAG) Reform Council. From July 2000 to March 2003, he served as the Secretary to Cabinet and Head of the Cabinet Policy Unit reporting directly to the Prime Minister, and as Chairman of Cabinet, with responsibility for supervising Cabinet processes and acting as the Prime Minister's most senior personal advisor on strategic directions in policy formulation.

Shelley H. Metzenbaum is the founding President of the Volcker Alliance and former Associate Director for Performance and Personnel Management, Office of Management and Budget, Washington DC. In 2009 she was appointed by President Obama as the Associate Director for Performance and Personnel Management at the White House Office of Management and Budget, where she was responsible for setting and implementing the Obama Administration's approach to improving the performance of federal programs. She previously served as Associate Administrator for Regional Operations and State/Local Relations at the US Environmental Protection Agency, and Undersecretary of Environmental Affairs and Director of Capital Budgeting for the Commonwealth of Massachusetts.

Michael O'Donnell is Professor of Human Resource Management in the School of Business, University of New South Wales, Canberra. Prior to this he was Associate Professor in the College of Business and Economics at The Australian National University. His research interests include human resource practices and employment relations in the public sector, executive remuneration in the private sector and international employment relations. Michael has acted as a chief investigator on large ARC funded projects exploring management strategy and employment relations in the Australian and United Kingdom public sectors, and executive remuneration and corporate governance in Australian listed companies.

Janine O'Flynn is Professor of Public Management at the University of Melbourne. She holds an Adjunct Professorship at the Australia and New Zealand School of Government and was elected onto the Executive Board of the International Research Society for Public Management in 2012. Her research focuses on public sector reform and relationships and she has published widely on topics such as how government organisations work with external parties, joined-up government, and public value. She is currently engaged in a collaborative project with the Australian Public Service Commission to design and implement new performance management principles across the Australian Public Service.

Andrew Podger is Professor of Public Policy, The Australian National University and Adjunct Professor, Griffith University and Xi'an Jiaotong University. His expertise lies in public management and social policy, particularly health financing. Highlights of a long career in the APS include being the Public Service Commissioner for three years, following six years as Secretary of the Department of Health and Aged Care. He has also headed the Departments of Housing and Regional Development and Administrative Services. Before retiring from the Australian Public Service in 2005, he chaired a task force for the Prime Minister on the delivery of health services in Australia.

Peter Shergold is the Chancellor of the University of Western Sydney. He has enjoyed a distinguished academic and public service career spanning three decades; as the Secretary of the Department of the Prime Minister and Cabinet from 2003–08, he was the nation's most senior public servant. In two decades as a senior public servant he served four Prime Ministers and eight Ministers in both Labor and Coalition governments and was Secretary of several government departments.

Gary Sturgess holds the Premier's Australian and New Zealand School of Government (ANZSOG) Chair in Public Service Delivery, University of New South Wales. He has worked in public sector reform for the past three decades, contributing in the fields of functional federalism, the design and management of public service markets, the commercialisation and regulation of government business enterprises and the use of economic instruments in environmental protection, among others. In 2011 he was appointed as an Adjunct Professor at the Centre for Governance and Public Policy at Griffith University, and the NSW Premier's ANZSOG Chair of Public Service Delivery, based at the Australian School of Business, University of New South Wales.

Doug McTaggart is the Commissioner of Queensland's Commission of Audit and Chair of Queensland Public Service. In 2012, he retired after 14 years as Chief Executive of investment solutions company QIC. Prior to this appointment, he held roles including Professor of Economics and Associate Dean at Bond University, and Under Treasurer of the Queensland Department of Treasury. He has been a member of the COAG Reform Council, a Councillor on the National Competition Council, and Chairman of the Economic Society of Australia.

Simone Walker is Director of Out-of-Home Care, NSW Department of Family and Community Services (FACS). She has extensive experience across policy development, program management and service delivery in Community Services, in both the government and NGO sectors. Since joining Community Services in 2006 as Director of Policy Development and Service Planning, she has taken on a number of roles including Director, NGO Engagement, Service Delivery Improvement and, most recently, Acting Executive Director, Service System Delivery, where she was responsible for reforms relating to contract management for the transition of out of home care and the development of Social Benefit Bonds in FACS.

John Wanna holds the Sir John Bunting Chair of Public Administration at the Research School of Social Sciences, The Australian National University, and is Director of Research for the ANZSOG. He was also until 2012 Professor of Politics and Public Policy at Griffith University, and formerly principal researcher with the Centre for Australian Public Sector Management and the Key Centre for Ethics, Law, Justice and Governance at Griffith University. Professor Wanna has written numerous monographs, including two textbooks on policy and public management.

Damian West is Group Manager, the Australian Public Service Commission (APSC). He has a lead role in implementing a number of the key reform projects at APSC which originate from the report 'Ahead of the Game: Blueprint for the Reform of Australian Government Administration'. This includes streamlining recruitment and improved induction, performance management and mobility. He also has responsibility for the Commission's growing international capability development work program, the Commission's regional network, communications and client engagement, and a number of other Commission programs and services.

PART ONE: THE IMPERATIVE TO IMPROVE PRODUCTIVITY AND PERFORMANCE

1

DELIVERING UNDER PRESSURE: PUBLIC SERVICE, PRODUCTIVITY AND PERFORMANCE

John Wanna
The Australian National University

We have no money. Economic circumstances are driving the imperatives for change in government and the search for alternative approaches in behavioural incentives.

—David Halpern, UK Cabinet Office, Behavioural Insights Team, 2013

Austerity should be used as a springboard to explore new models, productivity and innovation.

—Director-General, Australian State Government, 2013

Productivity isn't everything, but in the long-run it is almost everything.

—Nobel Prize Winner, Professor Paul Krugman, 1994, p. 11

This volume of essays is focused on public sector renewal in the context of 'austerity'. Previous Australia and New Zealand School of Government (ANZSOG) volumes have explored implementation and project management in the public sector; collaborative governance and working collaboratively with the non-government organisations (NGOs) and third sector; inter-jurisdictional and intergovernmental policy relations; managing the Global Financial Crisis (GFC); attracting political interest in delivering policy reform and making it 'stick'; citizen engagement and putting citizens first in service delivery; and learning from disaster management to future-proof the state and society. In all of these books ANZSOG has striven to be relevant and engaging to governments, public sector executives, policy practitioners and service deliverers. The latest edition is no less aimed at relevance and engagement, but has a harder managerial edge. It will examine in practical ways how governments can best respond to the ongoing conditions of austerity. It is also an agenda with which most Western societies will have to wrestle for some time: perhaps the 'new normal' for modern government into the future.

At the onset of the GFC, most Western governments thought it would likely be a short-term correction and that expedient Keynesian and regulatory initiatives would avert global recession. However, the nature of the global crisis kept changing, morphing from one type of crisis to another. It began as a sub-prime housing mortgage crisis, then became a banking credit freeze, leading to a broader credit crisis, then a macro-economic crisis lowering investment, confidence and creating higher unemployment and finally into a fiscal crisis impacting on government budgets.

Today, most advanced nations are locked in various fiscal straitjackets that have caused a near-universal resource squeeze on public sector provision and government policy appetites. The resource squeeze is close to a worldwide phenomenon. Governments are experiencing sustained structural deficits, expenditure overhangs, increasing levels of debt and debt-servicing charges, bringing in turn renewed pressures to privatise public services and increase user-charging. There is growing concern that these austerity strategies may perversely reinforce the economic downturn and continuing fiscal crisis. Moreover, fiscal problems have also led to crises of confidence among constituencies and increasing questions as to the sustainability of many areas of public policy. The value, funding and management of policy and program areas is widely coming under scrutiny with calls for circuit-breaking change and a transformation in the ways of doing business. So how do we respond in such circumstances?

Responding to the new fiscal context: New pressures, new modes of governance

Governments worldwide have responded to their cash-strapped predicaments in various ways: some political, some fiscal, some technical or managerial. Some have tightened entitlements and eligibilities for selected constituencies; or they have deferred spending on projects or programs. Many have imposed severe budgetary disciplines across their own public sectors and the services provided (including where possible broadening revenue bases). Some governments have radically downsized.

Australasian governments have not yet had to resort to the deep austerity measures that many southern European nations have been forced to implement. Nonetheless, our governments are still imposing expenditure reductions, reducing the size of the public sectors, de-scaling activities in agencies, and increasing revenues by using various forms of co-payment and special levies, and exploring the possibilities of shifting areas of responsibility back to citizens and communities themselves (shifting costs). And changes in government may produce further edicts to reduce spending or implement agency cutbacks.

We are also seeing a reassessment of government itself. The mid-2010s may be heralding in fundamentally new thinking about governments' roles, responsibilities and the ways of achieving its desired outcomes. We may be transitioning into a new mode of governance, marking a distinct departure with previous ways of thinking about the nature of government. Broadly, we may characterise these previous eras as ones of leap-frogging providence and managerial reform, whereas today we may be heading in a direction of radical re-engineering, with innovation founded on frugality.

- The 1960s was an era of government expansion, programmatic investments and seemingly endless policy possibilities (the so-called 'great society' reforms); governments still struggled to manage budgets.
- In the 1970s, expansionary governments hit the first wave of crises (oil shocks, post-Vietnam debts, the end of Bretton Woods, stagflation); governments talked of 'hard times' but often carried on business as usual.
- The 1980s was an era of structural reform and managerialism (new public management (NPM)) within public agencies; budgetary surpluses were produced across Australasia and in many other Organisation for Economic Development (OECD) nations.
- In the 1990s reforms stalled, outsourcing and contact management were increasingly favoured for services giving known 'prices' for program delivery.
- By the 2000s revenue growth was considerable, and there were few internal disciplines on government or pressures for reform; non-discretionary spending became a very significant component of public finances (up to 80 per cent of expenses in some nations such as Australia).
- The 2010s—post-GFC and some fiscal stimuli; governments begin to consolidate their fiscal position, belt-tightening, downsizing, allowing programs to lapse; there is mounting pressure for significant innovation and functional reforms.

Paradoxically, while embracing notions of austerity, there remains scant evidence that governments have developed an appetite to be doing less. Governments continue to want to intervene in society—formulate new programs and tackle new challenges—often with their own political survival in mind. Their political instincts remain activist, interventionist and regulatory; and heightened community expectations continue to impose pressures for additional services, qualitatively improved services and spending augmentations. Whereas once the rationale for government intervention was 'market failure', we are now also addressing perceived new complex community failures in many areas of social provision. This has become a present-day global conundrum of governance— governments trying to do less but still wanting to do more, and becoming more comprehensively enmeshed into new and emerging policy sectors (e.g. aged care, vocational training, early childhood education, climate change, and environmental issues).

Hence, in the current context and for the foreseeable future, governments are going to have to manage more smartly, for improved efficiency and greater productivity. Demands for better or additional services will require governments (and the policy process more generally) to find improved ways of doing business. This challenge will affect policy design, program management and administration, and a reconsideration of processes and procedures.

To date, existing reform efforts in the public sector have tended to focus on high-level reform blueprints, initiated from the centre and focused on policy, accountabilities and system-wide changes. Often the *capacity* of the public service to implement reform efforts is ignored or shown lip service. Many reform initiatives have failed to acknowledge service delivery imperatives, and indeed some have arguably disrupted operations, diverting attention away from the efficacy and efficiency of service delivery. Various efficiency dividends, ostensibly imposed to improve efficiencies, have reputedly eroded actual capacities. A corresponding thickening of monitoring and oversight processes has mired frontline personnel in red tape and compliance issues.

So, how do we improve productivity in public agencies and harness innovation across policy areas, and what impediments stand in the way of better efficiencies? How do we realistically and sustainably deliver better services for government and the community? What practical and achievable ways can we pursue to meet increasing expectations in a highly constrained environment? How can we reposition ourselves internationally to meet global challenges, making ourselves more adaptable, leaner and competitive? These are the fundamental questions we are addressing in the latest ANZSOG collection of essays, *Managing under Austerity, Delivering under Pressure*.

The volume will canvas such issues under six themes:

1. How should governments crystallise their core choices to maximise their input and value for money?

2. Why and how should we use the current era of austerity as an opportunity or springboard to improve policy and delivery?

3. Can we find ways to enhance the adaptive capacities of government and its delivery systems (adapting its provision), including new models of provision (adopting models from other contexts or jurisdictions)?

4. How can the productivity of government providers and hybrid provider networks be improved?

5. In what way can experimentalism and frugal innovation as ways to improvement be encouraged?

6. How can we find ways to manage community expectations and make expectations more realistic in the current austerity context?

Enabling governments to crystallise their core choices requires them to exercise forms of self-discipline by asking a series of basic questions. For what purpose does government wish to act or intervene? Where and how does government seek to have an effect? Are governments forced to act through various market or community failures or do they choose to act themselves? What roles or partial roles do the government wish to fulfil? How can governments ensure effective delivery systems especially involving complex value chains? Governments will thus have to be far more explicit in defining and defending where they choose to have an impact. They will need to articulate some overarching strategic directions with long-term sustainability in mind, choosing their preferred scale of responsibilities carefully. In many ways, and especially given our recent histories, this represents a huge task for elected governments.

Austerity measures and downsizing are often deeply painful exercises; but they are also opportunities for re-examining how we do business. Even as governments impose such measures, they know that the present strictures will be insufficient to rebalance the books as well as meet the new demands for additional services. Maybe the old ways are no longer adequate or appropriate to the new circumstances—especially given the combination of new technologies and more educated and skilled communities. Limits on budgets or staffing in public agencies are not necessarily limits on policy impacts, but searching for alternative modes of provision will call for new thinking and more open mindsets. The challenge for public managers is how to build a positive and inventive culture contemporaneous to downsizing planning or after going through the downsizing exercises. In many agencies this calls for new types of leadership and managerial mentalities. The agenda of austerity makes imperative a fundamental rethinking of the ways in which public services are delivered, innovations are identified and adopted, outcomes are measured and the quality and responsiveness of services are assessed.

Going forward, governments will have to be less monolithic, hierarchic, conservative, inertia-ridden, risk-averse and controlling, and explore new ways to enhance the adaptive capacities of delivery systems. There are many viable new models of provision and incentive structures (including greater involvement from the community through social benefit investments, greater community ownership, crowdsourcing, etc.). But such adaptive capacities cannot readily prosper under traditional constraints and narrow accountabilities. Alternative models will require sharing power and responsibilities, granting more autonomy to providers, accepting more diversity and customisation in provision. These qualities in turn raise new challenges for governments motivated by conformity and standardisation.

There are major impediments to improved efficiencies and effectiveness in program delivery in the existing public sector. Productivity improvements will involve policy redesign and business re-engineering, not merely to improve input ratios but to enhance service quality and the effectiveness of outcomes. This is a complex iterative process involving allocative and technical efficiencies, lowest cost, scale and specialisation, effectiveness indicators, and analysis of the determining causes of net changes in performance. It will require the greater involvement of hybrid provider networks, especially to deliver heterogeneous services such as health, education, social services, defence and even regulatory and public order services. Above all, an emphasis on productivity involves governments being prepared to drive reform through 'performance accountability' rather than remain preoccupied with 'process accountability'.

Alongside the importance of productivity lies the capacity to innovate and experiment. Innovation in the public sector is less motivated by the imperatives to bring new commercial products to market, but rather to transform the nature of production processes or service provision to radically change their form for the better. Innovation is a process of discovering latent potential or hidden possibilities, or a 'perpetual search for new capabilities'. In public agencies, innovation tends to rely on conducive cultures, supportive leadership, learning and nurturing, autonomy and a preparedness to learn from failures, as well as in responses to crises and major challenges. Innovation can occur with the *instruments* used to deliver some value (e.g. technological developments, software innovations, improved human resource management, budgetary flexibilities), or with the *output/services* themselves (e.g. co-production, product redesign, radical re-engineering).

We can also think of stimulating innovation in various phases of the public service *value chain* (agenda-setting, formulation, consultation, implementation, etc.). The vast majority of innovations are 'new to business' rather than 'new to world' initiatives. In the current context of austerity, agencies may be encouraged to explore forms of learning from others (including *frugal* innovation, experimentalism, contestable or randomised trials, forms of 'nudging' and other behavioural incentives as ways to improvement).

In some cases, innovation can spur productivity improvements and create so-called 'radical efficiencies' (different services at much lower cost), but in others innovations can create additional work or consume more resources (perhaps to enhance an output or service, such as enhanced information technology (IT) services). Hence, the challenge for governments today is to imagine service systems that unleash the potential for innovation—harnessing the energy, knowledge and networks of local providers to improve services, while also ensuring high standards of accountability and appropriate risk management.

Our final theme concerns the gulf between what governments can sustainably deliver and community expectations of what governments ought to deliver (within prevailing fiscal parameters suggesting no increases in taxation and little tax reform). Despite the GFC, it is not apparent that community expectations have become more realistic or de-scaled—and, indeed, in new areas of policy they have become more ambitious. Governments have not been good at managing expectations and indeed have often contributed to their inflation. Managing in the current context of austerity implies that expectations have to be contained—not only for the legitimacy/credibility of elected governments but also for the levels of satisfaction and trust in public delivery systems more generally.

Practical and feasible strategies to deliver better under pressure

These themes strike at the very core of the relations between government and the community. As public officials what should we do in this challenging new setting? Arguably, we need to think of ourselves as stewards of sustainable public outcomes investing in more efficient and effective modes of delivery. In addressing these themes *Managing under Austerity, Delivering under Pressure* will explore four key strategies that are practicable and feasible in constrained resource contexts, and which can be used to assist the necessary future adaptations and transformations. These are:

1. Strategies to assist governments embrace smarter thinking to deliver better value for money, offering alternative modes of delivery and involving an array of incremental improvements to business practices ('doing a thousand things a bit better than yesterday').

2. Strategies to engage the real 'doers' in experimentation and innovation— taking devolution seriously to empower the frontline providers and local deliverers in producing innovation and making practical transformations (including non-government deliverers).

3. Strategies to encourage bottom-up input and creative suggestions about how greater productivities can be achieved (harnessing 'great ideas' from the coalface or the frontline counter).

4. Strategies to test the appetite for more radical transformational change in public policy delivery—asking how far governments are prepared to reconceptualise or re-engineer their delivery options.

These strategies may not sound all that radical, but on closer inspection they pose major challenges to many traditional government departments and public organisations used to the incremental expansion of their roles and responsibilities, working from standard operating procedures, displaying defensive cultures and risk-adversity, as well as assuming that additional resources and staffing would follow increased policy responsibility. Some of these challenges are inevitably cultural in nature, some philosophical in origin, some confronting institutional norms and conventions, and some involving threats to bureaucratic hierarchies or executive power. For example, cutting across all of these domains are the challenges of promoting local innovation and encouraging other areas to 'adopt or adapt' acknowledged successes.

To progress these strategies we need to re-examine the question of what distinctive contributions a plethora of institutions and actors can make to deliver improved outcomes and where they can best make these contributions. These institutional actors include government, the private sector, the not-for-profit organisations and voluntary organisations and various community bodies and groups of citizens. They are all institutional forms of organisation made up of people operating within incentive structures. This requires us to understand the benefits and costs of new forms of service delivery, free of the historical biases dictating which policy instrument has typically been given carriage of delivery—public bureaucracies, markets or community associations. We will need to re-examine our normative presumptions and choices, and begin with a fresh look at possibilities guided by efficiencies and effectiveness.

Clearly, in some quarters we will need to overturn old cultures of 'in-house' autarky and complacency in public bureaucracies—in particular to gain a better alignment between citizen expectations and service provision. This will impact on incentive/disincentive exchanges between institutions and actors; managerial discretion and initiatives; labour market flexibilities and the relaxation of imposed rigidities; the exploration of forms of hybrid integration between public and private providers in delivery chains; and collaborative partnering between complementary actors. We may also need to overturn the pervasive community mindset that governments *can* and *should* be expected to solve every passing problem society identifies, and in particular find ways to improve communication between government and the community to enable a better understanding of priorities, context, circumstance and mutual responsibilities.

The overriding intention of *Managing Under Austerity, Delivering Under Pressure* is to find practical ways to gain more value from inputs and resources in delivering effective outcomes across our various domains of public policy. It is a challenge we hope to share with the reader, so they can take back these concepts, ideas and practical ways of doing the business of government under today's more productive imperatives.

Reference

Krugman, Paul. 1994. *The Age of Diminishing Expectations*. Washington: The Washington Post Company.

2

GETTING LEANER, SMARTER AND MORE EFFECTIVE: OPPORTUNITIES AND CONSTRAINTS FOR GOVERNMENTS UNDER AUSTERITY

Doug McTaggart
Queensland Commission of Audit
and Queensland Public Service

I would like to approach this topic both from my perspective as a Commissioner of the Queensland Commission of Audit, and from my perspective as Chair of the Queensland Public Service Commission, sitting on the Public Sector Renewal Board. In these roles, I have been involved with my colleagues in trying to drive reform and renewal in this sector. Unfortunately 'trying' is the right word—because it is not easy, and because we are asking people to do some very different things.

The economy and fiscal austerity in Queensland

Where do we start? We know that governments around the world and in all Australian jurisdictions face two major problems, and I think these two problems get conflated. The first is how to balance the budget in the short term, over the next one to four years. The second and much more important problem is how to keep the budget balanced in the longer term without drastically reducing the quantum or quality of the services delivered.

The first problem arose with the global fiscal profligacy fostered by an extended period of strong economic growth, abruptly ending when the resulting financial bubble burst and brought about the Global Financial Crisis (GFC) in 2008–09. Pre-GFC strong economic growth delivered strong revenue growth and with the fiscal shackles removed government spending increased, the large part of it being discretionary.

In Queensland in the decade to 2005–06, revenues were growing at 10 per cent per annum on average, and expenses at 7 per cent—a happy place for a government to be. In 2005–06 to 2010–11, this was reversed—revenues grew at 7 per cent per annum and expenses at 10 per cent, resulting in unsustainable deficits. And, of course, the ability of governments to fund deficits has met its limits—there are limits to a government's ability to tax, particularly in the states, and the size of the accumulated deficits to be funded by borrowing pushes past the tolerance of the markets. This has led to credit downgrades and subsequent increases in funding costs.

Now you might ask whether it matters that governments borrow and/or run deficits and that credit ratings get downgraded. As the Commissioner of Audit noted in Queensland's case, the interest bill paid on accumulated general government debt rose from $173 million in 2005–06 to $1.9 billion seven years later in 2012–13 (Australian Bureau of Statistics (ABS) 2013, Table 1). This is a rate of increase of over 40 per cent per year and the bill is rising to approximately $2.5 billion in 2015–16 (Queensland Commission of Audit 2012, Chart 1.6). This is by far the fastest-growing component of general government expenses, all of which must be paid from general revenue.

The opportunity cost (an economic concept, but a very important one) of this debt payment to foregone government services is very large but is often not questioned. As to the credit downgrade Queensland incurred in 2009, the accumulated cost of the margin spread—that is, the difference between an AAA and an AA rated borrower—has pushed past $330 million to date and is increasing by about $150 million per annum (Queensland Commission of Audit 2012, Chart 2.9; see also Queensland Treasury updates). This is occurring in a low interest rate environment that will not last, and while the Queensland government remains on negative credit watch. Simply adding these up shows that the cost of the credit downgrade alone will soon be more than half a billion dollars. Again, what services could half a billion dollars fund?

In its June 2012 interim report, the Commission of Audit (2012) recommended the Queensland government act quickly to stabilise the growth in debt and deliver a fiscal surplus that met all operating expenses and all current and planned general government capital expenditure in the budget timeframe. In an accrual sense, this means an operating surplus sufficient to cover all operating capital expenditure. Consequently, of course, a period of fiscal repair—what we call 'austerity' here in Queensland—was implemented, culminating in the loss of 14,000 public sector positions in a short period of time. Looking at the recent budget projections, the result of this fiscal repair is that the government has accomplished an astonishing feat in bringing about a turnaround; expenses that were growing at 10 per cent per annum now show almost no growth within the current and forward estimates period. The expected rate of increase in expenses in this most recent budget was the lowest since 1998. This brought about an abrupt and painful episode of fiscal austerity. It was to some degree indiscriminate, a blunt instrument—but it had to be done. The growth in debt will be stabilised at a significantly lower figure than previously anticipated.

But let us not confuse fiscal repair or forced austerity with reform. It was cost-cutting, and in some cases cost-cutting can be inimical to productivity growth. Still, it has set the platform and focused minds on the large-scale reform of public service delivery that must lead to significant productivity increases.

This brings us to the second and more important problem. As the Commission of Audit described, and as governments around the world are discovering, the next decade almost certainly will not yield the revenue growth of the pre-GFC decade. In Queensland's case, lower economic growth caused by declining interstate migration, an ageing population increasing demand for some services and slowing growth in Commonwealth tax receipts (which of course flow through all the states) are factors that put increasing pressure on the budget. The audit report produced a chart showing that on a 'no policy change' basis, or on a 'business as usual' basis, the expenditure gap manifesting a budget deficit would be 3 to 4 per cent of gross state product (GSP) by 2025, rising to around 15 per cent of GSP by 2050 (Queensland Commission of Audit 2013, Volume 1, Chart 2). Of course, we will not get to that position because neither markets nor the electorate will allow it: credit downgrades and election losses would precipitate action through crisis management and fiscal repair, or forced austerity would come into play long before such apocalyptic scenarios emerged. Then Queensland would very quickly find itself in the same position as last year, looking at equally draconian measures.

But this is precisely the point. Governments today have the opportunity, as they have always had, to cut calmly and with forethought—to plan now for a measured and reconsidered reform of the way services are being delivered. The key message from the Audit Commission report is that 'business as usual' is not an option. The report shows that productivity improvements in government service delivery of 0.8–1.1 per cent per year will be required to maintain a stable fiscal position, given the current and expected level of demand for public services. This is equivalent to reducing the unit cost of service delivery in 2050–51 by one third of what it would be on a 'business as usual' basis—that is a big ask.

Improving public sector productivity

This is not just an issue for Queensland. Work produced by Accenture (2012) in conjunction with Oxford Economics shows that by 2025, the expenditure gap across a range of countries will be between 1.5–5 per cent of gross domestic product (GDP), averaging around 3 per cent. In other words, the fiscal position of many countries on a 'business as usual' basis is not sustainable. Accenture notes that the average annual productivity or public sector efficiency increase required to bring about fiscal sustainability is about 1 per cent each year. So there is widespread agreement that ongoing efficiency and productivity improvement is necessary in the delivery of public services, and this is the challenge.

Yet even here there are voices of dissent. One prominent critic dismissed the recommendations for sustained productivity improvement as wishful thinking, claiming that it's been tried before on many occasions and failed each time (Quiggin 2013). Moreover, there was a good theoretical reason as to why, enunciated by William Baumol in the 1960s and now known as the 'cost disease' (see e.g. Baumol and Bowen 1966). As an example, it is difficult to get productivity improvements out of a symphony orchestra—the orchestra can only play so fast. Looked at another way, an orchestra might have four trombones. It is not really feasible to dispose of trombones 2, 3 and 4, and say, 'We are going to work trombone 1 harder and smarter'.

And so goes the argument—many if not most public services are similarly delivered, therefore it is impossible to get productivity improvements in the public sector, ergo the Commission of Audit was a waste of time. Even worse— and here is where the 'cost disease' comes in—if wages are driven at the margin by productivity growth in other, more flexible industries then not only will productivity not rise in the public sector but wages *will* rise—the result of an economy-wide labour market. So costs of public service delivery, and of our philharmonic orchestra, will also inexorably rise without concomitant productivity increase.

It all sounds too easy to simply accept the status quo with no other options but to increase taxes or cut services. This is simply wrong because at a minimum there are benchmarks available that indicate that productivity can improve. The Commission of Audit report is replete with examples of where the private sector is demonstrably more efficient than the public sector at delivering the same services. Gary Sturgess, in a speech to the Victorian Institute of Public Administration, suggests that from what benchmarking and market testing data we do have, the average increase in productivity available to the sector is in the order of 20 per cent. He goes on to say that 'a quarter of the national economy—that is the public sector—is capable of making productivity gains of that order over the short to medium term should be a national scandal. It isn't' (Sturgess 2013, 1). We know a significant proportion of public service delivery is already provided by the non-government sector, but even here, with better and more contestable outsourcing arrangements, we can improve efficiency.

If the above is debatable, the following fact is not: some jurisdictions are better at some activities, or are more productive on average. This suggests that simply learning from each other, picking the best means of production, will yield benefits. On Commonwealth Grants Commission data, Queensland is 5 per cent more costly in terms of service delivery than the national average, and 10 per cent more costly on average than New South Wales (Queensland Commission of Audit 2013, Volume 1, Chart 5). Using Australian hospital statistics from the Australian Institute of Health and Welfare (AIHW 2012), in 2010 Queensland was 8.2 per cent more costly than the national average when it came to cost per case with adjusted separations, and nearly 20 per cent more costly than Victoria (Queensland Commission of Audit 2013, Volume 1, Chart 7). So without much thought about new delivery methods, simply adopting existing best practice should yield significant gains.

So, let me come back to 'cost disease' and test the underlying assumptions. I think we recognise that the basic structure of a philharmonic orchestra is a given. These are what an economist would call *fixed coefficient processes*—the capital to labour ratio cannot change without a significantly diminished quality of output. To produce more output requires proportionately more of every input. Is this true for most public services? I don't think so. Is the doctor to nurse to equipment to administrator ratio for each patient in each medical service fixed? Is a given class size the only determinant of education quality? Do sworn police officers have to operate speed cameras? Is there only one way to deliver the myriad of other services as mandated by the public sector? Again, I don't think so. This means there are different, perhaps more flexible, production processes to get the necessary outputs into the hands of the public who demand them.

Asking what the taxpayer actually wants is probably a good start; allowing the purchaser some say in what they get will probably help. Catering for increased demand by simply expanding current activities using current processes (as if the production processes were fixed) will drive us to an unsustainable fiscal outcome more quickly. This is what the Commission of Audit meant by its key theme: 'business as usual' is not an option.

By all means, every jurisdiction should avail itself of best practice from other jurisdictions or the private sector. This will bring about a one-time reduction in costs or increase in productivity. There is no excuse for not doing this. But this will not deliver a sustained increase in productivity growth, and given all jurisdictions are in the same long-run boat toward fiscal unsustainability, new and different methods of service provision are required.

Perhaps the difference here is the following (and here I will slip into public sector language): it is commonplace in the sector to think of inputs through a production process as delivering measurable outputs. Outputs, we believe, have a predictable effect on achieving desired outcomes, but outcomes themselves are often hard to quantify. By adopting best known production processes from other jurisdictions or the private sector, we get an increase in outputs per use of given inputs. This is a one-time rise in productivity. We can then think about changing and improving the production processes to get the same outputs for fewer inputs, producing an improvement in productivity. This, I think, is what Sturgess (2013) refers to as the 'how' of improving productivity. If this latter activity can be sustained we have ongoing productivity growth, but I suspect there are limits to how far any given production process can be pushed.

Now we come to the 'what'. More radically, we can think about how to use our inputs to get better outcomes by delivering *different outputs*. This is harder, but it is true reform. For example, we might improve the operation of juvenile detention centres, perhaps by outsourcing to the private sector to reduce costs and thus getting better productivity. Or we might incentivise an operator (public or private) to, while securely detaining juveniles, undertake appropriate interventions or case management so that individuals are less likely to reoffend, with repayment related to the rate of recidivism. How they do this may not be rigorously prescribed, leaving the design and the operation of the centre with the operator—but payment could be by outcome, which in this example would be the reduced rate of recidivism. In a case such as this, we would need to think about whether or not a public operator could deliver the same response as a private operator. I think it would be harder for a public operator.

'Business as usual' versus public sector reform

This brings me to the big question: can the public sector, on its own account, radically reform? I think this is also very hard. We know that governments and the public sector exist to deliver outcomes when the market itself breaks down. Because market failure arises from a variety of possible sources, the public sector of necessity fills the gap. But this creates the sector as a monopoly provider with no competitive discipline from the market. The monopoly provider is not under constant external pressure to reduce costs and so to innovate, and it becomes very difficult for the sector to discipline itself on an ongoing basis. As others have noted, it often takes a crisis or a threat of crisis to precipitate action. However, threats and their crises eventually dissipate and the sector is very good at outlasting crises. 'Business as usual' generally prevails.

This is what led the Commission of Audit to recommend much greater use of the non-government sector in actually delivering services. The Commission recommended that the public sector become a *facilitator* rather than a *doer* wherever possible. If the public sector were accountable for ensuring that other non-government providers deliver promised outcomes, it would be less likely to be captured by its own investment in a particular way of delivering services. Of course, government providers will always have a key role in providing services that have large 'public good' components, where markets generally fail. But the range of services that fall into that category is surely much more restricted today than it was in even the recent past. Advances in contracting practices, effective regulation, and risk management, mean that non-government providers can, with confidence, be tasked to do more. This is especially true if the public sector can direct its creative skills toward clever market design, thus ensuring that outsourced activities continue to be subject to cost competition and innovation (both to reduce costs and to yield better outcomes).

The key here is that the public sector, which has always had an administrative approach, finds it hard to be at the same time commercial. What usually happens is that commercial practices themselves become administrative and so fail to be commercial. Even if the public sector periodically shakes itself up there is no ongoing competitive or other pressure to continue to shake the sector. I think there should be a conscious decision by the public sector to willingly step back and commission others to do the work. The sector can then focus on designing policy and administering the contractual basis of non-government provision in accordance with that policy. The contracted providers can be constantly subject to competitive pressures related to quality, cost and the effectiveness of outcomes delivered. Competition will drive productivity growth through innovation.

Improving ourselves out of a job

There are 60 recommendations in the Commission of Audit report, designed to push the boundaries of public sector service delivery thinking. These cover the entire gamut of government service delivery, including health and hospitals, aged care, education, vocational training, disability services, police services and corrective services. There are instances where more rather than less government involvement may be required. For example, suppose all bus services in a given area were put out to tender for private provision. It might make sense for the government to step in and buy all the depots so that none can be used as a source of monopoly power. Alternatively, if a current government service competes in the market with two private duopolists, it might make sense for the government to encourage or facilitate a third private player into the market to promote greater competition. Both these examples are what I would class as creative market design—an area where the public service needs greater expertise.

The Commission of Audit implementation in Queensland has now been combined with a public sector renewal process where agencies are being asked to fundamentally re-evaluate their reason for existence. They are being asked to consider the following: Who are our customers? What services have they been promised? What is the best way of delivering on that promise? Beginning with and embracing the customer is important. Embracing contestability of service provision will drive much of this thinking.

Here, perhaps I disagree with those who maintain that we will always have large government. Is it too far-fetched to imagine a sector that has become so creative it actually works itself out of a job? Or something close to that, where a much reduced public service facilitates the non-government sector in bearing the delivery load while maintaining and improving quality and value for money? To me, that would be a measure of success. As a chief executive officer (CEO), I've always believed that a good CEO works himself or herself out of a job by building processes and a senior management that can make the CEO redundant.

Perhaps that is how the public sector should think about itself. Engaging in further program cutting, zero-based budgeting or other measures to reduce inputs and therefore reduce costs might not be the best way to go, particularly if we do not have a clear idea of what is the best way of delivering services to the public. Agencies need to address the question of why they exist and what they should do before they decide on how to do it.

Difficulties in the reform of public sector delivery

Let me address the difficulties and obstacles to reform I have noted over the past 12 to 18 months.

First, the capacity and capability constraints within the sector: moving from doing to facilitating and overseeing requires different skill sets and capabilities, which have been poorly developed in the past. Queensland has committed to buy, borrow and build the requisite skills in procurement, contract negotiation, contract management and innovative market design to progress its agenda.

It has also become apparent that the capability of the non-government sectors needs improvement. Although willing, NGOs and the private sector are still building capability and capacity and cannot currently handle the full extent of government outsourcing that could emerge. Growing capability will be a joint endeavour.

Second, and equally importantly in the public sector, is creating the capacity to think about planned implementation of change. In an austerity environment it is easy for an agency to say, 'We simply don't have the resources'. But is it really credible, in a sector with around 220,000 people (as in Queensland), where performance management has not been exercised for decades, that people or funds cannot be found or released from other duties to undertake the task? If we do not create the capacity to seriously think about reform then it will be relegated and squeezed into 'business as usual' activities, as I think we are seeing in Queensland. 'Business as usual reform' is an oxymoron.

Third, we are discovering that we really do not know how to specify many of the outcomes, and the outputs that deliver these outcomes, with sufficient clarity for the purposes of contracting. This is not an excuse for not introducing contestability and outsourcing, nor is it a reason to not engage in recommissioning services that are already outsourced. But it is an indication of just how poorly defined many current in-house activities are if they cannot be quantified. If they cannot be quantified, how can we ever measure productivity or value for money? Here, I think, is an area where the Australia and New Zealand School of Government (ANZSOG) can significantly contribute by helping to define and build the tools that enable us to measure the compendium of services currently provided to the public.

Fourth, reform must come from the centre. It is a whole-of-government activity. Trying to think about and implement reform within any given agency setup would limit the extent of reform because so much actual service delivery cuts across well-defended agency boundaries. The Queensland government recently set up a social services subdivision of cabinet as one way of dealing with this issue, requiring the respective directors-general to similarly interact. There needs to be more of this. In Queensland, every agency—from police to emergency services, health and disabilities, and housing—operates under a different regional breakdown of the state. Each goes about piloting new activities in different regions. With a consistent regional structure and a consistent implementation of pilot studies we would get a much better picture of the overall outcomes because we would internalise the mutual dependencies that are currently largely ignored. At the centre, we ourselves are still learning how to promote, encourage and direct the task of approaching reform.

Fifth, we need a new approach to risk-taking. If 'business as usual' is not an option then innovation must prevail. However, innovation requires taking risks, which is not something that sits easily within the current culture of the sector. The perceived approach of auditors-general also needs to change. I am advocating for the development of a risk framework that encourages sensible risk-taking, and it would be helpful for auditors-general to provide guidelines on sensible, managed risk-taking that allows, under very measured circumstances, for the prospect that innovation might not work.

More generally and more importantly, we must actively prepare the hearts and minds of the sector to embrace a culture of reform. If all public sector employees do not accept the need for reform they will not actively participate and may well passively resist. While it is vital to have CEOs and senior management on board—which I think is largely the case in Queensland—we also need the people at the coalface. This requires a massive change in culture and values, and we know this does not happen spontaneously.

As an example, we have produced a manual for introducing contestability into the Queensland public sector. It is 40 pages long and I was aghast when I heard this. Having read it and recognised the low base we come in on, I now believe that in the hands of a passionate advocate for reform this is a powerful and comprehensive tool. However, in the hands of someone *not* committed to reform it is 40 pages of reasons why contestability cannot and will not work.

Culture change must be driven within a believable context, an all-encompassing narrative. In the public sector—an industry with one of the highest labour-to-capital ratios of all industries, and which professes constantly that people are its most important asset—the complete absence of a strategic human resources capability across the sector and in most agencies astonishes me. How will we effect the necessary change to bring about sustained productivity increases and enhance value for money outcomes if we cannot equip our people to do so? I see little evidence that we have made much progress in this direction, and it must occur now. If it doesn't, all the measures we peddle about reform, all the processes we push out to encourage reform, will be seen as just that—new processes to be put alongside all the others we have dreamed up over the years.

To conclude, there is a dire need to generate sustainable productivity growth in the delivery of public services. This cannot come from doing things the way we have always done them. Short-term gains should be accessed by adopting best practice from other jurisdictions and the private sector, but sustainable productivity growth can only come from doing things differently. This requires a fundamental introspective analysis of why the sector exists, at an agency and a whole-of-government level, as well as a search for the best way to deliver the defined services. Moving from a doing role to a facilitative role will be a good start.

This will not be easy and many challenges need to be addressed along the way. The public sector needs to be prepared to embrace and chase change to deliver productivity growth, and I think ANZSOG has a very important role in helping lead that chase.

References

Accenture. 2012. *Delivering Public Service for the Future: Navigating the Shifts*. Online: www.accenture.com/SiteCollectionDocuments/PDF/Accenture-Delivering-Public-Service-for-the-Future-112812.pdf (accessed 9 July 2014).

Australian Bureau of Statistics (ABS). 2013. *Government Finance Statistics, 2012–13*. Cat. 5512.0. Canberra: ABS.

Australian Institute of Health and Welfare (AIHW). 2012. *Australian Hospital Statistics: 2010–11*. Health Services Series No. 43. Canberra: AIHW. Online: www.aihw.gov.au/WorkArea/DownloadAsset.aspx?id=10737421722 (accessed 9 July 2014).

Baumol, William J. and William G. Bowen. 1966. *Performing Arts, the Economic Dilemma: A Study of Problems Common to Theater, Opera, Music, and Dance*. New York: Twentieth Century Fund.

Queensland Commission of Audit. 2012. *Interim Report – June 2012*. Online: commissionofaudit.qld.gov.au/reports/interim-report.php (accessed 14 January 2013).

Queensland Commission of Audit. 2013. *Final Report – February 2013*. Brisbane: Queensland Government. Online: commissionofaudit.qld.gov.au/reports/final-report.php (accessed 14 January 2013).

Quiggin, John. 2013. The Queensland Commission of Audit Final Report: A Critical Review. RSMG Working Paper Series. St Lucia: University of Queensland. Online: www.uq.edu.au/rsmg/WP/Australian_Public_Policy/WPP13_1.pdf (accessed 2 July 2015).

Sturgess, Gary L. 2013. 'If your only tool is a hammer ....' Speech to the Victorian Institute of Public Administration, Melbourne, Victoria, 25 June.

3

PUBLIC SECTOR PRODUCTIVITY: PUZZLES, CONUNDRUMS, DILEMMAS AND THEIR SOLUTIONS

Patrick Dunleavy
London School of Economics

This chapter will discuss four aspects of productivity in the public sector. First, why do we have so little public sector productivity information? After all, productivity has been an important concept in the private sector for approximately 80 years, and has been much talked about since the early 1970s when President Nixon set up a Productivity Council in the US. However, what we have known about it up until now has been relatively restricted.

I want to try and explain why, on the whole, a lot of people in society—mostly economists and the right-wing press—tend to think of productivity as being completely flat in the public sector, and sometimes even declining. I will argue that we have no evidence for that. In fact, I will show that public sector productivity can grow spectacularly—and quickly—in some cases; and it can be flat, or even declining, in other cases. We need to look at this in a consistent way, and I will use three narratives running through some very big UK departments to tell these different stories.

Then I will pull together content from my book with Leandro Carrera (Dunleavy and Carrera 2013), as well as the academic literature on factors that shape government productivity. Many people have faith-based views of this—they say that the private sector is more productive than the public sector, and consequently they assume that we need more contestability and competition. There is zero evidence that competition and contestability make any difference to the public sector's productivity, for very good and strong reasons. I believe that rather than making faith-based decisions on how we set up the public services, we should look at the empirical evidence.

Finally, to round off our discussion, I will look at eight steps that our book suggests are important; four of them are rather immediate, and four are more long-term.

Productivity and the public sector—what is 'productivity'?

I am a conservative minimalist when it comes to how we define public sector productivity. It is a really simple concept and we should keep it that way: productivity is outputs divided by inputs. *Outputs* are not the same as *outcomes*—they do *not* include all the things we are trying to achieve in life, or the social transformation or public value that we may be trying to achieve, but rather they are the things that are relatively easy to measure and under our own control. An output would be a teacher delivering a lesson, or a fire service answering an emergency call. We could limit them to activities, but fundamentally outputs are things that an organisation provides and controls.

To measure productivity, we do not have to cover all of these outputs; it is usually sufficient to look at just a few of them. For example, for our research we looked at the productivity of the tax agency in the UK, Her Majesty's Revenue and Customs (HMRC). One of the biggest agencies in the UK government, it comprises a quarter of the staff in the entire UK civil service, and we needed to measure 14 different indicators to understand HMRC's productivity. In contrast, in studying most organisations we can obtain sufficient information by examining just two or three indicators of primary outputs or kinds of activities.

The next issue is measuring the value of outputs. In the private sector, when we have a firm that is producing lots of widgets, and an industry that is also producing lots of widgets, we can see how much they sell for, and we can weigh the overall output of the organisation by the prices that they sell for in the market. That is a very easy way of determining an overall level of output for the firm.

We cannot do that in the public sector, where we have a sizable problem determining the value of outputs. If our private sector firm produces a 'super widget' compared to last year's widget, and then sells it at a higher price, we can draw the welfare implication that somebody felt it was worth paying that extra price (or they would not have bought it). This means that in the private sector we can cope with technological and other types of change, and we can think about the welfare implications more easily. We cannot do any of that in the public sector, and consequently for the best part of the last 80 years, economists and national statisticians have treated government productivity as completely flat. They have reasoned that we cannot measure outputs, so instead of outputs we use inputs, and we divide inputs by inputs—with predictable results. This sounds very crude, but that is the way national statistics have been done and are still being done over most of the world.

Some progress on this matter can be attributed to economist Sir Tony Atkinson, who in a nutshell argued that we can get to grips with the overall output of a public sector organisation by looking at the things that it does and weighting them in relation to administrative costs rather than prices (Atkinson 2005). For example, if it is 10 times more expensive to collect Tax A than Tax B, then Tax A must count more in the overall output weight of the organisation.

Another problem in the public sector is that when somebody says 'productivity', everybody says, 'Yes, that's a great buzzword, I like that. Productivity means basically everything good.' So we tend to take this useful concept and inflate it. Productivity is a small concept that is part and parcel of what every organisation is doing—but it is not the whole story. If anybody says something like, 'We're looking at the social productivity of an organisation', it does not actually mean anything at all.

Issues in measuring public sector productivity

The next set of problems with public sector productivity relate to the fact that it is difficult to measure. It would be ideal to measure public sector productivity at a local level, or at a state level in a big federation like the USA, and so compare different sorts of units; hopefully the units would be doing pretty much the same sorts of things. That kind of data would be very useful. Unfortunately, if something has been done at the local level, or even at the state level, it is usually because it is not easy to standardise—it may be a personalised service, or needs to be delivered directly to people, because quality makes an enormous difference to whether the service is delivered correctly.

We could, for example, easily get perverse effects. Imagine a patient checks into Hospital A, and is treated very well. He/she is kept in hospital for just the right amount of time (e.g. four days), is released upon improvement and recovers. That counts as one unit of output. On the other hand, another patient suffering a similar complaint checks into Hospital B and is treated badly, discharged after only two days, and needs to be readmitted later on. Hospital B can then claim two units of output, even though they are doing a worse job than Hospital A. So we should be aware of possible perverse effects, and should also think about what we are trying to do. If one fire service answers a lot of fire calls, and another answers fewer fire calls because it does better fire prevention work, it is easy to misread the data and get the wrong signals. As a result, although it would be best to study productivity comparatively, it is often quite difficult to do.

At the national level, we often have just one agency—one defence agency, one tax agency, one social security agency, and so on. It is consequently hard to make comparisons, and the international data on productivity is substandard, despite years of work by the UN and OECD and other bodies. We do not have big N data sets; we have this single organisation. So the question is how can we measure productivity here?

It is also difficult to think about productivity patterns over time. Sometimes productivity will go up or down for reasons that are not under our control. If demand goes up, most organisations can cope with that for a year or two by cramming in more people and working the staff hard. But this is not really sustainable. Sometimes demand goes down—for example, we might roster extra staff to assess passports, but if fewer than expected foreign visitors come in then productivity drops before we can de-roster some of our staff.

There tends to be a very high level of resistance towards measuring productivity by politicians and civil servants at the national level or the state level. People dream up lots of excuses about why we should avoid measurement, many of which are based on the idea that the public service is really complicated. But I disagree—I do not think that public sector organisations are more complicated than private sector organisations.

As you can see, there are a lot of problems with measuring productivity, which is another reason not to get into things like outcomes. Keep it simple—it is hard enough to assess productivity correctly in the first place without bringing in extraneous elements.

Three case studies from the UK

In our five-year study, Leandro Carrera looked at six big agencies in Britain. This chapter will discuss three of them. I will focus primarily on some of the 'over time' evolution of productivity: if we want to know how an organisation is doing, and we can assemble some data that goes back even five years, we will begin to see patterns. We can then begin to think about why certain things are moving in particular ways, and why the ratio of outputs divided by inputs changes.

In our study, we focused on the big departments, but also ones with fairly standard outputs so that we had access to consistent, reliable data. We did not really look at effectiveness, or at the issue of how a department responds to a new government. Instead, we examined issues like how many tax forms were returned, how many staff there were, and so on—we kept it fairly simple. We also did not want to introduce quality changes unless necessary. For example, at the start of the period we were studying, only about 10 per cent of people were filling in their tax forms online. Now it is 84 per cent, and public servants at HMRC argued that this increase should count as a quality improvement. We decided that this does not count as a quality improvement because the rest of society has changed—filling in a 50-page paper form is no longer what anybody is doing anywhere else in society. Everybody is doing it online, so there is no extra quality credit for doing the same thing that everybody else is doing, and somewhat behind the pack at that.

What we need to do then is look at a detailed narrative for each agency. We suggest agency leaders should do this, because they know a lot about their own agencies, and where all the outputs and inputs are—they will know how many people are on staff, how much capital has been invested, the number of intermediate outputs they are getting from contractors, and so on. From this data, we can create an overall measure of output, weigh that output by the cost of doing different things, and so start to obtain an overall measure of productivity by dividing these figures by our inputs.

I will use three case studies to illustrate how these techniques can be useful:

- British Customs;
- HMRC, our new integrated tax agency created in 2005; and,
- Department of Work and Pensions (WAP), which handles social security.

HMRC and WAP between them account for half of the British civil service.

British Customs

Volume (2001/02=100)

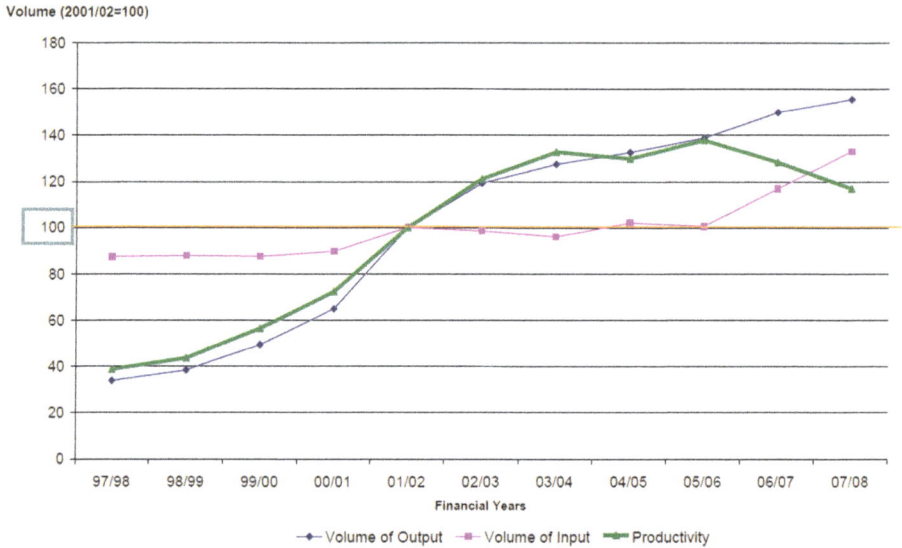

Figure 3.1. Total factor productivity in the UK Customs regulation on trade, 1997 to 2008

Source: Patrick Dunleavy.

Figure 3.1 shows Customs regulating imports and exports. The volume of output is shown by the dark blue line, the volume of input is shown by the pink line, and the overall productivity index is shown by the thick green line. Over this period there was not much staff growth until 2005—so for 10 years the staff was constant. Meanwhile, the amount of containers coming into the UK, that is the amount of trade to be looked at (the green line), went up significantly because of the boom years before the Global Financial Crisis. When outputs are going up but there is no increase in inputs, productivity rises—and it rises very dramatically. If you looked at the USA you would see the same pattern in US Customs.

How did that happen? Firstly, Customs made a very big decision in the mid-1990s to introduce a computerised system. A pre-internet system for tracking all imports and exports, where everything was done online, this allowed Customs to make huge steps forward throughout the next 10 years without increasing their staff numbers—they were simply able to get more done. Of course, technology on its own does not really help unless you make other kinds of changes. British Customs used to operate on a volumetric basis; the general practice was to open up every 20th or 50th container to see what was in it. The containers were opened blind, and sometimes problems were found, and sometimes they were not. It was not a very sophisticated way of doing things.

Over time, British Customs more than any other customs organisation in the world transformed its processes into a risk-based and intelligence-based way of looking at import and export trade—despite the fact that they open far fewer containers now than any other country in the European Union.

One reason they managed to achieve this huge change is the technological investment discussed earlier, and the other is the managerial changes that made a significantly more effective use of the same number of people. Even here we can see in Figure 3.1 that towards the end of the period, there is a bit of an increase in inputs, and productivity begins to tail off a little. But the overall change is very dramatic—any private sector organisation would be very pleased to achieve the same threefold increase in productivity over time.

Her Majesty's Revenue and Customs

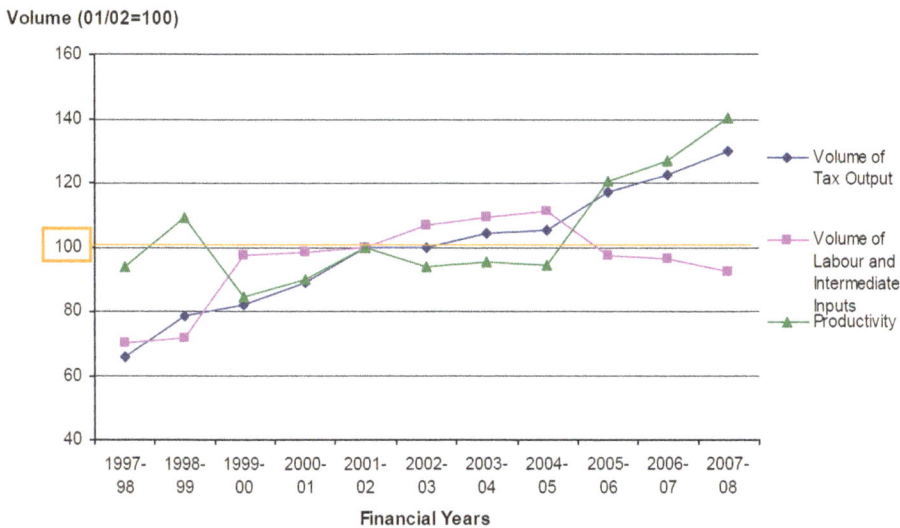

Figure 3.2. Labour and intermediate inputs productivity, UK taxation, 1997 to 2008, using tax collection activity data
Source: Patrick Dunleavy.

Unfortunately, we do not have complete data on the capital investments for HMRC, so we used a measure looking only at staff and contractors—there is no capital investment reflected in the charts. While this is a bit of a limitation, we can still observe in Figures 3.2 and 3.3 that there is a more complicated pattern with HMRC.

Volume (2001/02=100)

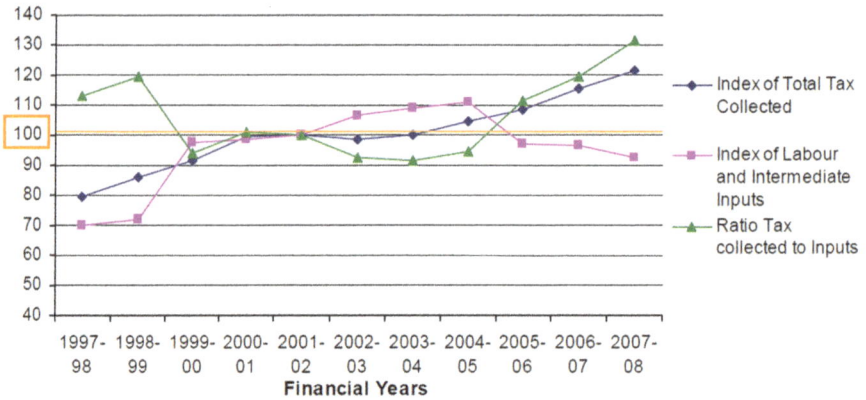

Figure 3.3. The ratio of the deflated amount of tax collected to labour and intermediate outputs for HMRC and predecessor departments, 1997 to 2008
Source: Patrick Dunleavy.

The volume of tax demand had been steadily increasing, but for a long time the green line indicating productivity hovered at just around 100, and had not quite reached 100 in 2001. There was quite a big increase in staff from 1997 to the middle of the Blair Government period (1997–2007), but subsequently a reorganisation of the tax agencies in Britain resulted in a merging of Inland Revenue and Her Majesty's Customs and Excise to create HMRC. At that point, we can observe the staff savings being accumulated and the inputs coming down. Staff numbers, which had totalled about 115,000, were reduced to about 70,000 at the time of the merger.

During this period, the tax agency became a lot more successful in getting people to use online forms, and made some other big technological changes. These took a long time to come properly into effect, but eventually led to a sharp increase in productivity. The increases caused by the merger and the new technology continued until about 2011.

By 2011, there had been overcutting. The tax agency failed to answer 44 per cent of phone calls made to it, which had a negative effect on public legitimacy. So there was a period of long stagnation (which became a big growth period), there was continued growth for a few years, and then a few problems emerged.

If we look at this in relation to tax raised per staff member, or staff input and contractor input (Figure 3.3), we see essentially the same pattern—the green line remained static near the productivity line for quite a long time, and then following the reorganisation and the IT developments, it began to significantly improve.

Department for Work and Pensions (WAP)

Volume (99/00=100)

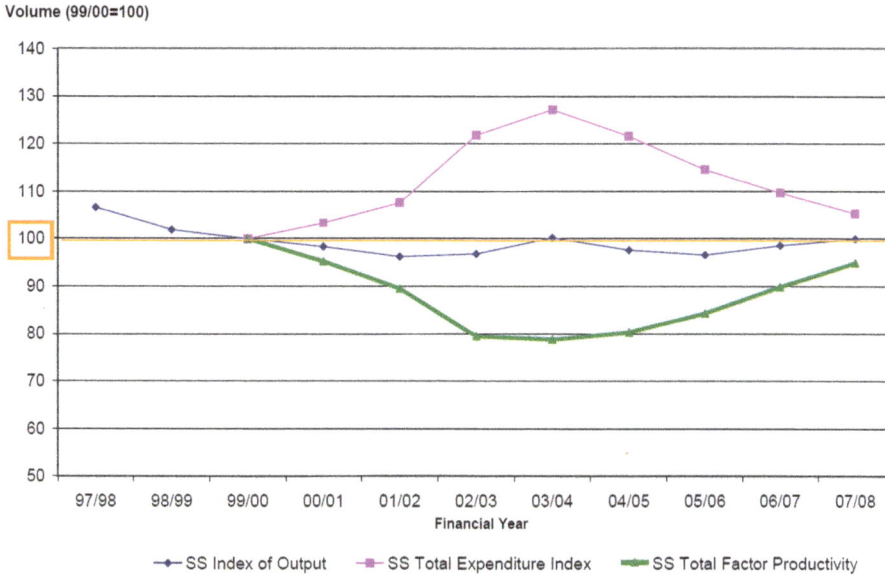

Figure 3.4. Total factor productivity in UK social security, 1997 to 2008
Source: Patrick Dunleavy.

The third agency I will discuss is the Department for Work and Pensions, which is responsible for all the UK's social security. Figure 3.4 indicates that output throughout this period was fairly static, only going down a little as Britain came out of recession. However, there was a big increase in inputs (staff and contractors), and as a result the overall productivity slumped significantly in the period from 1999 to 2003–04.

This stemmed from two big decisions. First, there was a merger in 2001 (primarily a combination of the Department of Social Security and the Employment Service), after which the agency decided to fundamentally change the way in which it did technology. It moved away from paper, but not towards online services—the departmental leadership did not believe that welfare clients would ever use the internet, so they built the whole department around a telephone-based model. This tripled the number of phone calls it received. Unfortunately, however, most of these phone calls were not useful—they were just cluttering up the call centres. Clients were complaining about things, while staff did not know what was happening and could not help. The department made a very good effort to cut the number of phone calls over the next three years but, as can be seen in

Figure 3.5, it consequently used more postal services and more paper forms than it had in the beginning (although it did save some money by cutting face-to-face contacts).

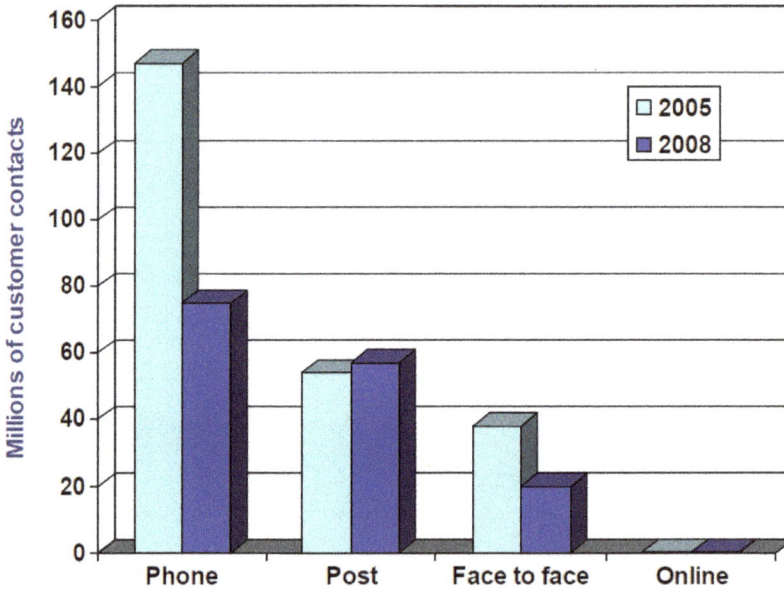

Figure 3.5. The changing pattern of the WAP's customer contacts, 2005 to 2008

Source: Patrick Dunleavy.

Note the online story shown in Figure 3.5; only 0.5 per cent of customer transactions were done online in 2005, and the same in 2008. By the time we conducted our study for the National Audit Office, 51 per cent of UK welfare recipients had broadband access, yet only 0.5 per cent were doing online transactions. Subsequently, the department has made a huge change in policy, moving towards what is called 'digital by default'—the vast majority of transactions to be conducted online. It was a belated move, but at least the department has now come into the twenty-first century. Fundamentally, the decision not to go digital was a strategic 'mis-decision': management miscalculated where society was going to go, made the wrong decision, and put a lot of effort into what was a doomed strategy.

Second, the Labour Government wanted to overhaul and modernise welfare benefits. They may have had very good reasons for that, and they certainly improved the flow of money to various disadvantaged groups, especially the elderly. However, the introduction of new policy requires more staff; and when the policy does not work terribly well, more people need to be hired. As a result, policy change is associated with a large increase in staff inputs. The productivity measure does not tell us that it was not a good idea *socially*, but it does indicate that in simple productivity terms there was a big slump.

Factors influencing productivity

So what shapes productivity? What things work? What things don't work?

One thing that clearly works is going digital—taking it seriously, recognising that society is going digital and that 10 years from now we need to have essentially digital public services, born digital, delivered to citizens who are digital natives. It is not enough to layer a little bit of digital on top of paper-based or pre-existing twentieth-century systems. We must think about how we can do digital in a really radical way.

In the same vein, the second thing that works is thinking about restructuring services, really studying our services, really understanding them, really seizing control of them, really trying to change them and deliver public value as cheaply and as effectively as we can—including making major investments.

What *does not* work is bringing in consultants who do not adequately know the agency's service, and so give them off-the-cuff solutions that worked somewhere else but may not be appropriate for that agency. On its own, outsourcing does not do anything for productivity. An agency might try outsourcing for one of any number of reasons—because the minister tells them to, because they have faith in economic solutions, because they want more diversity—but we cannot expect it to improve productivity.

Going digital

It was very difficult and time-consuming to get enough good data on investment in IT—it took my co-author and me three or four years just to get the data and we have not got many data points. Figure 3.6 is not as good a graph as we would like, but it does provide some idea of how IT investment affects productivity. It shows a positive association between investing in IT now as a percentage of administrative costs, and what happens to productivity two years from now. The graph does not display very strong clustering but there is nonetheless evidence that it is working. Dunleavy and Carerra (2013) contains more detailed descriptions of this dynamic, including at the local level.

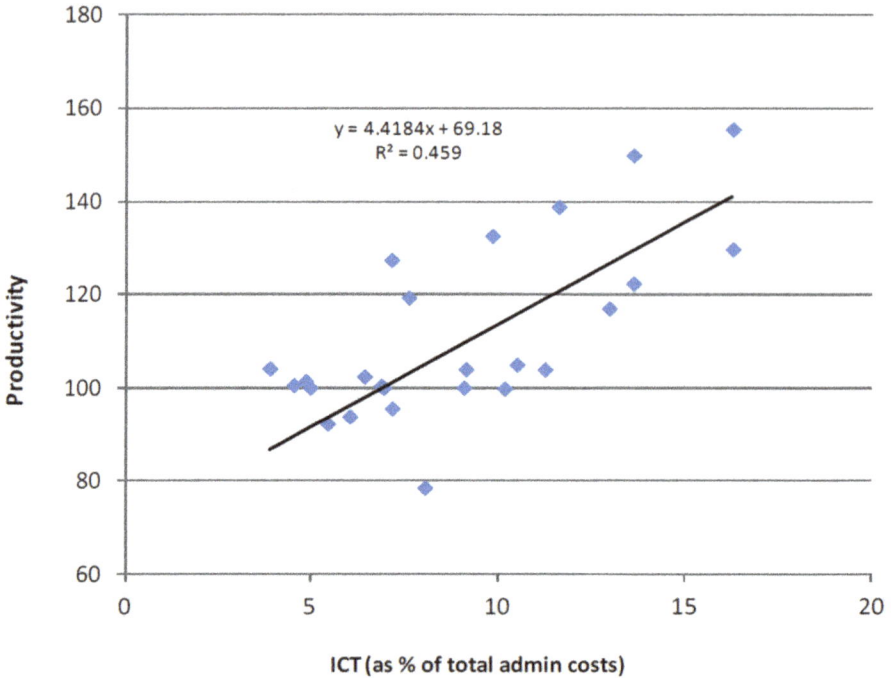

Figure 3.6. Productivity versus lagged ICT spending across UK welfare, tax and customs, 1999 to 2008

Source: Patrick Dunleavy.

Restructuring

The second thing that works is a major think-through and restructure of what an organisation is doing. The measure used in Figure 3.7 is investment in Private Finance Initiative (PFI) projects; when the Blair government came to power there was a lot of investment in new offices, new processes and new work processes. When we build or open a new building, we tend to reorganise the staff a lot more fundamentally than we would otherwise. Again, there is a positive relationship here—on the whole, the more new construction there is, the more we reorganise our work processes, the more our productivity tends to go up. There are a few troubling outliers here, but it is quite a strong clustering otherwise.

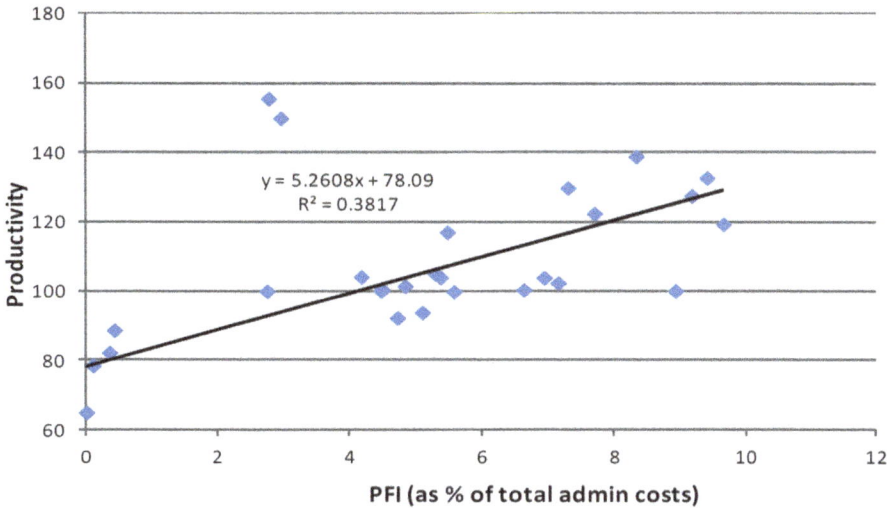

Figure 3.7. Productivity versus lagged construction PFI spending as proxy variable for major reorganisation; UK welfare, tax and customs, 1999 to 2008
Source: Patrick Dunleavy.

Consultants and outsourcing

We also looked at the impact of consultants, and it is very inconsistent (see Figure 3.8). There is no relationship between spending on consultants and productivity. If there is a relationship, it is negative.

So, why does outsourcing not work? It is because government service offices are highly imperfect and they are not going to stop being highly imperfect if two or three contractors are brought in. The markets created are oligopolistic. In Britain we have large problems with our IT sector—62 per cent of the market is dominated by the top contractor, and the top five contractors have 95 per cent of the market. There are usually only two or three tenders for any given contract, and the tenders are very expensive. The idea that more firms can bid is not feasible, because a firm needs to have a large governmental relations unit and a contracting unit just to understand the e-procurement system; this will always be the case. Contract specification works directly against productivity because an organisation needs to specify what it wants the contractor to do. It has to fix a whole service specification and then as needs change, and demand changes, and society changes, it has to go back to the contractor and renegotiate.

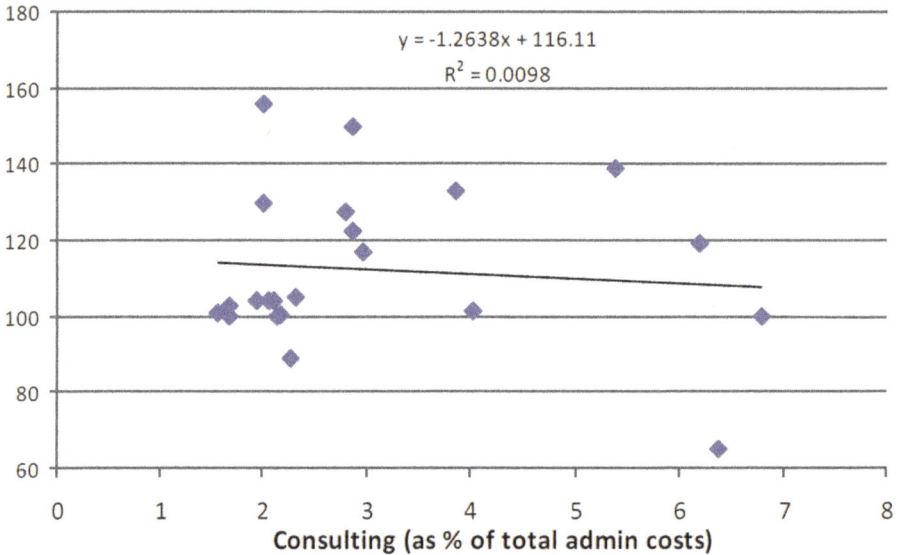

Figure 3.8. Productivity versus lagged consulting spending; UK welfare, tax and customs, 1999 to 2008

Source: Patrick Dunleavy.

In the British government IT market, the famous rule was 'six for one', meaning that if you had open competition for £1 million worth of business, you knew that over the life of the contract you would in reality get six times as much because of the renegotiation that would be forced by political or social changes. There are some outrageous examples of contract fixing. The current IT contract for British tax is an 18-year contract for IT services—and IT changes five times faster than normal life, so it is the equivalent of a century-long contract for a normal area of business.

Public servants also tend to use outsourcing in a very rational way—if we have better business to be attending to and there is something that we really hate doing, we tend to outsource it. This means that nothing changes in that area. The contractor will not want to change—as soon as we outsource it to them, they will want to freeze the technology and keep things exactly the same. This may seem irrational, because at the end of the contract they will have to re-tender, but it is actually cheaper for contractors to work that way.

When we have genuine cost reductions, it is likely to be a signal that lower contractor prices require a sacrifice in performance. For example, the UK progressively outsourced all its hospital cleaning. Fifteen years later, the UK had a hospital-acquired infection rate 15 times greater than the European average, and

40 times greater than field-leader Denmark. We then had to re-internalise this area and also reallocate work back to a few expensive, oligopolistic contractors, in order to fix the problem.

One final note—*contestability* is a great word, and it may do some good when trying to introduce product diversity, or when attempting to engage different kinds of contractors. The arrival of mutuals might make a difference, but keep in mind that mutuals only have 1/70th of the outsourcing market in the UK, so they are not a serious threat to the big outsourcers yet. On the whole, outsourcing contestability will not grow government productivity.

Eight steps to improving public sector productivity

So what can we do? From our recent book and the work we have been doing for the last 20 years, we can draw four immediate steps and four longer-term steps.

Short-term recommendations

1. Talk about it, look at it, measure it, and try to improve it. If we are not doing that with our organisation, we're not in the game. We need to have a viable minimal definition of productivity; we need to keep it simple. Perhaps as we get better we can make it more elaborate by bringing in more quality weights and starting to think about outcomes. But that's optional, and my recommendation is to keep it simple, try to get some measured productivity going in our organisation, and then build it up over time. Keep the definition stable, rather than constantly changing how we define everything. Try to obtain a time series and then build up a narrative about what it is that drives productivity in our organisation.

2. Public sector innovation is the lifeblood of productivity. Early private sector estimates said that 60 to 70 per cent of productivity gain in an industry was produced by displacement—that is, by customers leaving a firm that was less efficient or had an inferior product and moving to a firm that was more efficient and had a better product. That ratio has come down over time, and nowadays home-grown innovation is far more important in private sector productivity gain. But 50 per cent of all productivity gain still comes from people moving from the worst firms to better firms, while the bad firms go out of business.

This is an effect that cannot be reproduced in the public sector. People have been trying to produce supplier succession in the new public management period for the last 25 years. These efforts are feeble because there can be no supplier succession, and most public sector agencies are immortal, and will continue to be immortal—that is the good news for public servants. Consequently, the public sector will not see the same displacement as the private sector, certainly not in the short term under current arrangements. This means that home-grown innovation produced by managers—particularly medium managers, lower managers and staff themselves—is the lifeblood of change in the improvement of productivity.

3. Take digital seriously. I know everybody thinks they are taking digital seriously, but government websites across the world are vastly out of date, few are using blogs or Skype, and Twitter use is still rare. The IT world changes constantly; government has to be proactive and stick with what citizens and companies are doing. We should be thinking about moving to a future in which digital services are the core of what we are doing, and other things are add-ons. In the area of personal services, or professional services at the local or state levels, there must still be a lot of digital enhancement occurring.

4. Bring the workers with us. The people who know how to improve things are the people who are doing the job. But why do they not now tell us how to improve things? My feeling is that they do not trust us. There is a concern that if they offer up information, management will say, 'Thanks very much! Okay that's a great idea. We'll start doing that, and then we'll fire one of you, or we'll speed up the work process.'

This is the fundamental problem inside public sector organisations. I have been to organisations where consultants have found that staff are using two different computer systems—an old one and a new one. The new one is much more time-consuming than the old one, but management are really dependent on their expert workers, who are doing it on the old system in unrecognised ways. And this is the only way that things are being done. These are large organisations that have spent a lot of money on change, but they have spent it poorly because they have not talked to their workforce.

Management consultants will tell you their job is to go into organisations, talk to the managers who do not really know how the organisation is working, then talk to the workers that the managers have not bothered to consult (or feel that they cannot because it is 'beneath their dignity' to go and spend time with the workforce). The consultants then write down what the workers tell them, and tell it to the managers—that is what management consultancy is all about, in a nutshell.

Longer-term recommendations

1. The question is, can we have genuine demand transfers across suppliers? Can we get genuine supplier succession, genuine competition or contestability? I think we could if we had public sector suppliers who could scale up their services; who could move from one area to another and enlarge. More mixed public/private competition could also improve the situation, and mutuals may help in a small way here.

2. We must try to persuade the public to stop supporting big state policies from the late twentieth century that really are not working anymore, and to have enough trust in politicians and managers to embrace the new kinds of service patterns that would work better.

3. We need to exploit digital to focus public services, again, on free services. We can get free services from a company like Google—but can we get a genuinely free service from the state? There is a lot of potential to develop this area in the next few years.

4. Citizen co-production: we have tended to focus on producing a fully specified, very finished public sector product—one which is fully controlled. We need to move towards producing more part products that citizens can use for their own purposes.

But these are all longer-run changes. Nevertheless, there is enormous potential in them, especially in difficult areas such as health, social care and education.

References

Atkinson, Anthony B. 2005. 'Measurement of UK government output and productivity for the national accounts.' *Journal of the Statistical and Social Inquiry Society of Ireland* 34: 152–60.

Dunleavy, Patrick and Leandro Carrera. 2013. *Growing the Productivity of Government Services*. London: Edward Elgar.

Osborne, Stephen (ed.). 2002. *Public Management: Critical Perspectives*. London: Routledge.

4

MEASURING AND IMPROVING GOVERNMENT PERFORMANCE: LEARNING FROM RECENT US EXPERIENCE

Shelley H. Metzenbaum
President of The Volcker Alliance

In late September 2009, about 10 months into President Barack Obama's first term, I started work as the Associate Director for Performance and Personnel Management in the White House Office of Management and Budget (OMB). In this position, I was responsible for setting and implementing the Obama Administration's policy governing management practices that US federal government agencies (Cabinet departments, their components, and other organisations reporting to the President) would use to improve performance on their mission-focused objectives. I held this position until May 2013 when I left government to launch The Volcker Alliance, a new organisation dedicated to working for more effective and trusted government.[1]

---

1   The Volcker Alliance was launched by former US Federal Reserve Chairman Paul A. Volcker in 2013 to rekindle intellectual, practical, political and academic interest in the implementation of policy—in the 'nuts and bolts' and, increasingly, the 'electrons' of government. The Alliance seeks to be a catalyst for change—encouraging public, private and educational institutions to give sustained attention to excellence in the execution of federal, state and local policies in the US and abroad. The author would like to thank Kaeleigh R. Forsyth and Peter D. Morrissey for assistance in writing this chapter.

The Obama Administration's performance objective was straightforward—help the federal government improve along multiple clearly identified dimensions. The ones on which my office focused were to increase the positive impact of government action on the outcomes that touch people's lives (mission-related objectives); improve return on spending and the quality of people's interaction with government; and strengthen accountability. To strengthen accountability, we aimed to improve transparency and public understanding of what government was trying to accomplish, why, how (strategies chosen to make progress on a goal and why those strategies were chosen), how well they were doing, and adjustments made to planned actions as experience was gained. Other management offices within OMB focused on improving performance relative to mission-support, including acquisition, financial management and information management.

This chapter explains the approach taken, why it was selected, what worked, and what issues were encountered. It also suggests next steps and identifies challenges that could threaten future progress. These lessons should be helpful for both national and sub-national governments in Australia, New Zealand, the United States, and elsewhere in the world. Further, this chapter will, it is hoped, spark ideas about opportunities for cross-government collaboration and co-investment and for cross-country research, education and learning, including benchmarking, to find ways to improve.

The remainder of the chapter is organised as follows. The next section describes the Obama Administration's approach to performance improvement and why this approach was chosen. A review of how the approach worked follows. The final section of this chapter offers recommendations for further improvement. An Appendix elaborates on the experiences and evidence that informed the approach with an in-depth look at two cases: crime reduction in New York City and water quality improvement in Massachusetts.

Blueprint for action

I was hired as the Associate Director for Performance and Personnel Management at the US Office of Management and Budget because of a report I had written, 'Performance Management Recommendations for the New Administration' (Metzenbaum 2009). This report, which reviewed past US federal government efforts using performance goals and measurement, recommended which past US federal governments' current performance practices to continue and which to change. It also looked at noteworthy developments around the world to identify new practices worth adopting. The report served as our blueprint for action.

The IBM Center for the Business of Government had asked me to write this report because of my prior work as executive director of the Harvard Kennedy School's Executive Session on Public Sector Performance Management and as the author of two Center-published studies on the subject (Metzenbaum 2006; Metzenbaum 2003). The Executive Session produced an Open Memorandum for New Executives on public sector performance management, 'Get Results through Performance Management' (Executive Session on Public Sector Performance Management n.d.), which had caught the attention of key leaders in the Bush Administration.

Drafts of my report were shared with the Obama campaign and transition team. Even before I joined the Administration, the Administration was moving some of the report's recommendations forward, such as the recommendation that Cabinet secretaries and other agency heads set priority targets.[2]

Resetting the mindset: Improvement, not punishment

Learning from the Clinton and Bush years, state and local governments, and other countries, the Obama Administration aimed to reset the performance[3] mindset of US federal agencies. We wanted people across the US federal government focused on improving performance, not on getting higher ratings from budget examiners, attaining a higher percentage of targets met, or complying with reporting requirements for the sake of compliance.

Successful efforts to reduce crime in New York City and improve water quality in Massachusetts, as well as experience from the United Kingdom, New Zealand and multiple US state and local governments, all informed the Obama Administration's approach. Some of these experiences are described in greater detail in the Appendix.

US government agencies made progress setting outcome-focused goals and measuring performance during the Clinton and Bush Administrations, following passage of the Government Performance and Results Act of 1993 which required all federal agencies to set goals and measure performance, starting in 1997.

---

2   President Obama was already moving fast to implement his priorities, most notably stabilising the financial system, resetting American policy in the Middle East, and healthcare reform.
3   After starting work in the federal government, I stopped using the term 'performance management' as the primary way of describing the work we did because it became apparent that, for most federal employees, the term 'performance management' brought to mind the employee appraisal system that affects annual awards, a system that is badly broken and needs fixing.

In compliance with the law, agencies set strategic and annual performance goals, and included them in strategic and annual plans. They also prepared annual performance reports.

Few agencies, however, used the goals and measurement in the reports to improve. They did not tap the power of ambitious, outcome-focused goals to motivate, inspire innovation and enlist goal allies—all demonstrated benefits of effective goal-setting (Metzenbaum 2006, 15–21). Nor did they use frequent analysis and data-rich discussions to find promising practices worth promoting for broader adoption, nor problematic practices in need of fixing.

One reason for this was the Bush Administration's adoption of the Program Assessment Rating Tool (PART) as its primary means to motivate mission-focused improvement. OMB budget examiners used the 25-question rubric of the PART to score every government program with the intention of rating each program once every five years. While PART questions were by and large good questions and the rating effort was well-intentioned, PART reviews created numerous problems in practice. Reviewer bias was inevitable (Lavertu, Lewis and Moynihan 2013), for example, because a single reviewer rated each program, a problem that the Olympics and other scoring systems long ago recognised and addressed by using multiple reviewers. Additionally, the rating system penalised programs for problems beyond their control; no mechanism existed to encourage high-scoring programs to continue to improve; individual program ratings undermined cross-program management of problems needing cross-program attention; and a five-year review cycle for all but low-rated programs created a long-range planning mindset rather than an orientation toward immediate action based on experience. Perhaps most seriously, OMB's emphasis on PART caused agencies to devote their time to earning a good PART score rather than to finding ways to improve outcomes, return on spending, and the quality of people's interaction with government.[4]

Exacerbating problems associated with PART ratings, OMB had identified as a model a few agency performance reports summarising performance by using the percentage of targets met, which proved problematic. While focusing on target attainment rates can be useful for a manager intimately familiar with all of the targets and the reasons those targets were set, it does not work well as a public reporting mechanism. One report OMB spotlighted as a model, for example, showed an upward trend in the percentage of targets met, implying

---

4   During the Bush Administration, the Office of Management and Budget also issued a companion scorecard every quarter that graded agencies on their adoption of prescribed acquisition, information technology, financial management and human resource practices. Where the scorecard encouraged the adoption of practices backed by evidence of the value of those practices, it contributed to positive outcomes. In many cases, the scorecard suffered from problems similar to the PART; agencies report they learned how to game the system to 'get to green'.

that performance on the measured indicators was improving when, in fact, the underlying targets had become easier over time and actual performance was getting worse. Publicly reporting the percentage of targets met as an indicator of overall performance may tempt organisations to adopt timid targets that they know they can meet. Sometimes, it can also tempt them to add easy targets to the total number of targets reported so they offset those they are not likely to meet. A far better public reporting practice, also useful for internal reporting and management, is showing whether key indicators are trending in the right direction (US Department of Commerce 2011, 7; US Department of Commerce 2013, 9).[5]

To shift the emphasis from punishment to continuous (and sometimes breakthrough) improvement, the Obama Administration required federal government agencies to adopt several distinct but complementary performance measurement and improvement practices:

- **Priority outcome-focused goals with stretch targets selected by leaders.** Cabinet members and the heads of other large agencies were required to set outcome-focused goals, including a few ambitious, priority goals they would try to accomplish within two years without additional increments of funding or new legislation. We asked the 16 Cabinet members and heads of eight other large government organisations to set priority goals to make sure they thought about, communicated, and managed their delivery priorities.[6] Goals were set in consultation with OMB and White House policy offices; agencies were also expected to consult with key stakeholders.

- **Leaders named for each goal.** Agency leaders were required to designate a single accountable official, the goal leader who would be responsible for managing progress on each priority goal and be identified on Performance.gov.

- **Frequent data-rich, constructive performance reviews.** No less than once a quarter, the Deputy Secretary (or equivalent) was expected to conduct data-rich constructive performance reviews, examining with each goal leader progress on each priority goal, opportunities for improvement and risks. These meetings were intended to keep the pressure on the goal leader,

---

5   Getting agencies to stop focusing on the percentage of targets met proved easier said than done. Several years into the Obama Administration, one Cabinet department, the Department of Commerce, summarised its progress for fiscal year 2011 using a chart that suggested steadily improving trends over time. A closer look at the chart revealed that what the agency was actually counting, which seemed to be trending steadily upward, was the number of key performance indicators. By FY2013, the Commerce Department corrected this confusion by showing indicators trending in the right direction and those trending in the wrong direction.
6   Leaders of other organisational units, such as the Pension Benefit Guaranty Corporation, were encouraged but not required to set priority goals initially, although they were expected to adopt priority goals in later years.

not function as 'gotcha' sessions.[7] Rather, we urged data-rich discussions to find what worked and was worth continuing and possibly promoting for broader adoption, as well as what did not work and needed a 'deeper dive' to identify root causes. In addition, we urged brainstorming and field testing of new practices to accomplish more with available funds, inviting people inside and outside an agency working to accomplish the same or a similar goal to join the reviews, and allowing other agencies to attend reviews to learn from one another's experience and coordinate on shared goals.

- **Quarterly public progress reporting**. Agencies were required to report progress on their priority goals every quarter to OMB and to the public via Performance.gov.

- **Complementary evaluation and measured trials**. Agencies were expected to complement ongoing performance measurement with occasional, appropriately rigorous retrospective evaluations to isolate the impact of agency action from other factors influencing trends of interest. They were also encouraged to run prospective evaluations—measured trials with a control group or other adequately rigorous benchmark—to test new ways to achieve unprecedented performance gains.

- **Single performance portal**. A new website, Performance.gov, was created: to communicate to people in the federal government; to facilitate public understanding of agency goals, strategies, and performance; and to motivate adoption of this new way of doing business. In addition, Performance.gov was designed to support cross-organisational cooperation on shared goals, as well as cross-agency learning, investment, transparency and accountability to the public.

- **Accountability for improvement and cogent strategies rather than target attainment**. Accountability expectations were changed from meeting targets and earning a high score from OMB budget examiners to using stretch targets to inspire and encourage innovation; knowing whether key performance indicators were trending in the right direction and, if not, why; having a plan to address trends heading in the wrong direction; using data, measured trials, and other evidence to find ways to improve; and communicating to the public why a goal and strategies were chosen, progress, problems, their causes and proposed next steps.

OMB budget examiners were no longer expected to give programs PART scores but were expected to ask questions and address concerns when they reviewed proposed budgets. Budget submissions were to be accompanied by proposed annual goals for the budget year and updated prior-year goals, plans

---

7   To explain this approach across the government and to the public, Performance.gov provided an example of one Agency's approach to these data-rich constructive performance reviews. See HUDSTAT ca 2011.

for achieving the goals, proposed measurements to track progress and planned evaluations. Agencies also shared draft annual performance reports showing and discussing past trends. Every other year, agencies proposed a small set of goals with their budget submissions to be two-year implementation-focused priority goals. After the budget was finalised, budget examiners were also asked to review and assess that agencies' proposed action plans for implementing priority goals, quarterly progress updates, and planned next steps.

In addition, the Performance Improvement Council (PIC), composed of the Performance Improvement Officers of every federal agency and supported by a small staff, provided feedback on goals, how progress was being reported, and each agency's performance review and improvement process. The PIC reviews not only provided useful feedback to the agency being reviewed, but also helped those doing the goal-focused performance reviews to learn from other agencies' experiences. The PIC worked closely with OMB's Office of Performance and Personnel Management on these reviews.

We wanted outcomes. We wanted agencies, wherever possible, to measure, manage and improve the conditions and events affecting people's lives. Focusing on outcomes requires agencies to try to influence the actions of others, not just the actions of government. This requires agencies to choose indicators and other ways to gauge progress to achieve better outcomes and higher returns on spending, not default to indicators that are easy to measure.[8]

We also wanted agencies to track whether key performance indicators were trending in the right direction. When they were not improving or improving too slowly, we wanted them to analyse relevant data to find ways to improve, ferret out root causes of problems that could be prevented, and think more strategically about where to focus government efforts.

Similarly, we wanted people in government to communicate their organisational goals and explain why they were important to their workforce, other parts of government (including Congress), and the public. We wanted them to invite discussion about goal framing (were the goals understandable and 'actionable' and were they framed to encourage and inform action?) and goal appropriateness (was a goal sufficiently ambitious relative to prior and peer performance and did it make sense in the context of competing needs and limited resources?). We wanted agencies to communicate their strategies and why they were chosen to encourage suggestions about better options that might exist (did the strategies make sense in the context of evidence about relevant past experience,

---

8   It is not possible to gauge progress on all types of activities using performance indicators. For areas such as investment in basic research and development, agencies could propose alternative methods for gauging progress to inform future decisions and actions.

the operating environment, evolving technologies and other developments?). In addition, we wanted government officials to communicate their goals and share their data to enlist assistance and expertise from others with the potential to contribute to performance gains on specific goals.

The Obama Administration introduced these changes with the FY2011 budget (Office of Management and Budget 2010) and incorporated them into budget guidance (Metzenbaum 2010). The US Congress subsequently adopted the approach into law, the *Government Performance and Results Modernization Act* of 2010 (*Results Act*). The *Results Act* added a few additional requirements, including requiring the adoption of cross-agency priority goals and Congressional consultation.

Progress

This section briefly describes how this approach worked. It spotlights two of the five two-year, implementation-focused priority goals set by the Department of the Interior for FY2011: one to increase renewable energy and one to reduce violent crime on Indian reservations. A brief discussion of progress on other priority goals and the process follows, including a brief introduction to the US federal government's performance reporting website, Performance.gov.

US Department of the Interior renewable energy goal

The US Department of the Interior (DOI) manages one fifth of the landmass of the United States and 1.7 billion acres of the outer continental shelf. Leaders at DOI realised that with so much land under management, they could help America produce more energy at home, support a growing economy and job creation, reduce dependence on foreign oil and reduce greenhouse gas emissions (Department of the Interior 2013). Concurrent with the release of the President's Fiscal Year 2011 budget in early 2010 (along with the release of the priority goals of all major federal agencies), DOI announced that one of its two-year implementation-focused priority goals would be to:

> Increase approved capacity for production of renewable (solar, wind, and geothermal) energy resources on Department of the Interior managed lands, while ensuring full environmental review, by at least 9,000 megawatts through 2011 (Office of Management and Budget 2010, 43–90).[9]

---

9   The first set of agency priority goals and the performance improvement approach was announced in the President's FY2011 budget, Chapter 7 of the Analytical Perspectives (Office of Management and Budget 2010, 43–90). DOI's goals can be found on printed p. 82. For progress on DOI's FY2011 performance goals see US Department of the Interior 2012.

DOI's goal was not to produce renewable energy itself, but to expedite permitting to facilitate private sector development. To appreciate how much of a stretch this target was, over the prior 20-year period, DOI had authorised capacity to produce 1,500 megawatts of renewable energy on Interior land.

To reach its stretch target, DOI had to move quickly down a steep learning curve to figure out how to approve requests more quickly without compromising environmental quality. Through the first year, DOI authorised less than 200 megawatts. By year two, though, it had clearly worked out the kinks in its review system and approved nearly 4,000-megawatt capacity (US Department of the Interior 2013, see the Data & Explanation button at the Indicator List tab).

DOI did not meet the 9,000-megawatt stretch target by the end of FY2011. It did, however, permit 6,064 megawatts of renewable production capacity, enough to power over 1 million homes.

OMB did not chastise DOI for failing to meet its target; the goal had clearly achieved its motivational intent. Instead, OMB celebrated the progress DOI made by spotlighting this goal as an example of success. We wanted to signal that OMB would not attack agencies that did not meet all of their ambitious targets if they were clearly making progress at a healthy pace and were aggressively trying new strategies, assessing their impact, and adjusting agency action quickly based on what they were learning. Further, OMB explicitly warned agencies that if they met all their targets all the time, it would prompt OMB to ask if the agency was setting sufficiently ambitious targets. OMB guidance explained that OMB review of agency progress would focus on whether performance was trending in the right direction at a strong pace, not whether the agency was meeting all of its targets (Office of Management and Budget 2013).

Despite its failure to meet its target by the end of FY2011, DOI did not get discouraged. In the President's FY2013 budget, DOI renewed its commitment to this goal by setting a new two-year implementation-focused goal of 11,000 megawatts (cumulative from 2009) by the end of FY2013 on 30 September 2013. Having figured out how to get the job done, DOI was able to beat this target, approving cumulative capacity of 12,573 megawatts. DOI again renewed its commitment to this target for FY2015, setting a goal of 16,500 megawatts of renewable energy permitted since 2009 (Kornze n.d.).

US Department of the Interior goal to reduce violent crime in Indian communities

Another DOI priority goal for FY2011 and FY2013 was reducing violent crime on four, and subsequently six, high-crime reservations in Indian country. While focusing on such a small number of reservations may seem like a timid target considering the hundreds of tribal communities nationwide, it was in fact an ambitious goal because when it was set, DOI did not know how to reduce violent crime on even one reservation.

DOI began this crime reduction effort by building a better measurement system and teaching tribal members how to collect and report crime data. It then initiated weekly phone calls and data-driven reviews.

Double-digit crime reduction was accomplished, but not without some problems, as the goal leader reported on Performance.gov at the end of the goal period, 30 September 2013 (Washburn 2013):

- The strategy employed with this priority goal has been effective, achieving an overall 38 in violent crime incidents in four tribal communities with long-standing community policing programs, and a reduction of 8 per cent in one of two new communities. These experiences have been documented in a *Crime-Reduction Best Practices Handbook* (Bureau of Indian Affairs, Office of Justice Services 2012a), which has been distributed throughout Indian country. The members and officers of the Bureau of Indian Affairs' Office of Justice Services were using this handbook.
- Progress was hampered by limited housing resources available for officers.
- Progress was also impeded by an inability to secure full engagement in one of the new sites.

To help other federal managers learn from this experience, the US Office of Personnel Management created a training video in which the goal leader talks about the power of this priority goal for bringing about change (Bureau of Indian Affairs, Office of Justice Services 2012b). A retrospective review of the ups and downs involved with managing the crime reduction goal was nicely captured in an article written in late 2013 (Lunney 2013).

Progress on other priority goals

The experience of the US Department of the Interior was not unique. It was, in fact, more the rule than the exception. By the end of FY2013, US agencies made progress on most of the 117 agency and cross-agency implementation-focused priority goals for that period, documented in the archived section of Performance.gov ('Clear goals: Using goals to improve performance and accountability'). For example, exports increased ('Cross agency priority goals: Exports. FY2013 Q4 Status Update'), energy efficiency improved (Utech 2013), the patent application backlog and wait times declined (although the goal was not met) (Rea 2013), nearly 1.7 million homes were weatherised with projected savings of $16.4 billion in energy costs and reduction in greenhouse gases of

85 million tons (Poticha 2013), and an additional 120,000 families were served in US government-supported affordable housing without additional funding, bringing to just over 5.4 million the total number of families served (Kolluri 2013). In addition, the US Department of Treasury reduced paper benefit payments from 131 million in 2010 to 39 million in 2013, getting money out to beneficiaries and into the economy faster, and raised electronic collections from 85 per cent of total collections in 2010 to 97 per cent in 2013 (Gregg 2013). Social security similarly increased online applications, with more than 2.2 million retirement and disability applications submitted online during FY2012, an increase of 55 per cent over FY2009 with 1.4 million online submissions (Snyder 2013). For both Treasury and the Social Security Administration, the rate of improvement (slope of the curve) accelerated after the priority goal was set.

Tentative yet promising progress was evident elsewhere as well. For example, the US Education Department (ED) aimed to turn around the 500 persistently lowest performing schools (Delisle 2013). This goal was very challenging because ED first had to determine how to define these schools, then identify effective turnaround practices, and, after that, successfully promote adoption of these practices in 500 schools—not a simple undertaking in the US system where local governments, not the federal government and not even the states, manage schools. Other goals that seem to be moving in the right direction, but where progress was not yet certain at the end of FY2013 because of reporting lag times, include goals to reduce foodborne illness (Wagner 2015)[10] and hospital-acquired infections (Tavenner 2013).[11]

There were, of course, goals where progress was not trending in the right direction or trending too slowly as of the end of September 2013. Performance.gov shows, for example, that the US Department of Defense was not doing well procuring a higher proportion of its energy from renewable sources (Sikes 2013), and that the US Department of Transportation was wrestling to find effective ways to bring down general aviation fatalities (Gillian 2013) and reverse a one-year uptick in roadway fatalities following a steady decline since 2005

---

10 For FY2015 goals, see Wagner 2015; and Almanza 2013.
11 See, for example, the Partnership for Patients led by the Department of Health and Human Services to reduce hospital-acquired infections and hospital readmission rates. See Tavenner 2013; 'A partnership to save thousands of lives and billions of dollars.' n.d. Since this is an archived site, some of the links are dead. For updated information as of November 2014, see Centers for Medicare & Medicaid Services 2015.

(Friedman 2013).[12] Similarly, the Veteran's Administration was clearly struggling to bring down the backlog of disability and pension claims. While it was successful in improving the accuracy rate of determinations, it did not show progress in reducing average days for claims until the last two quarters of FY2013, following a steady rise in backlogged claims in prior quarters (Rubens 2013).

Progress on goal-setting and measurement

Many agencies struggled to frame their goals in meaningful ways. The US Department of Agriculture (USDA), for example, sought to protect water resources and wanted to measure the effectiveness of its conservation investments. In the first round of priority goal-setting for FY2011, the USDA set a goal of increasing the number of acres agreeing to adopt high impact targeted practices to improve water quality rather than a goal of improving water quality affected by those lands. But the USDA did not have a robust evidence base about the impact of the treatments it was promoting. To address this problem, for FY2013, it updated its priority goal to be the identification of a better way to measure the impact of the treatments it was promoting (Mills 2013).

The US Office of Personnel Management (OPM) similarly needed to find a better way to measure progress on one of its priority goals—reducing the large backlog of pending retirement claims from former federal employees. Wait times were so long that it provoked Congressional ire (Lapin 2012). Accordingly, the OPM set as one of its FY2013 priority goals: 'By July 31, 2013, Retirement Services will have reduced its case inventory so that 90 per cent of all claims will be adjudicated within 60 days' (Zawodny 2013a).

While this goal was sensibly framed as an outcome (the number of days each claimant would have to wait to get a claim amount determined and full payment started), OPM did not have an inventory management (ageing) system that allowed it to calculate the age of claims in the system at the time this goal was set. It therefore started by measuring what it could measure: claims received, claims processed, and claims pending in the system. By measuring and managing these indicators, and using overtime and other management tools, OPM was able to reduce the claims backlog from over 61,000 pending claims in January 2012

---

12   In 2012, as DOT reported on Performance.gov, 'An estimated 34,080 people died in roadway crashes. This represents an increase of about 5.3 per cent compared to the 32,367 fatalities that occurred in 2011. It is the first year with a year-to-year increase in fatalities since 2005. Traffic fatalities had declined steadily over the previous six years by about 26 per cent from 2005 to 2011. It is too soon to speculate on the contributing factors of any increase in deaths on our roadways, however the historic downward trend in traffic fatalities in the past several years means any comparison today will be to an unprecedented low baseline figure. This also fits the pattern of previous economic cycles, where as the economy improved, so did traffic fatalities, likely due in part to higher levels of discretionary and recreational travel' (Friedman 2013).

to 36,000 in January 2013 to 14,000 in October 2014 (Zawodny 2013a, 2013b, n.d.). By its own projection, however, OPM expected the backlog to start to rise again because of the normal January–February seasonal surge in incoming claims (Office of Personnel Management 2015).

OPM did not, however, have any way to manage progress on the goal itself—reducing claimant wait times. It fixed that problem in May 2014 when OPM started to measure the 'age' of pending claims, a better outcome indicator of progress than the numbers of claims pending because it captures the claimants' experiences. In May 2014, OPM processed 76.6 per cent of all claims received within 60 days. Between then and October 2014, the number of pending claims processed within the target time frame steadily improved. As of October 2014, OPM improved the percentage of claims processed in 60 days to 83.2 per cent, short of its 90 per cent goal but moving in the right direction.

It is interesting to note that the key indicator OPM had previously used as its primary metric—claims pending—might show a worsening trend in months when the number of claims received surges. OPM needs to track claims received, processed and pending to help it anticipate and prepare for variations in the number of claims, but measuring and managing claimant's wait times is a more appropriate key outcome indicator that captures the claimant's experience.

Over time, OPM would be well-advised to complement this indicator, showing wait times for all claimants, with wait times for different claimant categories. More complicated claims, such as those for claimants who worked in multiple federal government personnel systems or those involved in contested divorces, tend to take longer to process. Sharing information about these distinctions would help claimants plan better and OPM manage better. In addition, to make sure claims older than 60 days do not get cast aside because they are already over target, the average and distribution of times for claims that missed the target should be tracked and managed as well.

The US Department of Justice (Justice) has similarly made progress, not just in developing more meaningful measures but also in setting more focus on goals. Still, it struggles to find more meaningful ways to measure progress on those goals. As with traffic fatalities, Justice often wants to prevent bad things from happening and keep their costs as low as possible when they do. However, the unwanted incidents Justice wants to reduce, such as drug trafficking, human trafficking and civil rights violations, are harder to count than traffic fatalities or fires because crime perpetrators work hard to hide the incidents they create. For its FY2011 goal, Justice started counting the size of its caseload in different areas and the percentage of cases resolved in targeted areas where it was using enforcement to try to deter crime. For FY2013, it added greater specificity about the categories of crimes it was pursuing (Gannon 2013). For FY2015, Justice added a more outcomes-focused indicator for its effort to protect vulnerable people. In addition to counting the number of cases, it is tracking and trying to increase the percentage of children recovered within 72 hours of an (Amber) alert.

Progress on constructive performance reviews

Another area where progress was made is in the conduct of constructive performance reviews, which must occur at least once a quarter. As a way to promote this practice to other parts of the federal government, the promising approach used by the US Department of Housing and Urban Development (HUD) was described in detail on Performance.gov (HUDSTAT ca 2011). In addition, Performance Improvement Officers started annual peer reviews, providing feedback to other agencies on their review processes. In doing this, they also accelerate the peer reviewers' learning.

Progress linking performance measurement and other evidence-based management tools

Another area where progress was made was integrating performance measurement and other evidence-based management tools, such as regression analyses, randomised control trials and matched samples.[13] The US Department of Labor hired a chief evaluation officer to work closely with the Deputy Secretary and the performance improvement office to identify relevant past research and support program offices in identifying and designing future research (United States Department of Labor n.d.). HUD experimented with a matched sample to compare how residential vacancy rates in neighbourhoods hit hardest by foreclosure receiving help from the department compared to those that did not receive assistance (Chavez 2013), while the US Internal Revenue Service explored a number of 'test and learn' measured trials in areas as diverse as reducing improper payments associated with paid Earned Income Tax Credit preparers, small business income under-reporting, and fraudulent returns.[14]

---

13   Discussion of the need for and approach to integration was first set out in the Analytical Perspectives to the President's FY2013 Budget, see Office of Management and Budget 2013.

14   Personal correspondence with Dean Silverman, Senior Advisor to the Commissioner in the IRS's Office of Compliance Analytics, 29 December 2014.

Progress on transparency

Performance.gov was created as a single website to report performance on US federal government goals for current and past agency goals,[15] as well as for cross-agency priority goals. Performance.gov also introduced the key elements of the Obama Administration performance improvement approach to people in the federal government.[16] As at the end of 2014, each of the 16 Cabinet departments and eight other large US government federal agencies report on four different types of goals on Performance.gov: longer term **strategic goals**; **strategic objectives** supporting each strategic goal; two-year **priority goals** for the goals that agency leaders designated for near-term performance acceleration and focused senior leadership attention; and **annual performance goals**.

Each agency's **strategic goals and objectives** can be found in its strategic plan, accessible from Performance.gov. The strategic goals and objectives can also be seen on the site itself in three locations: the Performance.gov home page, the agency 'home page', and by sorting on budget themes (e.g. energy, national defence, health).

Agencies' **annual performance goals** can be found in their annual performance reports, again available via Performance.gov. All agencies release their annual performance plan with their budget request and justification, laying out the goals they hope to accomplish with their requested budget. Many combine budget justifications and annual performance plans into a single document. Agencies report progress on their annual performance goals in their annual performance reports. Some, but not all, combine their annual performance reports with their annual performance plan. Performance.gov makes all of this information readily accessible, although improvements are needed to make goals, trends and strategies easier to find and interpret in context.

Performance.gov provides more detail on **agencies' two-year priority goals** and a small set of **cross-agency priority goals**. Progress on both sets of priority goals is updated no less than once per quarter.

Each priority goal has its own 'home page' with the following information:

- **Goal leader:** identifies the 'goal leader', designated by the agency Secretary or chief operating officer (COO), who is responsible for driving progress on

---

15   Progress on FY2013 priority goals can be found at the archived section: 'Using goals to improve performance and accountability.' Performance.gov. Online: archive-goals.performance.gov/goals_2013 (accessed 15 June 2015).

16   To see the original public site introducing the key components of the Obama Administration approach, see 'Delivering a high-performing government.' 2013. A non-public beta version of Performance.gov introduced the key concepts to all federal employees in advance of the public site launch.

each priority goal and appropriately adjusting planned actions if problems or new opportunities arise.

- **Overview:** explains why the agency selected this goal.

- **Strategies:** describes strategies chosen to achieve the goal and explains why they were chosen. Agencies are encouraged to discuss relevant evidence, such as past evaluations and insights from peer benchmarking in this section.

- **Progress:** discusses progress made since the goal was set and for the most recent quarter, including trends and milestones completed during the quarter, and likely reasons for progress and for problems.

- **Next steps:** describes the next set of actions planned to achieve the goal, updated as experience is gained and lessons learned.

- **Indicators:** shows trends on the key performance indicators for each goal, as well as for other indicators. All agencies must have *performance* indicators, but can also show *other* indicators. Other indicators could include whatever measures the agency found useful and wanted to share with the public, such as *demand-side indicators* of incoming claims or applications, *productivity indicators, precursor indicators* that can act as a warning sign, *unwanted or beneficial side effect indicators*, or *outcomes indicators that lag agency action*. The 'Data & Explanation' button in this section shows quarterly targets and allows more detailed explanations of each quarter's performance. The 'Indicator Details' button provides the metadata.

- **Contributing programs tab:** shows programs contributing to the goal's accomplishment. Agencies can list programs within the agency or in other parts of government, as well as external delivery partners. This tab makes it possible for goal leaders to show the reality and complexity of managing across organisational boundaries.

- **Learn more:** agencies have the option to add 'Learn More' buttons wherever they choose. For example, for its renewable energy goal, the Department of the Interior used the 'Learn More' button to link to a list of active renewable energy projects and a list of projects approved since the beginning of the calendar year of 2009. DOI also used the 'Learn More' button to share a handbook on crime reduction in Indian communities based on lessons learned from working with the initial four Indian communities to reduce violent crime.

- **Feedback:** the public can click on this button and offer suggestions for improvement using a 'Feedback' button.

Factors contributing to progress

I made the case in the preceding section that the Obama Administration's approach to performance measurement and management achieved noteworthy and, in some cases, breakthrough progress on goals, with progress on priority goals most readily apparent. We also made significant progress on key processes such as outcomes-focused goal-setting, measurement, data analysis, data-rich performance reviews, and complementing measurement with evaluations and measured trials to find ways to improve. In addition, we put in a place a system designed to strengthen accountability by making more readily transparent agency and cross-agency priority goals, progress, problems encountered, two-year strategies, near-term planned actions and accountable officials.

Perhaps this progress is not surprising because the approach was based on a careful look at lessons learned during the Clinton and Bush Administrations, and from other governments in the United States and abroad. That look identified a common set of practices contributing to progress: setting ambitious outcome-focused goals; measuring frequently to get timely intelligence; analysing the data to look for problems and promising practices; searching for root causes contributing to progress and problems; applying insights from analysis to improve practice; complementing retrospective analysis with occasional measured trials to find more effective new practices; clearly designating responsibility for managing progress on each goal; frequent, constructive performance reviews with each 'goal leader' led by a senior person in each department; and accountability for significant improvement and cogent strategies rather than for target attainment.

Other likely reasons for this progress include a shift in the emphasis of central office oversight from punishment in the form of a potential bad rating (and fear of consequent funding reduction) to encouragement for improvement along multiple dimensions (outcomes, return on the taxpayer's spending, government's interaction quality and accountability). Budget examiners remained involved with the process, but not as graders. They were, however, given multiple opportunities to raise concerns and encourage new practices.

Likely reasons for progress also include strengthening the community of performance improvement leaders across government, engaging them more aggressively in identifying and sharing better practices, providing specific feedback on agency performance measurement and management processes, and developing common performance improvement tools needed by many agencies. In addition, likely reasons include tapping the power of two key tools used during the Bush Administration—goals and measurement—not just to meet reporting requirements but also to enlist ideas and assistance from across and outside an agency to speed progress on goals.

Finally, an attitude change about accountability expectations may have contributed to progress. We tried to move away from a 'gotcha' attitude, implying that those who did not meet all their targets would be punished, to expecting every goal leader to know if key performance indicators were all trending in the right direction at rapid speed and, if not, to know why and have a cogent plan to deal with the problem.

Observers may appropriately question whether the progress described here, especially on the goals, would have occurred in the absence of the changes described here. It is an important question to ask and a good question to study. Such studies would help government determine which management and communication practices make a difference. It would also help identify which practices, in isolation or with others, make the most difference. It is worth noting, however, that several of the practices worthy of study, most notably goal-setting and measurement, don't just contribute to better outcomes but also facilitate objective analysis by academics and others.

Future challenges and opportunities

While progress was made, problems did arise and more progress is needed. Ten recommendations for near-term improvement are:

1. **Link organisational goals to social indicators.** The President's Budget (Analytical Perspectives) has long included a chapter on social indicators. The value of this information would be greatly enhanced if Performance. gov was updated to show trends in social indicators and link agencies' goals, strategies and programs to them. Performance.gov already links the strategic goals and objectives and the priority goals to budget themes. Linking to social indicators is an obvious next step and should not be too costly or difficult.

2. **Communicate and consider long-term trends.** Performance.gov gives agencies the option to show long-term historic trends for priority, annual and strategic goals, but few take advantage of this option. This is unfortunate for several reasons. First, long-term trend lines provide a quick sense of directional and rate changes. Also, and perhaps more importantly, government spending and action long ago contributed to dramatic improvements in a variety of policy areas such as public health, public safety and transportation. Continued funding is often needed to sustain past progress, but the public no longer remembers many of those gains. Whenever possible, trend lines should start early enough to show key performance indicators starting from 'before' key government actions were initiated, noting on the trend line when significant government actions took place and what they were (Bloomberg 2008, 17). When displayed with information about dates of government action, this

provides a sense of whether government action had the intended effect, even though it cannot control for other factors possibly influencing what is being measured. Complementary analysis and evaluation is needed for that.

3. **Link to relevant studies and evaluations.** Performance measurement and program evaluation are complementary tools, each enhancing the value of the other. Performance measures are essential to ongoing, real-time continuous improvement, but often cannot answer key questions that independent evaluations can, such as whether changes in performance measures were likely to have occurred in the absence of government action. The Overview section for each priority goal on Performance.gov should clearly describe data and other research about problems (and opportunities) that informed priority setting, while the Strategy section should discuss evaluations and other information that informed strategy selection. Some agencies provide this information in their narrative discussions on Performance.gov. Others, such as the US Department of Labor, have created dedicated websites to facilitate access to relevant evaluations (United States Department of Labor n.d.). Both practices should become standard practice for all agencies.

4. **Link to relevant data sets.** The Obama Administration made 'open data' a priority, opening over 100,000 data sets to the public ('The home of the US Government's Open Data' n.d.). It also opened up opportunities for the private sector to create new economic ventures with 'Datapaloozas' (White House Office of Science & Technology Policy 2014). A next logical step would be to create a link between the social indicators in the budget, and the goals and indicators on Performance.gov, and relevant data sets to make it easier for researchers to find relevant data and amplify government's analysis about priorities and effective practices. In addition, an effective but safe way to expedite researcher access to government data is needed.

5. **Invite constructive feedback.** Performance.gov includes a feedback button. In the era of social media, however, the government should test new ways to get constructive feedback from the field, from current and potential delivery partners, and from outside experts. It could start by asking targeted audiences the kinds of questions addressed in PART questions. Some of the starter questions might be: Are the goals outcome-focused enough? Is it clear why the goals were chosen? Are they sufficiently specific and ambitious? Are there better ways to measure progress? Is there relevant research or related experience that could accelerate outcome and productivity gains? Most PART questions touched on important issues, but asked them in a yes/no format without suggesting ways to improve and, as noted earlier, were limited in value because they reflected the views of only a single rater. PART-like questions should be asked and answered, but by a larger group of experts.

6. **Enlist and engage national and local partners.** Government seldom improves outcomes through its own actions. It usually needs to collaborate with

others for that purpose, whether through formal or informal collaborations. Goal-focused partnerships, supported by data to inform everyone's decisions, should be the norm rather than the exception. Recently, the Department of Health and Human Services used specific goals to enlist organisations and individuals to join its Partnership for Patients to reduce hospital-acquired infections and readmission rates. It has long done this with its decennial Healthy People effort. Other agencies should do the same, and experiment with better ways to share data and crowdsource improvements.

7. **Support continuous learning and improvement communities and build frontline intelligence.** Structured, managed continuous learning and improvement communities should be created and financially supported for common mission-support functions, for similar program types, and for mission-focused goals. Leaders for these improvement communities should be clearly designated and supported. This has already started to happen for common mission-support functions, such as human resources and information technology management, with cross-agency priority goals ('Cross-agency priority goals' n.d.). Sporadic progress has been made creating improvement networks for similar program types, such as benefits processing, permit approvals, grants management, and research and development, but far more is needed.[17] Similarly, some progress has been made creating continuous learning and improvement communities on mission-focused objectives, but not enough, especially in federal grant-giving agencies that depend on state and local governments or non-profit organisations to accomplish their objectives. These agencies and their grant-giving programs should be authorised, and arguably mandated by law, to support structured, managed continuous learning and improvement communities that fully engage the frontline delivery agents (Metzenbaum 2008, 209–42).[18]

8. **Use constructive comparison.** The private sector has long used comparison to peers running similar processes and comparisons across similar field units to find more effective, efficient practices. Some federal agencies routinely

---

17 During the Clinton Administration, as part of the National Performance Review, communities of practice evolved around some similar program types, such as regulatory programs, research and development and programs dependent on states and locals. Change agents from different agencies came together to learn from and share each other's experience and work on similar problems, such as finding effective measurement methods. The Bush Administration established a set of program types for PART reviews (listed in Metzenbaum 2009, 56), which provide a good starting point for creating these communities. During the first term of the Obama Administration, a benefits processing working group was supported that decided to focus on reducing improper payments. The Obama Administration subsequently devoted significant work to speeding infrastructure permit processing building on lessons learned by the Interior Department with its renewable energy goal. See Cobert 2015.

18 This describes early federal learning leadership efforts at mission-focused agencies, such as the National Highway Traffic Safety Administration. Anthony Bryk (2010) at the Carnegie Foundation for the Advancement of Teaching has recently developed the concept much further, building networked improvement communities to improve community college education.

compare with others to find better practices and to motivate,[19] but not enough. More systematic attention should be given to identifying agencies and programs that would benefit from more sophisticated internal and external comparisons and benchmarking.

9. **Promote effective, evidence-based accountability structures.** Continued efforts are needed to reinforce accountability expectations likely to encourage continuous improvement, with breakthrough progress in a few areas. Evidence on effective individual and organisational incentive systems with minimal dysfunctional responses should be shared, used and strengthened in grant programs, contracts and personnel reviews. Often, the most effective incentive systems do not involve financial incentives. In fact, motivational systems with financial incentives often backfire, leading to measurement manipulation or the selection of timid targets.

10. **Add other agencies and major components to Performance.gov.** When Performance.gov was launched, it included performance information for 16 Cabinet and eight other US federal agencies, but not for smaller agencies such as the Nuclear Regulatory Commission and the Pension Benefit Guaranty Corporation. It is time to add performance information, including priority goals, for all but the smallest federal agencies and pilot ways to show the priorities, progress and practices for the largest components of the 16 Cabinet departments already reporting, such as for the Federal Aviation Administration, the Centers for Disease Control, and the US Coast Guard, and for some regional offices.

Appendix

Experience informing our performance improvement approach

A large body of experience informed our thinking in the Obama Administration about what to do and what not to do. Tony Blair's Prime Minister's Delivery Unit, for example, showed that intensive data analysis brought into discussions with program managers can lead to dramatic reductions in hospital wait times (without compromising medical care) as well as better health outcomes (Kelman 2006; Kelman and Friedman 2009; Barber 2007, 380–89). New Zealand's earliest ventures into performance measurement and management warned us that linking

---

19   See, for example, HUD's comparison of voucher use to serve veterans (HUDSTAT 'Using data to understand the problem to be solved: Where are these homeless veterans located?').

senior executive pay to target attainment can cause a retreat to output (rather than outcome) targets, making it less likely that conditions will improve and that the cost and consequence of unwanted incidents will decline (James 1998).

At the state and local level in the United States, DC Mayor Tony Williams showed how public posting of agency scorecards can be used to motivate department heads to set comprehensible goals and manage progress on them. He also used web-based scorecards to enlist public assistance in identifying community (e.g. pothole) priorities and data problems (Scott 2002; Winkler 2001). Other departments in New York under Mayor Rudy Guiliani and Baltimore Mayor and subsequently Maryland Governor Martin O'Malley demonstrated that 'Stat' meetings, modelled after New York Police Department *CompStat* sessions described below, also work well in other parts of government (Behn 2014). Washington State Governor Christine Gregoire built on the performance measurement foundation established by her predecessor, Gary Locke (Washington State Office of the Governor 2004), and added to that televised, taped, data-rich program performance reviews (Krieger 2005). At the beginning of her second term, Gregoire pioneered a statewide outreach effort to invite the public to inform the state's goal-setting process (Patton 2006). Virginia Governor Mark Warner, term-limited by law to one four-year term, enlisted the assistance of the university to create a single performance portal, *Virginia Performs*, which survived his tenure and has been used by several successive governors ('Virginia Performs' 2015). Indiana Governor Mitch Daniels, fresh off his experience running the US Office of Management and Budget during the first term of President George W. Bush, created a counterpart Indiana OMB, which adopted a more sophisticated approach to performance-informed budgeting, including encouragement of cross-agency management of problems, such as rising methamphetamine use (Horst 2005).

Several agencies pioneered goal-focused, data-rich management in the US federal government, producing steadily improved results. The US National Highway Traffic Safety Administration system adopted an injury epidemiology framework, often referred to as the Haddon matrix that helped drive down both the traffic fatality rate and fatality numbers (Maddox n.d.; Sleet 2011). The US Department of Health and Human Services adopted the goal-focused, data-supported Healthy People campaign to enlist state and local partners in setting national, state and local health goals and using them to inspire improvement (Metzenbaum 2008). The Coast Guard, too, has long made effective use of goals and risk management for better results (United States Coast Guard 2010 and n.d.).

The following two cases, pertaining to crime reduction in New York City and water quality improvement in Massachusetts, illustrate in more detail some of the practices we prescribed.

Case 1: New York City policing and *CompStat* to reduce crime

In 1994, New York Police Commissioner William Bratton created the *CompStat* (computerised statistics) program to reduce crime in New York City (Bratton with Knobler 1998; Smith with Bratton 2001; Henry n.d.). He publicly announced a specific outcome-focused goal (a 25 per cent reduction in crime in two years, with a 10 per cent reduction in year one); made clear that precinct commanders were accountable for managing progress on the crime reduction goal in their precinct; increased the frequency of crime reporting; and convened frequent data-rich reviews with each precinct captain to discuss strategies,[20] progress, problems and future plans.

After setting the goal, Bratton needed to find data to gauge progress and decide next steps. He discovered that the New York Police Department (NYPD) collected data about police response primarily to submit in quarterly reports to the US government, a condition of its federal funding. These data were due six months after the close of the quarter, so could be as much as nine months old and seldom fewer than six.

Bratton wanted more actionable information and these data were too dated to be useful. He wanted crime statistics collected, reviewed and delivered to headquarters weekly. At the time, before the days of near-instantaneous electronic transmission, this meant someone from each precinct had to drive a floppy disk containing a Lotus 123 spreadsheet of crime data into headquarters each week.

Bratton used the data for what he called *CompStat* sessions, a frequent process of in-person reviews of precinct-level data. Before each *CompStat* session, an analytics team would review the data to look for interesting or unexplained patterns and relationships, and suggest questions to be asked of the precinct

---

20 One of the most well-known theories informing Bratton's choice of strategies is referred to as the 'broken windows' theory, based on the writings of respected scholar James Q. Wilson. The name comes from the theory that broken windows and other signs of neighbourhood disorder create citizen fear and that inattention to these signs indicates that no one cares, leading to more disorder. Bratton felt that these kinds of small problems need to be reduced in highly visible ways, relying on citizens for legitimacy and assistance. For further discussion of Bratton's view on 'broken windows', see Bratton and Knobler 1998, 152. See also Nagy and Podolny 2008.

The 'broken windows' theory and police use of 'stop and frisk' practices, which became an issue during the New York City 2014 mayoral campaign as a cause of police abuse, are sometimes erroneously equated. While stop-and-frisk may be one tactic for reducing 'broken windows', it is not the only one nor necessarily as effective over time as it might be originally. See Rose 2014; and Golding 2014.

To make sure that police abuse did not rise as efforts to reduce broken windows did, the NYPD introduced statistics about civilian complaints and patterns of police misconduct into *CompStat* review meetings. See Smith with Bratton 2001, 453–82, 463.

commander. Questions might be general, such as: 'What's going on with crime in your community? If crime is up, why and what are your plans to deal with it? If it is down, why and did you take an action others might want to take, too?' They could also be much more specific, such as 'What is happening in this area?'

The precinct commander was accountable for knowing his or her statistics and for having well-informed plans to address problems and make improvements. During the meetings, other precinct commanders and departmental experts with relevant experience might offer suggestions. In addition, the meetings afforded a convenient venue that savvy precinct commanders could use to seek assistance from those they did not directly supervise, such as detectives, and to get fast feedback on ideas.

Penalties and rewards were not directly linked to crime reduction or target attainment. Deputy Commission for Crime Control Strategy, Jack Maple, who worked closely with Bratton to develop *CompStat,* would say, 'Nobody ever got in trouble because crime numbers on their watch went up.... [T]rouble arose only if the commanders didn't know why the numbers were up or didn't have a plan to address the problems' (Maple and Mitchell 1999, 33; Godown 2015). Still, precinct commanders who did not like this way of doing business tended to look for other work or left the department of their own volition, while those who liked to use the data to make more informed decisions found opportunities to advance their careers.

Prior to the introduction of *CompStat*, the person responsible for bringing crime rates down in different locations was unclear. Was it the borough chief or the precinct commander? *CompStat* clarified the answer: the precinct commander was on the line.

In fact, prior to the introduction of *CompStat*, when Bratton talked to the police about crime reduction, most argued that they should not be held accountable for outcomes—for reducing the crime rate—because they could not control it. They could only *influence* it, so felt they should only be held accountable for what they *could* control: response times.[21]

Bratton disagreed. He felt the police were responsible for public safety, and made clear that under his command the objective of the police force was to reduce crime. While this does not seem controversial today, it was then. Response times can be important for customer perceptions and public safety, but they are a means and not an objective. It is better to explain to a resident that the police

---

21   According to Smith with Bratton (2001), long before he offered the 'broken windows' theory, James Q. Wilson argued that police could not assess the impact of their actions to reduce crime, likely lowering the police's own expectations regarding what they could accomplish. Bratton clearly did not subscribe to this theory when he chose to measure and manage crime reduction.

might be delayed if more pressing incidents demand immediate attention than to respond to less pressing calls that will keep response time indicators looking good. Bratton wanted his police force to focus on reducing crime.

CompStat, focused on a crime reduction goal, helped him shift the focus. Not only was the goal met, but the *CompStat* approach has spread across policing in the United States and the world. It also spread to other parts of city government, including the management of city parks and correctional facilities.

In a separate chapter in this book, Gary Sturgess writes about fire services spending less time fighting fires. This is because, years ago, firefighters similarly focused on an outcome as their objective: reducing fires and their cost and consequence. They also gathered and analysed data from past fires to find ways to prevent future ones. In the United States and I presume across the world, many of the outcome-focused, data-rich aspects of *CompStat* have long been applied to fire reduction. In the US, the National Fire Protection Association and other national organisations collect data about every significant fire, their characteristics, their costs and their causes. They analyse frequency, patterns and causes to identify the most common and consequential causes of fires and to inform recommendations for model codes, such as mandating the preventive practice of installing sprinkler systems in large buildings. Thanks to this disciplined, data-rich approach to understanding the problem, firefighters have almost been put out of business (Metzenbaum 2007). At least in US communities, this has allowed them to change the nature of their work, picking up emergency response responsibilities. This dual responsibility works well because it allows firefighters to maintain capacity distributed geographically across many different locations to be ready to respond to the increasingly rare fires that do occur and to continue, through inspections and other means, to prevent future fires (Bloomberg and Flowers 2013).

Case 2: The US Environmental Protection Agency and cleaning up the Charles River

In 1995, during the presidential term of Bill Clinton, the regional administrator of the US Environmental Protection Agency (EPA) New England regional office, John DeVillars, initiated a variation of what Bratton had done in New York City. He set a public goal, designated someone to manage progress on the goal, and made clear he expected progress on the goal as well as public reporting about that progress. His team also quickly discovered the value of frequently gathering and analysing data (Metzenbaum 2002).

On the eve of the Head of the Charles Regatta, a major event that at the time brought a quarter of a million people to the Boston metropolitan area, DeVillars announced an ambitious, outcome-focused goal: the lower Charles River (running between the cities of Cambridge and Boston in Massachusetts) would be swimmable in 10 years. To give you an idea of how ambitious that goal was, rowers who fell into the river at the time of the announcement were advised to get a tetanus shot.

DeVillars' announcement won front-page news coverage. Six months later, on Earth Day, he gave the river a grade, once again garnering media attention. By picking a recurring annual event to announce the first grade, DeVillars signalled his intent that the initial goal announcement not be a one-time media story but something EPA actively managed and for which it would publicly report progress at least once a year.

DeVillars also designated a lead accountable official, Ken Moraff. A staff lawyer, Ken reached out to two of his engineering colleagues and, together, the three of them, all working part-time on this assignment, assumed responsibility for getting the Charles River to achieve swimmable status within 10 years.

Moraff and his colleagues started this effort by looking for useful data to inform their actions and to achieve measurable improvement in water quality before the next Earth Day. Finding useful data proved harder than expected. The state, long considered a national leader in using a watershed management approach to improve water quality, gathered water quality data for the watershed once every five years. Local governments also lacked water quality data EPA could use to find new ways to accelerate progress on the goal. Local governments collected data frequently to make sure there were no permit violations, but only about the quality of the discharge water released by permit holders, not about the quality of the receiving water. Fortunately, the Charles River Watershed Association had begun gathering data more frequently. Every month, volunteers collected faecal coliform and dissolved oxygen samples at 37 points along the 80-mile stretch of the river, posting the data online for all 37 locations. Moraff and his colleagues wisely decided to look at this information and found it useful for triggering focused follow-up questions that not only pointed them to problems needing attention but allowed them to gauge progress more often than once every five years.

Every month, the EPA team could quickly scan the watershed association data to look for anomalies in the data. When a downstream reading was worse than an upstream reading and could not be explained by a permitted discharger between the two sampling locations, it naturally prompted the question 'Why?' and focused the EPA on trying to understand the causes of the unexpected readings.

In the case of one anomaly, EPA called the state Department of Environmental Protection (DEP) to ask if the state knew why water quality was worse in that particular area. The DEP did not, nor did the local government (the Boston Water and Sewer Commission). So EPA called colleagues at the Boston Water and Sewer Commission and asked them to grab their maps and, with EPA, 'walk the pipes'. This revealed an illicit hook-up to the storm sewer system sending untreated contaminated water that should have been flowing into the sanitary sewer system for treatment directly into the river.

This example illustrates why setting outcome-focused goals and measuring changes in outcomes, not just measuring and managing activities and outputs believed to affect outcomes, is so important. To improve water quality, the staff of EPA and other regulatory agencies issue permits establishing allowable conditions for permitted discharge. Inspectors check if permit holders are in compliance with permit conditions. When non-compliance is suspected, enforcement staff follow up and levy penalties where warranted. These are all sensible activities and tracking them is helpful; trying to improve their productivity can also be useful.

EPA also receives complaints and needs to determine those warranting further attention. It had heard from rowers that disgusting stuff was flowing from pipes into the river but chose to put those complaints aside, thinking they were not as important as the other cases on which they were working. It was only after EPA set a specific outcome-focused goal, and started using frequent measurement to manage water quality, that EPA detected arguably some of the most egregious violators in its regulatory system, those who had not bothered to get a permit in the first place.

To accelerate progress on the goal, the EPA team embraced data-rich brainstorming. It looked for data anomalies and asked why they were happening. When it found an answer—illicit hook-ups—the team wanted to look for other illicit hook-ups. Someone suggested lifting manhole covers on days when it was not raining to look for water running through storm sewers. EPA instructed local governments across the states to do this and search up-pipe for sources when they found running water on dry days. One illicit hook-up detected this way was a 90-bed dormitory, sending untreated outflows directly into the Charles. Through this data-rich decision-making process, EPA and local governments were able to improve the water quality from being swimmable 19 per cent of the time in 1995 to being swimmable 59 per cent of the time in 2000, five years later.

The EPA team did not meet its goal of a swimmable Charles River by 2005, nor had it attained the goal by 2013. But through three different presidents and even more politically appointed regional administrators, EPA's New England regional office has continued pressing for and making progress toward a swimmable

Charles River ('Region 1. EPA New England. Charles River Report Cards' 2014). In September 2014, EPA reported that the Charles River was swimmable 70 per cent of the time in 2013 (United States Environmental Protection Agency n.d.).

One interesting note of special import for those who fear that public adoption of a specific, ambitious goal will provide fodder for those eager to attack government: the EPA has not come under serious attack for missing its target. One possible reason for this is that EPA updates the community on progress made, problems encountered, and plans for further improvement every year ('Charles River 2013 Report Card Reflects Cleanest Water in Decades' 2014). It also uses the goal to enlist assistance and expertise from others—including other governments and the private sector—to make progress on the goal.

References

'A Partnership to Save Thousands of Lives and Billions of Dollars.' n.d. Performance.gov. Online: archive-goals.performance.gov/videos-and-feature-stories/partnership-save-thousands-lives-and-billions-dollars (accessed 18 May 2015).

Almanza, Al. 2013. 'Reduce the number of foodborne Salmonella illnesses that are associated with USDA's Food Safety and Inspection Service (FSIS)-regulated products—meat, poultry, and processed egg products.' Online: www.performance.gov/node/3355?view=public#overview (accessed 18 May 2015).

Barber, Michael. 2007. *Instructions to Deliver*. London: Politico's Publishing.

Behn, Bob. 2014. *The PerformanceStat Potential*. Washington, DC: Brookings Institution Press.

Bloomberg, Michael R. 2008. *The Mayor's Management Report Fiscal 2008*, Online: www.nyc.gov/html/ops/downloads/pdf/mmr/0908_mmr.pdf (accessed 17 June 2015).

Bloomberg, Michael R. and Michael Flowers. 2013. 'NYC by the numbers: Annual report.' *NYC Analytics*, 12–16. Online: www.nyc.gov/html/analytics/downloads/pdf/annual_report_2013.pdf (accessed 18 May 2015).

Bratton, William and Peter Knobler. 1998. *Turnaround: How America's Top Cop Reversed the Crime Epidemic*, New York: Random House.

Bryk, Anthony S. 2010. 'Getting ideas into action: Building networked improvement communities in education.' *Carnegie Foundation for the Advancement of Teaching*. Online: cdn.carnegiefoundation.org/wp-content/uploads/2014/09/bryk-gomez_building-nics-education.pdf (accessed 15 June 2015).

Bureau of Indian Affairs, Office of Justice Services. 2012a. 'Crime reduction best practices handbook: Making Indian communities safe.' *US Department of the Interior*. Online: www.bia.gov/cs/groups/xojs/documents/text/idc-018678.pdf (accessed: 18 May 2015).

Bureau of Indian Affairs, Office of Justice Services. 2012b. *Reducing Crime in Indian Country through Analytics,* video. Online: www.youtube.com/watch?v=agSi5AK2oWs (accessed 8 May 2015).

Centers for Medicare & Medicaid Services. 2015. *US Government*. Online: partnershipforpatients.cms.gov/ (accessed 4 June 2015).

Chavez, Yolanda. 2013. 'Reduce vacancy rates.' Performance.gov. Online: archive-goals.performance.gov/goal_detail/HUD/416 (accessed 15 June 2015).

'Clear goals: Using goals to improve performance and accountability.' n.d. Performance.gov. Online: archive-goals.performance.gov/goals_2013 (accessed 18 May 2015).

Cobert, Beth. 2015. 'Infrastructure permitting modernization.' *Performance*.gov. Online: www.performance.gov/node/3393/view?view=public#progress-update (accessed 15 June 2015).

'Cross agency priority goals: exports. FY2013 Q4 Status Update.' n.d. Performance.gov. Online: archive-goals.performance.gov/sites/default/files/images/Exports_CAP_Goal_FY2013_Q4_Update.pdf (accessed 18 May 2015).

'Cross-agency priority goals.' n.d. Performance.gov. Online: www.performance.gov/cap-goals-list?view=public (accessed 15 June 2015).

Delisle, Deborah. 2013. 'Demonstrate progress in turning around nation's lowest-performing schools.' Performance.gov. Online: archive-goals.performance.gov/goal_detail/ED/354#eoa (accessed 4 June 2015).

'Delivery a High-Performing Government.' 2013. *Performance.gov*. Online: archive-goals.performance.gov/ (accessed 15 June 2015).

Department of the Interior. 2013. 'Increase the approved capacity for production of energy from domestic renewable resources to support a growing economy and protect our national interests while reducing our dependence on foreign oil and climate-changing greenhouse gas emissions.' Performance.gov. Online: archive-goals.performance.gov/goal_detail/DOI/379 (accessed 15 May 2015).

Executive Session on Public Sector Performance Management, to New Government Executives. n.d. 'Get results through performance management.' Harvard University, Kennedy School of Government. Online: www.innovations.harvard.edu/sites/default/files/7100.pdf (accessed 8 May 2015).

Friedman, David. 2013. 'Reduce the rate of roadway fatalities.' Performance.gov. Online: archive-goals.performance.gov/goal_detail/DOT/348 (accessed 18 May 2015).

Gannon, Anne. 2013. 'Protect those most in need of help – with special emphasis on child exploitation and civil rights.' Performance.gov. Online: archive-goals.performance.gov/goal_detail/DOJ/421 (accessed 15 June 2015).

Gillian, Margaret. 2013. 'Reduce risk of aviation accidents.' Performance.gov. Online: archive-goals.performance.gov/goal_detail/DOT/349 (accessed 18 May 2015).

Godown, Jeff. 2015. 'The *CompStat* process: Four principles of managing crime reduction.' *The Police Chief: The Professional Voice of Law Enforcement*. April. Online: www.policechiefmagazine.org/magazine/index.cfm?fuseaction=display&article_id=1859&issue_id=82009#2 (accessed 8 May 2015).

Golding, Bruce. 2014. 'Bratton: Kelley's stop-and-frisk caused minorities to fear cops.' *New York Post*. Online: nypost.com/2014/12/08/bratton-kellys-stop-and-frisk-caused-minorities-to-fear-cops/ (accessed 15 June 2015).

Gregg, Richard. 2013. 'Increase electronic transactions with the public to improve service, prevent fraud, and reduce costs.' *Performance.gov*. Online: archive-goals.performance.gov/goal_detail/TREAS/335 (accessed 18 May 2015).

Henry, Vincent E. n.d. Compstat *Management in the NYPD: Reducing Crime and Improving Quality of Life in New York City*. Online: www.unafei.or.jp/english/pdf/RS_No68/No68_11VE_Henry1.pdf (accessed 8 May 2015).

Horst, Adam M. 2005. 'Performance measurement and budgeting in Indiana.' Online: www.nga.org/files/live/sites/NGA/files/ppt/CJISHorst.ppt;jsessionid=3EFFB43F98B218106064D35CCF0C44CE (accessed 15 June 2015).

HUDSTAT. ca 2011. Performance.gov. Online: archive-goals.performance.gov/hudstat (accessed 8 May 2015).

HUDSTAT. 'Using data to understand the problem to be solved: Where are these homeless veterans located?'. Performance.gov. Online: archive-goals.performance.gov/hudstat (accessed 17 June 2015).

James, Colin. 1998. 'The state ten years on from the reforms.' *Leading a State Sector New Zealand is Proud of*, Occasional Paper No. 6, State Services Commission Te Komihana O Ngā Tari Kāwanatanga. October. Online: www.ssc.govt.nz/display/document.asp?NavID=82&DocID=2834 (accessed 8 May 2015).

Kelman, Steven and John N. Friedman. 2009. 'Performance improvement and performance dysfunction: An empirical examination of distortionary impacts of the emergency room wait-time target in the English National Health Service.' *Journal of Public Administration Research and Theory* 19(4): 917–46.

Kelman, Steven. 2006. 'Improving service delivery performance in the United Kingdom: Organization theory perspectives on central intervention strategies.' *Journal of Comparative Policy Analysis* 8(4): 393–419.

Kolluri, Lopa. 2013. 'Preserve affordable rental housing.' Performance.gov. Online: archive-goals.performance.gov/goal_detail/HUD/376 (accessed 18 May 2015).

Kornze, Neil. n.d. 'Renewable energy resource development.' Performance.gov. Online: www.performance.gov/node/382?view=public#indicators (accessed 18 May 2015).

Kriegerm, Matthew. 2005. 'Washington State Governor Chris Gregoire's Government Management Accountability and Performance Program.' *2005 NASCIO Recognition Awards Nomination Program*. Online: www.nascio.org/awards/nominations/2006Washington2.pdf (accessed 15 June 2015).

Lapin, Andrew. 2012. 'Senators express frustration over OPM backlog of retirement claims.' *Government Executive*. Online: www.govexec.com/pay-benefits/2012/02/senators-express-frustration-over-opm-backlog-retirement-claims/41108/ (accessed 15 June 2015).

Lavertu, Stéphane, David Lewis and Donald Moynihan. 2013. 'Government reform, political ideology, and administrative burden: The case of performance management in the Bush administration.' *Public Administration Review* (PAR) 73(6) (November/December): 845–57.

Lunney, Kellie. 2013. *Crime Scene: A Federal Program Reduced Violent Crime on Four Indian Reservations. Now Comes the Hard Part*, Government Executive. Online: www.govexec.com/feature/crime-scene-feature/ (accessed 8 May 2015).

Maddox, John. n.d. *United States Government Status Report*. Online: www-esv.nhtsa.dot.gov/Proceedings/22/files/22ESV-000465.pdf (accessed 15 June 2015).

Maple, Jack and Chris Mitchell. 1999. *The Crime Fighter: Putting the Bad Guys out of Business*. New York: Doubleday.

Metzenbaum, Shelley H. 2002. 'Measurement that matters: Cleaning up the Charles River,' in *Environmental Governance: A Report on the Next Generation of Environmental Policy*, ed. Donald F. Kettl. Washington, DC: Brookings Institution Press, 58–117.

Metzenbaum, Shelley H. 2003. *Strategies for Using State Information: Measuring and Improving Program Performance*. Washington DC: IBM Center for the Business of Government. Reprinted in *Managing for Results 2005*, ed. John M. Kamensky and Albert Morales. Lanham, MD: Rowman & Littlefield, 277–344.

Metzenbaum, Shelley H. 2006. *Performance Accountability: The Five Building Blocks and Six Essential Practices*. IBM Center for the Business of Government. Online: www.businessofgovernment.org/sites/default/files/Performance%20Accountability.pdf (accessed 8 May 2015).

Metzenbaum, Shelley H. 2007. 'Can environmental agencies make better use of accident, incident, and inspection information,' in *Ecostates* (Spring): 42–44.

Metzenbaum, Shelley H. 2008. 'From oversight to insight: Federal agencies as learning leaders in the information age,' in *Intergovernmental Management for the 21st Century*, ed. Paul Posner and Timothy Conlan. Washington, DC: Brookings Institution Press, 209–42.

Metzenbaum, Shelley H. 2009. *Performance Management Recommendations for the New Administration*. IBM Center for the Business of Government. Online: www.businessofgovernment.org/sites/default/files/Performance Management.pdf (accessed 8 May 2015).

Metzenbaum, Shelley. 2010. 'Performance improvement guidance: Management responsibilities and government performance and results act documents.' Memorandum. Executive Office of the President: Office of Management and Budget. 25 June. Online: www.whitehouse.gov/sites/default/files/omb/assets/memoranda_2010/m10-24.pdf (accessed 15 May 2015).

Mills, Ann. 2013. *USDA's High Priority Performance Goal for Water*. Online: www.nrcs.usda.gov/Internet/FSE_DOCUMENTS/stelprdb1101671.pdf (accessed 18 May 2015).

Nagy, Andrea R. and Joel Podolny. 2008. 'William Bratton and the NYPD: Crime control through middle management reform.' *Yale School of Management*. 12 February. Online: som.yale.edu/sites/default/files/files/Case_Bratton_2nd_ed_Final_and_Complete.pdf (accessed 15 June 2015).

News Releases from Region 1, 'Charles River 2013 report card reflects cleanest water in decades.' 2014. *EPA: United States Environmental Protection Agency*. Online: yosemite.epa.gov/opa/admpress. nsf/6d651d23f5a91b768525735900400c28/473e88ce3d5353a 485257d48005a4ea0!OpenDocument (accessed 9 May 2015).

Office of Management and Budget. 2010. 'Analytical perspectives: Budget of the U.S. Government.' Online: www.gpo.gov/fdsys/pkg/BUDGET-2011-PER/ pdf/BUDGET-2011-PER.pdf (accessed 15 May 2015).

Office of Management and Budget. 2013. 'Analytical perspectives: Budget of the U.S. Government.' Online: www.whitehouse.gov/sites/default/files/omb/ budget/fy2013/assets/spec.pdf (accessed 15 June 2015).

Office of Management and Budget. 2013. 'Strategic plans, annual performance plans, performance reviews, and annual program performance reports.' Circular No. A–11 Part 6. Online: www.whitehouse.gov/sites/default/files/ omb/performance/a-11_part-6_2013.pdf (accessed 18 May 2015).

Office of Personnel Management. 2015. 'Projected/Actual CSRS/FERS new claims, processed, and inventory.' Online: www.opm.gov/about-us/budget-performance/strategic-plans/retirement-processing-status.pdf (accessed 15 June 2015).

Patton, Zach. 2006. 'Persuasive performance.' *Governing: The States and Localities*. Online: www.governing.com/topics/mgmt/Persuasive-Performance.html (accessed 15 June 2015).

Poticha, Shelley. 2013. 'Retrofitting for families' – and the planet's – future.' Performance.gov. Online: archive-goals.performance.gov/videos-and-feature-stories/retrofitting-families%E2%80%99-%E2%80%93-and-planet%E2%80%99s-%E2%80%93-future (accessed 18 May 2015).

Rea, Teresa. 2013. 'Advance commercialization of new technologies by reducing patent pendency and backlog.' Performance.gov. Online: archive-goals. performance.gov/goal_detail/DOC/338 (access 18 May 2015).

'Region 1. EPA New England. Charles River Report Cards.' 2014, *EPA: United States Environmental Protection Agency*. Online: www.epa.gov/region1/charles/reportcards.html (accessed 9 May 2015).

Rose, Joel. 2014. 'Top NYPD cop: Stop-and-frisk is not 'the problem or the solution.' *NPR*. 3 June. Online: www.npr.org/2014/07/03/328120358/top-nypd-cop-stop-and-frisk-is-not-the-problem-or-the-solution (accessed 15 June 2015).

Rubens, Diana. 2013. 'Improve accuracy and reduce the amount of time it takes to process Veterans' disability benefit claims.' Online: archive-goals.performance.gov/goal_detail/VA/334 (accessed 18 May 2015).

Scott, Esther. 2002. 'Mayor Anthony Williams and performance management in Washington, DC.' *Harvard Kennedy School: John F. Kennedy School of Government*. Online: www.case.hks.harvard.edu/casetitle.asp?caseno=1647.0 (accessed 15 June 2015).

Sikes, Joseph. 2013. 'Improve energy performance.' Agency Priority Goals. *Department of Defense*. Online: archive-goals.performance.gov/goal_detail/DOD/408 (accessed 18 May 2015).

Sleet, David. 2011. 'Injury prevention, violence prevention, and trauma care: Building the scientific base.' *Centers for Disease Control and Prevention*. Online: www.cdc.gov/mmwr/preview/mmwrhtml/su6004a13.htm (accessed 15 June 2015).

Smith, Dennis C. with William Bratton. 2001. 'Performance management in New York City: *CompStat* and revolution in police management,' in *Quicker, Better, Cheaper? Managing Performance in American Government*, ed. Dall W. Forsyth. Albany, NY: Rockefeller Institute Press, 453–82.

Snyder, Roy. 2013. 'Increase use of our online services.' Performance.gov. Online: archive-goals.performance.gov/goal_detail/SSA/359 (accessed 4 June 2015).

Tavenner, Marilyn. 2013. 'Improve patient safety.' Online: archive-goals.performance.gov/goal_detail/HHS/375 (accessed 18 May 2015).

'The home of the US. Government's Open Data.' n.d., *DATA-GOV*. Online: data.gov (accessed 9 May 2015).

'Urban waters – The Charles River.' n.d. *EPA: United States Environmental Protection Agency*. Online: www.epa.gov/region1/charles/reportcards.html (accessed 15 June 2015).

US Department of Commerce, 2011, *Citizens' Report: Summary of Performance and Financial Results, Fiscal Year 2011*. Online: www.osec.doc.gov/bmi/ budget/DOCCitizensReport2011_021512.pdf (accessed 8 May 2015).

US Department of Commerce, *FY 2013 Summary of Performance and Financial Information*. Online: www.osec.doc.gov/bmi/budget/ DOCSummaryPerformancePlan_508_2013.pdf (accessed 8 May 2015).

US Department of the Interior. 2012. 'Annual performance plan & 2011 report.' *Report*. Online: www.doi.gov/bpp/upload/FY2012-2013-Annual-Performance-Plan-and-FY2011-Report.pdf (accessed 18 May 2015).

US Department of the Interior. 2013. 'Increase the approved capacity for production of energy from domestic renewable resources to support a growing economy and protect our national interests while reducing our dependence on foreign oil and climate-changing greenhouse gas emissions.' Agency Priority Goals. Performance.gov. Online: www.goals.performance. gov/goal_detail/DOI/379 (accessed 18 May 2015).

United States Coast Guard. 2010. *United States Coast Guard Fiscal Year 2009 Performance Report*. Online: www.uscg.mil/budget/docs/CG_FY2009_ Performance_Report.pdf (accessed 15 June 2015).

United States Coast Guard. 2014. *Performance Measures and Targets*. Online: www.uscg.mil/hq/cg5/cg531/LMR/OceanG/OG_AppD.pdf (accessed 15 June 2015).

United States Coast Guard. n.d. *National Maritime Center Performance & Analysis*. Online: www.uscg.mil/nmc/reports/ (accessed 15 June 2015).

United States Department of Labor. n.d. *CLEAR: Clearing House for Labor Evaluation and Research*. Online: clear.dol.gov (accessed 9 May 2015).

United States Environmental Protection Agency. 'Urban waters: The Charles River.' Online: www.epa.gov/region1/charles/reportcards.html (accessed 1 August 2015).

'Using goals to improve performance and accountability.' Performance.gov. Online: archive-goals.performance.gov/goals_2013 (accessed June 2015).

Utech, Dan. 2013. 'Increase energy productivity ($ GDP/energy demand) 50% by 2030.' Performance.gov. Online: archive-goals.performance.gov/ sites/default/files/images/Energy_Efficiency_CAPG_FY2013_Quarter_4_ Update_2013_12_19_final.pdf (accessed 18 May 2015).

'Virginia Performs.' 2015. *Virginia.gov*. Online: vaperforms.virginia.gov/ (accessed 15 June 2015).

Wagner, Roberta. 2015. 'Reduce foodborne illnesses in the population.' Performance.gov. Online: archive-goals.performance.gov/goal_detail/ HHS/372#details (accessed 4 June 2015).

Washburn, Kenneth. 2013. 'Reduce violent crime in Indian communities.' Agency Priority Goals. Performance.gov. US Department of the Interior. Online: www.goals.performance.gov/goal_detail/doi/381 (accessed 18 May 2015).

Washington State Office of the Governor. 2004. 'Governor Locke: Improve.' Online: www.digitalarchives.wa.gov/GovernorLocke/improve/improve.htm (accessed 15 June 2015).

White House Office of Science & Technology Policy. 2014. 'Fact sheet: White House safety datapalooza.' Online: www.whitehouse.gov/sites/default/files/ microsites/ostp/safety_datapalooza_factsheet_jan-2014.pdf (accessed 25 June 2015).

Winkler, Mary Kopczynski. 2001. 'Grading the D.C. scorecard commentary.' *Urban Institute: Elevate the Debate*. Online: www.urban.org/publications/900444. html (accessed 15 June 2015).

Zawodny, Jr., Kenneth. 2013a. 'Reduce Federal retirement processing time.' Performance.gov. Online: archive-goals.performance.gov/goal_detail/ OPM/392 (accessed 15 June 2015).

Zawodny, Jr., Kenneth. 2013b. 'PG1 Retirement claims processing improvements.' Online: www.opm.gov/about-us/budget-performance/strategic-plans/ retirement-processing-status.pdf (accessed 15 June 2015).

Zawodny, Jr., Kenneth. n.d. 'PG1 Retirement claims processing improvements.' Performance.gov. Online: www.performance.gov/ node/408?view=public#indicators (accessed 15 June 2015).

5

PERFORMANCE MANAGEMENT: CREATING HIGH PERFORMANCE, NOT HIGH ANXIETY

Deborah Blackman
University of New South Wales, Canberra

Fiona Buick
University of Canberra

Damian West
Australian Public Service Commission

Michael O'Donnell
University of New South Wales, Canberra

Janine O'Flynn
University of Melbourne

Anxiety about the evaluation of performance in the Australian Public Service (APS) affects both supervisors and those being assessed. We will explore some of the reasons for this anxiety, how it affects these organisations and the gap between the ideal of performance management and the more complex reality of practice. Our research suggests that we need a substantial change in the way we think about performance management conceptually and the way in which it should be implemented across the APS.

We believe that performance management systems could be reoriented to enable *high* performance across individual, group, organisation and system levels, rather than following a more typical focus on *under*performance. The preoccupation with underperformance in practice has, we argue, contributed to performance management being used as a pejorative term—something that is 'done to me', something I am going to 'do' to people, which leads to higher levels of anxiety in both employees and managers (see Kahneman and Tversky 1979 in Alford and O'Flynn 2012, 78; de Vos et al. 2003). Instead we will argue that by framing performance management as being about the more positive notion of high performance, we can reduce the associated anxiety.

Performance anxiety emerges when an individual is concerned about something to do with their employment and this affects the way that they perform. In an ideal situation, performance management systems are focused on encouraging high performance and supporting innovation through setting clear goals and identifying learning and development needs. This enables individuals to undertake more challenging work, thereby increasing the capacity of a workforce and reducing anxiety. However, in practice the processes involved in performance management systems could, in themselves, create anxiety.

The tensions between these points are important as they reflect the promise and pitfalls of performance management systems, enabling us to discuss the source of performance anxiety in organisations. We observed several sources of anxiety, including a lack of clear performance expectations, over-measurement, and a focus on process compliance rather than outcomes.

In the first part of this chapter we outline our research project,[1] explaining how it was established and the aims. In the second part we set out the data collection processes. The third part explains the reconceptualisation of performance management which developed from the project. In the fourth part we set out the key elements of the new performance management framework the project team developed, explaining how these can be used to manage and, potentially, reduce performance anxiety. In the final part we make the case that focusing on high performance and aligning individual and organisational goals can reduce anxiety and increase innovation in practice.

Why this project?

The project developed as part of the implementation of the *Ahead of the Game: Blueprint for Reform of Australian Government Administration* (AGRAGA 2010) report. The Blueprint set out a program of reforms, including attention to strengthening the performance framework and developing more collaborative relationships between academic and practitioner experts. A key driver for

---

1   This chapter is based upon a partnership between The Australian National University, the Australian Public Service Commission, the University of Canberra and the University of New South Wales, Canberra, which led to a new performance framework for the Australian Public Service. A partnership approach was seen as important to enable the partners to learn from each other and develop strong links between theory and practice. The three-year time frame enabled deep exploration of the literature, rigorous data collection and analysis, and ongoing interaction between academics and practitioners to develop a framework with practical implications.

the focus on performance management was emerging evidence—from both Australian Public Service Commission (APSC) (2012) research and scholarly literature (Grumana and Saks 2011; Truss et al. 2013)—linking notions of employee engagement with performance.

The APSC (2012), through its Employee Census (n=87,214), identified that performance management has a substantial influence on employee engagement. It observed a relationship between employees receiving quality feedback and other forms of support, including coaching on the one hand, and higher engagement, commitment and performance levels on the other. In Figures 5.1 and 5.2, the graph on the top shows that higher performance is associated with simply receiving feedback; the graph on the bottom demonstrates that higher engagement is achieved by receiving feedback that the employee views as positive or constructive (see APSC 2012a).

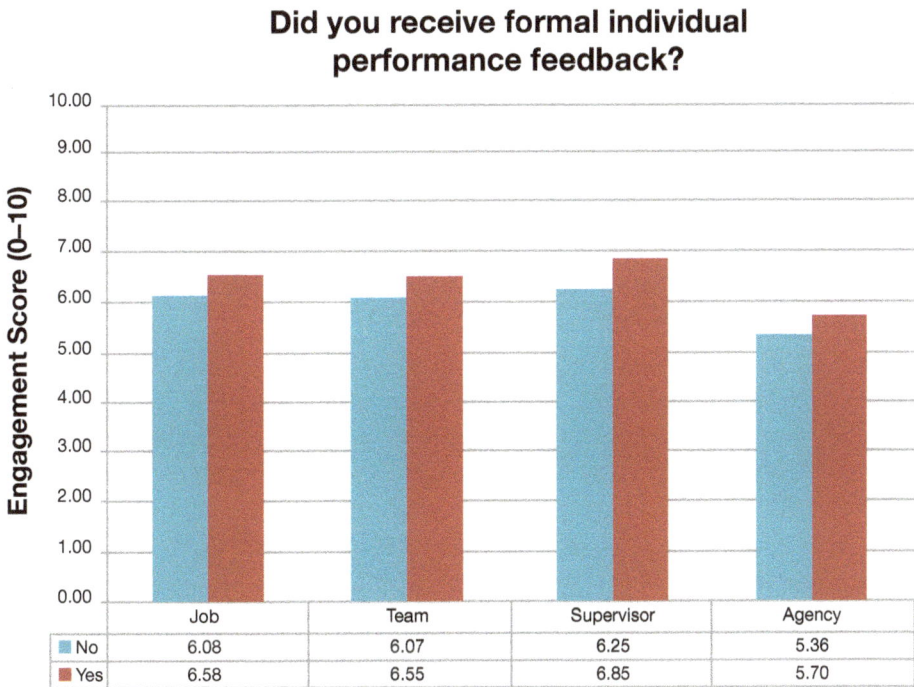

Did you receive formal individual performance feedback?

	Job	Team	Supervisor	Agency
No	6.08	6.07	6.25	5.36
Yes	6.58	6.55	6.85	5.70

Figure 5.1. Responses on performance feedback

Source: *State of the Service Report* (APSC 2012a).

Do you agree that is was useful?

	Job	Team	Supervisor	Agency
Str Agree	7.93	7.85	8.48	7.03
Agree	7.14	7.11	7.54	6.26
Neither	6.25	6.24	6.46	5.38
Disagree	5.49	5.47	5.45	4.62
Str Disagree	4.65	4.57	4.49	3.83

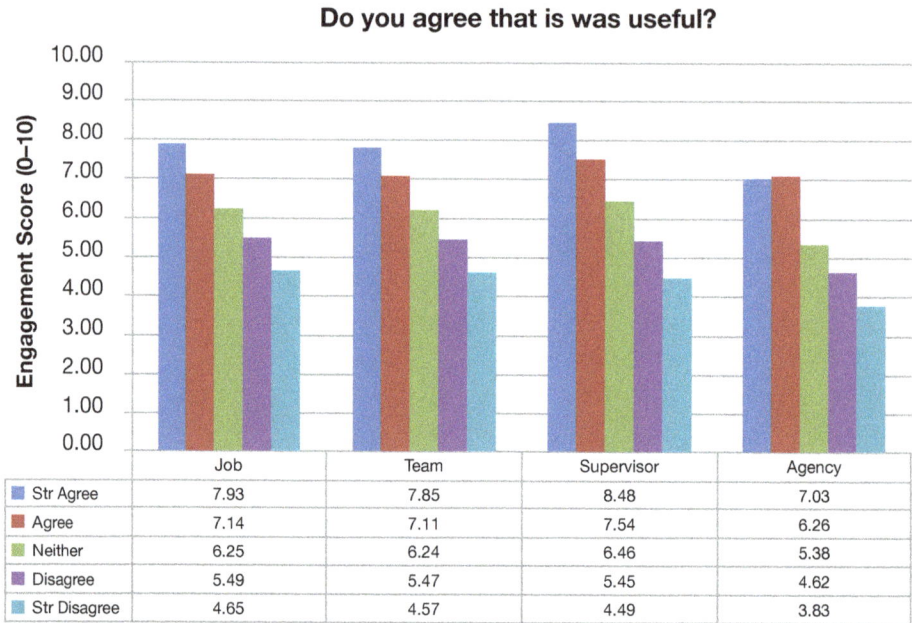

Figure 5.2. Responses on performance feedback

Source: *State of the Service Report* (APSC 2012a).

Findings from the Employee Census also emphasised the need for employees to receive feedback and support, with the return being greater engagement, performance and intention to stay (APSC 2012a).

These findings support those in the scholarly literature which illustrate the relationship between human resource systems and practices more broadly (beyond simple performance management), and employee engagement and performance (Alfes et al. 2013; Barbier et al. 2013). For example, some have found that trust felt by the employee in the organisation mediates the link between Human Resources (HR) practices and organisational performance (Patel et al. 2013; Mone et al. 2011). This highlights the importance of a productive employee–supervisor relationship and the provision of fair, regular and quality feedback, as these both affect and are affected by trust. Unfortunately, performance management is a tool that is not being used effectively for achieving productivity and performance gains in the APS, as demonstrated by ongoing reports that identify long-standing problems with the way performance is being managed (Blackman et al. 2012; Cheng et al. 2007; GAO 2004).

Research undertaken by the APSC and other organisations demonstrates that performance management is a long-standing issue for the APS (see, for example, ANAO 2004; APSC 2012a). The majority of organisations require all employees to have a performance agreement and most employees report receiving some form of performance feedback over the annual performance management cycle. Unfortunately, fewer than half of them report that this feedback will help improve their performance (see Figure 5.3).

Questions	2009–10	2010–11	2011–12
Agencies require employees to have performance agreement	93%	90%	92%
Employees receive formal performance feedback	88%	88%	79%
HOWEVER ...			
Percentage of employees who agreed that most recent performance review would help them improve their performance	51%	50%	48%
Percentage of employees who agreed that their agency deals effectively with underperformance	24%	23%	21%

Figure 5.3. *State of the Service Report* findings regarding performance management
Source: *State of the Service Report* (APSC 2012a).

This is one of the most concerning statistics for the APSC, particularly when other research identifies that most managers—there are between 30,000 and 40,000 in the APS—rate their own performance management abilities quite highly, but most employees rate their managers' ability to undertake effective performance management as quite low:

> The 2012 employee census showed that 80% of managers said they were confident in managing the performance of others. This is in sharp contrast to the virtually 80% of APS employees who did not respond positively when asked if they perceived their agency manages underperformance well. Managers who said they were not confident in managing performance agreed they would be helped through access to training on performance management (51%), improved guidelines on the performance management process (46%) and improved access to advice within their agency (51%) (APSC 2012a, 193).

Another issue which emerges in research undertaken by the APSC is the inconsistent implementation of performance management across the APS. The percentage of employees who report receiving feedback varied from just over 10 per cent to approximately 96 per cent. The variable implementation of performance management may be explained by additional research that demonstrates variability in managers' spans of control (i.e. the number of people they have to manage). This research demonstrates that the wider a manager's span of control, the more likely that they will report not having enough time to manage performance (see Figure 5.4).

I do not have sufficient time to manage the performance of employees

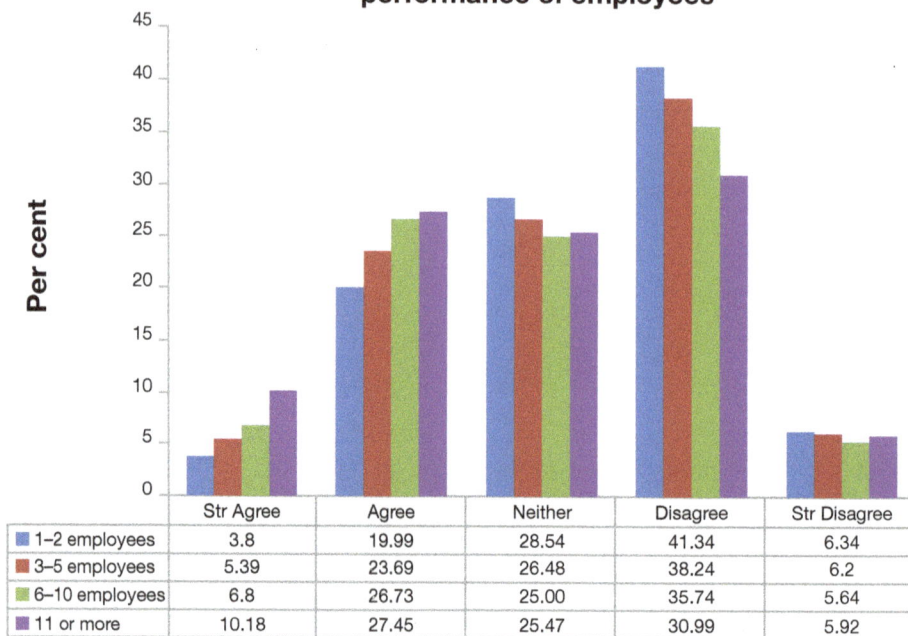

	Str Agree	Agree	Neither	Disagree	Str Disagree
1–2 employees	3.8	19.99	28.54	41.34	6.34
3–5 employees	5.39	23.69	26.48	38.24	6.2
6–10 employees	6.8	26.73	25.00	35.74	5.64
11 or more	10.18	27.45	25.47	30.99	5.92

Figure 5.4. Management responses to time availability for performance management

Source: APSC 2012b.

The APSC has recently completed 20 capability reviews of large APS organisations (APSC 2013), and its results reaffirm findings from the survey research discussed earlier. It is becoming clear that the implementation—not the design—of performance management systems is the critical problem. While many of the processes reflect current good practice, the implementation stage is where the promise of performance management dissipates. Here is the crux of the performance anxiety issue: many employees are not concerned about performance management *per se*, but rather the implementation of these systems, which creates uncertainty, confusion and stress. All of these have the potential to create anxiety around performance management practices and reduce their efficacy in organisations.

The issues discussed above led to three critical questions for the APSC in thinking about how to create an effective performance management framework and encourage a high performance culture:

1. Is people management valued appropriately if insufficient time is devoted to it?

2. Is performance management a managerial capability issue?

3. Is the potential of performance management more of a reflection of the way that management work is structured, rather than the competence of the individual manager?

These questions on performance management and engagement provided the impetus for the 'Strengthening the Performance Framework' project. To answer them, a team of practitioners and academics was formed. The team was to develop a new research foundation for performance management that would focus on developing high performance and implementing processes and procedures effectively. If a new perspective could be developed which would change the accepted norms in place, performance should improve and anxiety reduce. The co-production model was adopted in order to trigger innovation; since the more traditional models of consultancy had not delivered novelty, the research model itself needed to be different.

Revisiting the theory: Developing a new conceptual model of high performance

The first stage of this project was an in-depth review of the general performance management literature, with a specific focus on the high performance organisation, individual and work systems literature. We also looked at current practice in the Canadian Public Service, the United States Federal Public Service and reviewed studies undertaken by the Organisation for Economic Cooperation and Development (OECD) to establish what was happening globally.

We noted that the majority of the focus in the performance management literature is on the individual, with organisational performance as a secondary concern. There was fairly little literature that substantively considered these two levels of performance in a meaningful way and there was nothing (that we could identify) which then linked this more broadly to the overall system performance. Our first proposition was, therefore, that performance management needed to be reconceptualised as a four-tier model, with HR practices being used at each level to achieve high performance outcomes (see Figure 5.5).

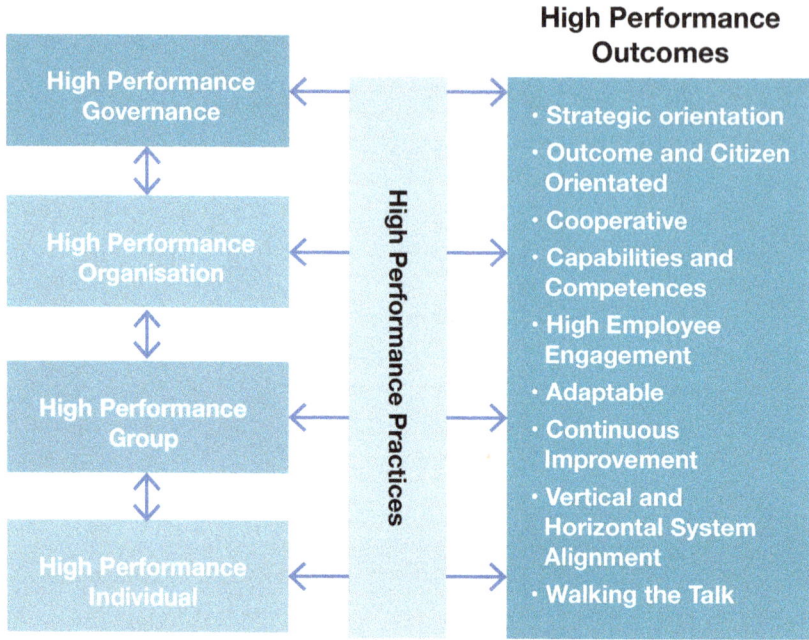

Figure 5.5. Achieving high performance outcomes through four levels of performance

Source: Blackman et al. 2012, 8.

The first level of our model is the *individual*, who is usually the focus of any conversation—we always talk about individual performance management, about agreements, about measurement. However, we considered that perhaps the gap between apparently good process and poor outcomes was related to the levels of analysis (for more details on this section of the work please see Blackman et al. 2012). We were struck by an example of a US organisation where everybody got a rating of 4 or 5 out of 5 for their individual performance agreement, yet the organisation was not achieving its outcomes. This confirmed that focusing solely on the individual is not a magic bullet for performance. In the US case it was apparent that there needed to be a clearer link between the individual goals and tasks, and the organisational imperatives; thus, the organisation became another level of the framework to ensure that there would be consideration of alignment.

The second level of the model was confirmed and clarified as we conducted the empirical research. The literature stresses the importance of teams and the relationships between rewards and team outcomes, but there is very little literature about performance management of groups more generally. It became increasingly clear that the *group* level is an important mediating factor between the individual and their organisation, even when an individual's work was not reliant upon other members of the group. So the second element of the model emerged as requiring performance to be at least harmonious with, and preferably supportive of, the group level.

The third level is that of the *organisation*. In the literature there are key outcomes that can be identified with high-performing organisations (Blackman et al. 2012). The performance management system needs to be designed (in conjunction with other HR practices) to enable the alignment of individual with organisational goals in order to achieve those goals. This is because the stated organisational outcomes and the ways they are to be measured will have a strong impact on performance management outcomes.

The fourth level—which we did not find in the literature—is about high performance *governance*. This links to ideas discussed by Glyn Davis in the Australia and New Zealand School of Government's (ANZSOG) Paterson Oration on 6 August 2013, when he raised the impact of the Dawkins Report: the related change in governance structure had a huge impact on all the universities because it changed the overarching system in which they worked. A high performance governance system is aimed at setting the system-wide architecture which enables high performance across a whole system, such as the public service. One reason for performance systems failing is that there are systemic issues inhibiting the changes needed for effective implementation. When governance is conceived of in this way, the orchestration of connections and actions between multiple actors becomes central.

The development of the four-tiered model highlighted several possible areas which could create performance anxiety. These include a mismatch of expectations between the individual and the organisation; tensions created within a group when performance systems are seen as unfair or creating competition within teams; structures which prevent performance from having the desired effect; or systems which either prevent the levels working together or create actual tension between them.

There is substantial literature about high performance work practices (see Becker and Gerhart 1996; Bullera and McEvoy 2012; de Waal 2012; Huselid 1995; Sung and Ashton 2005), almost all of which is targeted at the individual, despite being apparently relevant to the organisation. While there is some focus on the organisational level, most of the high performance work practices are geared toward establishing targets for the individuals in the expectation that they will change the organisation. This seems rather hit-and-miss, leading the research team to argue for something a bit more focused—this might be where performance management implementation was failing.

Faced with areas of potential performance anxiety, poor implementation and lack of system coherence, the researchers set out to consider empirically what could be done to support high performance in an ongoing way.

Data collection

The team undertook seven case studies. These were selected to ensure a range of small, medium and large organisations, as well as varying degrees of performance management effectiveness (according to *State of the Service Report* data; see APSC 2012a).

In case study research, multiple sources of evidence are collected (Yin 2003) to gain a deeper understanding of the studied phenomenon. This study employed semi-structured interviews to ensure consistency across interviews as well as adherence to the areas of interest, but still allow for sufficient flexibility for the participant to respond (Bryman 2004). Ninety participants were interviewed between August and November 2012. Exploratory focus groups (Dahlin-Ivanoff and Hultberg 2006) were also conducted, with 136 participants taking part in 22 discussions.

Interview and focus group participants were selected through a stratified purposive sampling technique, which involved the selection of participants from particular subgroups of interest ('strata') that were fairly homogenous. This facilitated comparisons across groups, enabling the researchers to capture variations and commonalities (Patton 1990). Invitations were sent to public servants within each case study based on their hierarchical level (senior manager, middle manager, operational staff) and geographical location (national office, selected state and regional offices). This led to an overall sample of 226 participants (see Table 3). Seventy-one were employees at the operational level, 113 at the middle management level, and 42 at the senior management level.

The primary qualitative data were complemented by:

* documentary analysis from agency reports and information about government processes;
* analysis of secondary data from the SOSR reports undertaken by the APSC; and
* an analysis of international systems gathered though interviews undertaken with senior government, ex-practitioner, think tank and international organisation officials in Washington (World Bank; IBM Center for the Business of Government), Ottawa and Paris (OECD) in 2012. All those interviewed were involved with advising on, developing and/or implementing performance

management policy and systems in public sector organisations. The objective was to establish global trends, good practice and challenges.

Empirical findings: What is going on in practice?

What is high performance?

One of the most important findings was the lack of shared understanding of what constituted high performance within organisations. When we coded our data, we could identify 125 different definitions of what high performance meant, with remarkably little agreement within or across organisations. Often during the interviews, we asked participants: 'Do you have conversations about what high performance in your organisation looks like if it is working?' 'No' was a common response. Many participants reported a focus on problems but limited attention on what denoted high performance in their individual, group or organisational setting.

So why does that matter? This lack of clarity about what high performance is has implications for performance measurement, evaluation and anxiety. It severely impedes the ability to establish clear performance expectations and this flows through to important aspects of performance systems, such as rating schemes. In our research, we found that people didn't know what was required to achieve high ratings, what differentiated the levels in the ratings scheme and how decisions were made regarding the allocation of ratings. The practice of performance management, therefore, resulted in considerable levels of performance anxiety amongst employees. For example: 'I'm given a 3 or a 4 but it's not clear to me why I'm a 3 or a 4. It's not effectively communicated to me how I become a 5'; and, 'I've had different ratings throughout time even though I've done nothing different'.

This lack of clarity extended beyond the individual to groups where, in some cases, generic performance agreements were put in place. We found instances where whole sections (groups) had identical agreements, because that was the approach their manager preferred. We also found instances where job descriptions were essentially 'cut and pasted' into the performance agreement. We argue that both of these examples, neither of which is an isolated incident, reflect a 'compliance' approach in practice: although the forms were completed on time and could be reported as an operational success, they were unlikely to lead to meaningful discussions or improvements in performance. Practices such as these create performance anxiety for both those completing the agreements and those undertaking the performance management discussions.

According to participants, anxiety also emerged because those involved did not feel equipped to undertake the process effectively. The reasons for this, which interviewees all thought were linked to the lack of clarity about high performance and/or clarity of desired outcomes, included:

- Supervisors were not sure how to rate employee performance, leading to tensions around the measurement systems.
- Capability of employees and managers to undertake effective performance management was low because nobody was sure what high performance meant at all levels of the model.
- Evaluation was difficult with no clarity regarding desired outcomes.
- Innovation was difficult, because the focus was on *tasks* and measuring the task as it was listed in the agreement.
- Performance agreements might, but often did not, link to the required outcomes.

Our empirical work also shed light on the narrowness of what constitutes performance management: there is an overemphasis on performance agreement writing and appraisals as a compliance exercise, but a lack of integration between performance management activities and other people management activities, such as recruitment, selection, probation and development. There is also a lack of integration more substantially into the other levels of the conceptual framework we developed—from individual to group to organisation to system. Hence, our identification of *role clarity* as being crucial for articulation and management of expectations. We argue that this is one of the critical aspects of performance management and a key driver for high performance (see Blackman et al. 2013).

The role of informal feedback

Despite initial assessments of performance management effectiveness at the organisational level implying that we should find better practices in some cases, the empirical work showed that both good and poor practice occurred in all the case study organisations. This was very much in evidence when considering the disconnection between managers' and employees' perceptions of informal feedback.

The importance of regular (often informal) feedback was widely discussed. Participants often focused on the importance of the informal conversations between managers and employees about various facets of the employee's work, what was required of them, how they were going and the provision of feedback on specific tasks. Interviewees emphasised how much this ongoing feedback helped to guide employees' on-the-job behaviour. Said one senior manager:

I think when [performance is] managed well there's no surprises for the individual, they understand how they're tracking because it's not waiting until a six-month performance cycle to tell them that they're not achieving whatever goal or benchmark they're expected to perform at.

Many managers claimed to provide employees with informal feedback on a regular basis, yet employees often did not appear to recognise informal conversations as a form of feedback. This led to the perception amongst some employees that they were *not* provided with regular feedback. A positive example came from one manager we interviewed, who was cited as an example of achieving good practice by several other interviewees. When a new employee arrived, this manager established what the desired group outcomes were, discussed them with the employee's group and changed the work patterns for all group members so that the right people were undertaking the right work and every employee was learning and growing. In this case they were receiving clear feedback, which they recognised, with no mismatch emerging between the manager's perception and that of the employees. This demonstrates the need to align the different levels of the model.

This type of practice was quite rare, despite general agreement that increased levels of informal feedback could reduce anxiety and increase high performance. The research highlighted the importance of informal performance conversations (rather than compliance activity), which provide timely and ongoing feedback and can link together the various levels of performance management.

Performance management is hard

The majority of participants, regardless of hierarchical position, thought that performance management offered great potential for organisational improvement and high performance. However, we found that for the most part it has developed into a largely negative, value-laden term, synonymous with 'underperformance' management. Many managers did not consider that performance management was core to their roles and found that it was overly time-consuming. This was partly because performance management was seen as something that was hard, involving 'difficult conversations', and often led to anxiety because of a perceived lack of support when addressing underperformance. Managers reported feeling 'abandoned' and unprepared to undertake such a process again. This led to a focus on compliance, rather than using the performance management system in a more positive and potentially performance-enhancing fashion.

The separation of performance management and core business appears to have been strengthened as a result of the over-focus on *compliance* with a performance management system and formal processes, rather than on performance management itself. We saw many examples of organisations focusing on 'improving' information technology (IT) systems, designing new forms and instituting extra conversations in the formal process, leading to the expectation that a new system might solve ingrained problems. We also heard about training and development on how to navigate the IT system, rather than how to implement it more effectively through better conversation, better feedback or greater clarity of the desired outcomes. In our US research, we observed a very large organisation spending half a billion US dollars on installing a new system and training people how to use the IT system, but providing no training on how using it could actually develop better performance.

These findings demonstrate some of the challenges associated with the effective implementation of performance management. If not addressed, these challenges can lead to increased performance anxiety, which can in turn impede the achievement of high performance. Conversely, good performance management can attenuate anxiety. To achieve this, performance management must have a clear purpose and be meaningful to employees.

From the findings discussed above, we established that for performance management to lead to high performance:

- There needs to be a shared understanding of what high performance means for the organisation.
- Performance measurements and ratings need to reflect the high performance definitions.
- There should be a shared understanding of what behaviours and attributes are required to achieve particular ratings.
- Performance management must enable alignment between organisational, group and employee goals.
- Performance management should help to establish role and goal clarity, enabling the articulation and management of expectations.
- Performance management must be integrated with other management practices, including rewards mechanisms and learning and development.
- Performance management should be used as a mechanism for monitoring and reviewing performance, in particular progress against performance expectations and goals.
- Performance feedback should relate to individual, group and organisational outcomes and be clearly articulated and understood.
- Performance management processes should be seen as core business.
- All those involved need to know how to make the performance process useful for themselves.

A new framework

As a result of our findings, and to assist this list of recommendations, the project team developed a new performance management framework. It is derived from both our empirical research and key ideas from the conceptual model. The new framework (see Figure 5.6) is designed to assist in the implementation of performance management approaches rather than set out a universal system to be adopted. In this way it is a flexible, system-wide framework that can guide tailored approaches at the organisational or sub-organisational levels.

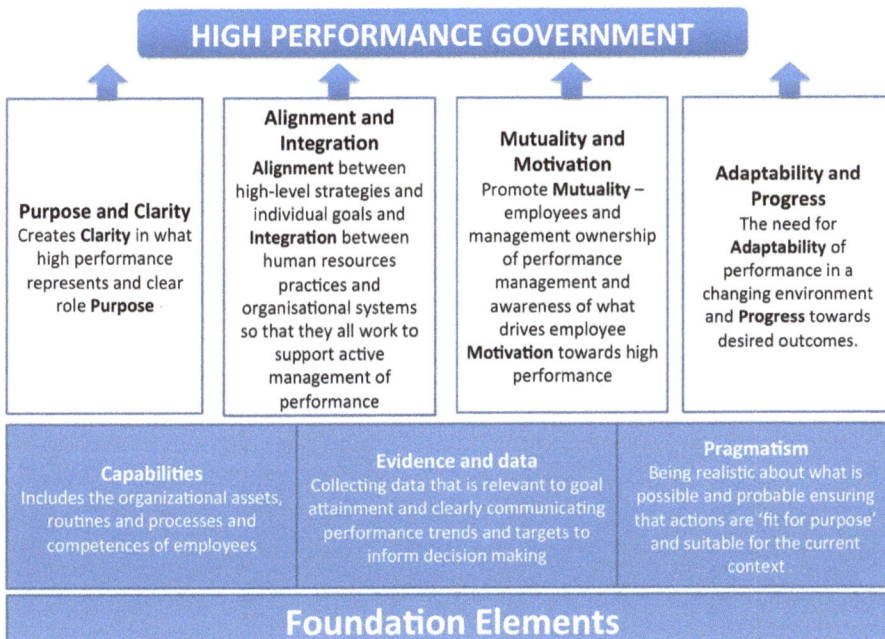

HIGH PERFORMANCE GOVERNMENT

Purpose and Clarity
Creates **Clarity** in what high performance represents and clear role **Purpose**

Alignment and Integration
Alignment between high-level strategies and individual goals and **Integration** between human resources practices and organisational systems so that they all work to support active management of performance

Mutuality and Motivation
Promote **Mutuality** – employees and management ownership of performance management and awareness of what drives employee **Motivation** towards high performance

Adaptability and Progress
The need for **Adaptability** of performance in a changing environment and **Progress** towards desired outcomes.

Capabilities
Includes the organizational assets, routines and processes and competences of employees

Evidence and data
Collecting data that is relevant to goal attainment and clearly communicating performance trends and targets to inform decision making

Pragmatism
Being realistic about what is possible and probable ensuring that actions are 'fit for purpose' and suitable for the current context

Foundation Elements

Figure 5.6. A framework for high performance
Source: Blackman et al. 2013, 5.

Our framework is designed to 'wrap around' the performance management process. We see it as the mediating level between the processes and systems that an organisation adopts and the emergence of outcomes. The objective is to focus on an outcome—high performance—rather than the inputs of processes, measurements or agreements for the sake of compliance. By concentrating on the implementation, not the process, the focus of both employees and managers can be on achieving the outcome of high performance. Stability of processes should reduce change anxiety. In addition, the attention to high performance should support a positive orientation that enables innovation through being clearly aligned with the organisational goals—and thus disposed to *outcome* rather than *process* aspirations.

The framework comprises seven components: four principles and three foundation elements. We argue that every performance management system requires these components in order to be implemented effectively. The four principles reflect what the framework needs to achieve, whereas we consider the three foundation elements to be critical factors underpinning the implementation of the principles. Any performance management system can be analysed against the framework to determine whether or not it fulfils each component. In the following discussion, we set out the principles and foundations and the key findings that emerged from them.

Framework principles

Clarity and purpose

A key factor that enables high performance relies on organisations, groups and employees having both role and goal clarity. Through our research, we found that many people did not feel their goals and roles were as clear as they could be. The risk with goal and role ambiguity is that it may contribute to increased levels of anxiety; hence the importance of providing clarity. Therefore, this principle focuses on the following questions: Is there a shared understanding of what constitutes high performance in different contexts? Does the organisation have a strategy comprising clear and simple goals, framed around the achievement of high performance? Do people understand what their specific role is about and how it contributes to the goals? Do they know what high performance means for them?

Alignment and integration

This principle focuses on illustrating why the work undertaken by groups and employees is important for achieving the organisation's goals. It was surprising how many of our participants did not really understand the relationship between what they did on an individual level and their organisation's priorities and outcomes. This can create real tensions, including inefficient prioritisation of work, thereby increasing performance anxiety levels. An example of the difference made when the goals are clear came from one of our case study organisations, demonstrating 'why the mail matters'. In this particular organisation, the manager explained to employees in the mailroom how what they did enabled the organisation—and more broadly the government—to achieve its desired outcomes. In doing so, employees learned why processing the mail in a timely manner was pivotal to organisational success, and thus why their individual roles were important. Performance increased and individuals not only knew the goal, but also how their individual tasks fitted into the bigger picture.

This principle also focuses on utilising HR and management practices in a complementary way to enable alignment and high performance. The right people should be in the right jobs at the right time, undertaking the right work in order to achieve organisational goals. In order to manage and control the growth of an organisation, there is a tendency to develop new policies and procedures to manage new parts of the system. But if the remainder of the system is not amended to fit the changes, or if the new part is not set up to be in harmony with the current system, effectiveness will decrease. One form of anxiety emerges when different practices or people are asking for apparently inconsistent or competing outcomes (for example, when a target for increased numbers and speeds of outputs is seemingly causing problems with an alternative call for increased quality). By seeing the organisation and the way that it is managed in a holistic way there will be less disconnection between new initiatives and ideas.

Thus, this principle focuses around the alignment and integration of the systems, both vertically and horizontally across the levels identified earlier in Figure 5.4. The questions here are as follows: Do groups and employees know how their role aligns with the organisational goals? Are organisational goals cascaded throughout the organisation? Do individuals and/or groups know how they align with the rest of the organisation? Are different parts of the organisation in alignment with other parts?

Mutuality and motivation

In our research, people talked about *being performance managed*—seeing performance management as something that was done *to* them—and stressed that, for the majority, the term was seen to mean *underperformance management*. The language indicated performance anxiety, uncertainty and often a rather adversarial view of the manager undertaking something negative. Yet the ability to motivate performance requires both employees and management to engage with performance management in a positive way. Mutuality means that there is a shared view that the outcomes will be of benefit to both the individual and the organisation. To achieve this there needs to be a common view on what is needed or wanted by the employee and the organisation.

However, one of the issues that came out strongly from management was: 'Well, if we can't reward people with money, we can't do anything'. At the same time the employees were saying: 'It's not about money. I want to know how my work is affecting other people'. It was apparent that these disconnected ideas meant that many organisations were not harnessing employee motivation: management thought financial rewards would increase employee motivation, overlooking techniques of alignment and ensuring that employees know why their job is important.

The key is that all those involved in performance management willingly engage in the process, meaning nothing is 'done' to anybody else and employees feel sufficiently in control so that anxiety levels are reduced. This principle emphasises the importance of employees taking ownership over their own performance and managers being held accountable for enabling employee performance.

Adaptability and progress

Our research suggests that the ability of organisations, groups and employees to adapt to change is critical for high performance. This is also important for reducing the anxiety commonly associated with change; employees must be supported in this process to reduce their anxiety and enable them to perform. The ability to track progress against performance targets is important for supporting the adaptability to change, however, it is difficult as performance agreements are often very static and reflect a particular moment in time. In addition, progress needs to be measured in ways that do not kill innovation, create fear or lead to undesirable results.

The first thing is to recognise what would be the *ideal* and what is *likely*; just because something has not yet been achieved does not mean it is a failure. The importance of establishing stretch goals at the organisational level was evident in the United States, where some organisations set themselves a very big stretch goal with the recognition that they were not necessarily going to achieve it. Crucial to this was a change in the way achievements were measured.

For example, in one organisation a senior manager reported that progress had been facilitated by moving from having '255 measurements … [and spending] every senior management meeting checking if we were getting there' to focusing on three key questions: 'Do we know where we're going? Are we there yet? … If not, how are we doing?' This was argued to be 'a much more useful conversation', which helped the senior manager to progress.

This highlights the importance of focusing on fewer, but critical, performance measures in order to facilitate adaptability to change, progress and high performance. The key for individual performance management would be to identify the stretch goal and then to clarify what would be acceptable progress that can be charted and recognised as an achievement while still working toward the overall goal. All of this should also help to reduce performance anxiety as it helps to clarify what employees need to focus on, particularly when priorities change.

Foundation elements

Evidence and data

Our findings suggest that the move toward high performance can be facilitated through the collection and provision of performance data that is directly relevant to goal attainment. This performance information can then be used to inform strategic and operational decision-making. In most case study organisations, however, participants highlighted that a myriad of data was collected and not necessarily used to inform decision-making. For example, the *State of the Service Report* provides rich data and the key is to establish which bits really add value in this context. In other words, what is the evidence that will help organisations understand what will support more effective performance?

In a similar way, once organisations and/or managers have identified specific targets, they will need to consider which questions or measures provide real evidence of progress. Evidence from the literature suggests that individuals will work to achieve whatever goal is set (Blackman 2006; Knight 1999; Norreklit et al. 2008). Participants agreed that they would focus upon the things that they knew were being assessed, as this would enable them to demonstrate good performance, thereby reducing one form of anxiety. Hence the choice of evidence is critical both for achieving goals and managing anxiety. However, what is measured is often just *what is measurable*, rather than what needs to be measured. Thus, those involved in implementing performance management need to consider what high performance will look like and what evidence will enable progress to be charted in a meaningful way.

Capabilities

Interviewees in Canada revealed that historically there had been so much focus on leadership that fundamental management skills needed by people were not being developed. Yet over time, managers' spans of control had been increasing, their resources were diminishing, the systems were becoming more complex and their teams needed more support and direction. Therefore, the Canadian Public Service decided that all managers would require certification before taking on managerial responsibilities. They also supported the development of managerial competencies through instituting a community of practice to support managers and ensure they had access to a support network.

Through ensuring employees, managers and leaders have adequate competencies, organisations can facilitate self-efficacy and reduce performance anxiety. This foundational element emphasises the importance of developing the capabilities necessary to achieve organisational goals. It highlights the importance of leveraging organisational resources, routines, structures, systems and processes to support high performance. It also highlights the importance of developing employee, manager and leader competencies—one of which is actually being able to undertake effective performance management.

Pragmatism

A common issue for the case study organisations was increased levels of performance anxiety and stress as a result of trying to do 'more with less', rather than reprioritising responsibilities as goals change. This is particularly important in times of austerity, highlighting the importance of questions such as: 'What is likely? What is possible? What is achievable?'

Another common problem was that of managers' and employees' identifying formal development opportunities in their performance agreement when the learning and development budget had diminished considerably. When formal development opportunities are identified but not taken up due to budgetary constraints, employees' expectations are not met, leading to cynicism regarding the performance management process. Thus this foundational element emphasises the importance of being realistic about what is happening and what is possible and, in particular, what can be achieved with the resources available.

Conclusion

In this chapter we have made a link between performance anxiety and performance management, arguing that poorly designed or implemented performance management systems will create or encourage performance anxiety. Such anxiety may emerge from measuring or focusing on the wrong things; over-focusing on what can be measured rather than developing alternative metrics to encourage desired outcomes; feeling unable to undertake the performance management system effectively; lack of transparency within a system; or a lack of understanding about what is actually required. We argue that focusing on high performance requires the development of a shared understanding of what is meant by good performance at different levels of the model throughout the organisation. This creates a more positive perspective, which can thus reduce performance anxiety.

However, we have presented data that highlights serious problems with the capacity of all employees and managers to undertake effective performance management. High performance is often not articulated clearly, feedback does not achieve the intended outcomes, and many managers and employees find performance management to be challenging and difficult. Indeed, performance management is often perceived as a negative thing. These findings supported our contention that the problem is with the *implementation* of performance management systems rather the systems themselves.

To overcome some of the problems we have presented a new performance framework which acts as a guide for implementing performance management systems. The framework is designed to enable organisations to self-evaluate: a) whether their systems will achieve the desired performance outcomes; and b) whether they have set in place foundations to support these outcomes. Our contention is that using the framework enables a more outcome-oriented approach. This should increase transparency, enable goal clarity and clarify what should be measured—and will thus reduce performance anxiety for both employees and managers, while supporting the development of high performance.

References

Alfes, Kerstin, Catherine Truss, Emma C. Soane, Chris Rees and Mark Gatenby. 2013. 'The relationship between line manager behavior, perceived HRM practices, and individual performance: Examining the mediating role of engagement.' *Human Resource Management* 52(6): 839–59.

Alford, John and Janine O'Flynn. 2012. *Rethinking Public Service Delivery: Managing with External Providers*. Basingstoke: Palgrave Macmillan.

Australian Government Reform of Australian Government Administration (AGRAGA). 2010. *Ahead of the Game: Blueprint for the Reform of Australian Government Administration*. Canberra: Commonwealth of Australia.

Australian National Audit Office (ANAO). 2004. *Performance Management in the Australian Public Service* (Audit Report No. 6 2004–05 Performance Audit). Canberra: Commonwealth of Australia.

Australian Public Service Commission (APSC). 2012a. *State of the Service Report 2011–2012*. Canberra: Commonwealth of Australia. Online: resources.apsc. gov.au/2012/SOSr1112.pdf (accessed 11 May 2015).

APSC. 2012b. *Census Survey of the Australian Public Service*. Canberra: Commonwealth of Australia.

APSC. 2013. 'Capability Review Program.' *Leading and Shaping a Unified, High Performing APS*. Canberra: Commonwealth of Australia. Online: www.apsc. gov.au/aps-reform/current-projects/capability-reviews (accessed 11 May 2015).

Barbier, Marie, Isabell Hansez, Nik Chmiel and Evangelia Demerouti. 2013. 'Performance expectations, personal resources, and job resources: How do they predict work engagement?' *European Journal of Work & Organizational Psychology* 22(6): 750–62.

Becker, Brian and Barry Gerhart. 1996. 'The impact of human resource management on organizational performance: Progress and prospects.' *Academy of Management Journal* 39(4): 779–801.

Blackman, Deborah Ann. 2006. 'Does measuring learning prevent new knowledge?' *Journal of Knowledge Management Practice* 7(3) September. Online: www.tlainc.com/articl117.htm (accessed 11 May 2015).

Blackman, Deborah Ann, Fiona Buick, Michael O'Donnell, Janine Louise O'Flynn and Damian West. 2012. *Developing High Performance: Performance Management in the Australian Public Service*. Crawford School Research Paper No. 12-09. Online: ssrn.com/abstract=2130232 (accessed 11 May 2015) or dx.doi.org/10.2139/ssrn.2130232 (accessed 11 May 2015).

Blackman, Deborah Ann, Fiona Buick, Michael O'Donnell, Janine Louise O'Flynn and Damian West. 2013. *Strengthening the Performance Framework: Towards a High Performing Australian Public Service*. Canberra: Australian Public Service Commission. Online: ssrn.com/abstract=2275681 (accessed 11 May 2015) or dx.doi.org/10.2139/ssrn.2275681 (accessed 11 May 2015).

Bryman, Alan. 2004. *Social Research Methods*. 2nd edn. Oxford: Oxford University Press.

Bullera, Paul F. and Glenn M. McEvoy. 2012. 'Strategy, human resource management and performance: Sharpening line of sight.' *Human Resource Management Review* 22(1): 43–56. Online: www.sciencedirect.com/science/journal/10534822 (accessed 11 May 2015).

Cheng, Mei-I, Andrew Dainty and David Moore. 2007. 'Implementing a new performance management system within a project-based organization: A case study.' *International Journal of Productivity and* Performance Management 56(1): 60–75.

Dahlin-Ivanoff, Synneve and John Hultberg. 2006. 'Understanding the multiple realities of everyday life: Basic assumptions in focus-group methodology.' *Scandinavian Journal of Occupational Therapy* 13: 125–32.

Davis, Glyn. 2013. 'Are public organisations trapped by their past? Reflections on Australian tertiary sector.' Australia and New Zealand School of Government's Paterson Oration. Canberra, 6 August.

De Vos, Ans, Dirk Buyens and René Schalk. 2003. *Psychological Contract Development during Organizational Socialization: Adaptation to Reality and the Role of Reciprocity.* Working Papers of Faculty of Economics and Business Administration, Ghent University, Belgium 03/194. Ghent: Ghent University, Faculty of Economics and Business Administration.

de Waal, André A. 2010. 'Achieving high performance in the public sector.' *Public Performance and Management Review* 34(1): 81–103.

Government Accounting Office (GA). 2004. *Human Capital: DHS Faces Challenges in Implementing its New Personnel System.* US GAO. Online: www.gao.gov/cgi-bin/getrpt?GAO-04-790 (accessed 12 May 2015).

Grumana, Jamie A. and Alan M. Saks. 2011. 'Performance management and employee engagement.' *Human Resource Management Review* 21: 123–36.

Huselid, Mark A. 1995. 'The impact of human resource management practices on turnover, productivity, and corporate financial performance.' *Academy of Management Journal* 38(3): 635–872.

Knight, Daniel J. 1999. 'Performance measures for increasing intellectual capital.' *Strategy and Leadership* 27(2): 22–27.

Mone, Edward, Christina Eisinger, Kathryn Guggenheim, Bennett Price and Carolyne Stine. 2011. 'Performance management at the wheel: Driving employee engagement in organizations.' *Journal of Business and Psychology* 26(2): 205–12.

Norreklit, Hanne, Marten Jacobsen and Falconer Mitchell. 2008. 'Pitfalls in using the balanced scorecard.' *Journal of Corporate Accounting and Finance* 19(6): 65–68.

O'Flynn, Janine, Fiona Buick, Deborah Blackman and John Halligan. 2011. 'You win some, you lose some: Experiments with joined-up government.' *International Journal of Public Administration* 34: 244–54.

Patel, Pankaj C., Jale G. Messersmith and David P. Lepak. 2013. 'Walking the tightrope: an assessment of the relationship between high-performance work systems and organizational ambidexterity.' *Academy of Management Journal* 56(5): 1420–42.

Patton, Michael Quinn. 1990. *Qualitative Evaluation & Research Methods.* Newbury Park, CA: SAGE Publications.

Sung, Johnny and David Ashton. 2005. *High Performance Work Practices: Linking Strategy and Skills to Performance Outcomes.* London: Department of Trade and Industry in association with the Chartered Institute of Personnel and Development.

Truss, Catherine, Amanda Shantz, Emma Soane, Kerstin Alfes and Rick Delbridge. 2013. 'Employee engagement, organisational performance and individual well-being: Exploring the evidence, developing the theory.' *International Journal of Human Resource Management* 24(14): 2657–69.

Yin, Robert K. 2003. *Case Study Research: Design and Methods.* 3rd edn. Beverly Hills, CA: SAGE Publications.

6

REVIEWING PERFORMANCE TO IMPROVE DELIVERY: KEY INSIGHTS FROM TWO AUDITORS-GENERAL

Andrew Greaves
Auditor-General of Queensland

Peter Achterstraat
Auditor-General of New South Wales

Andrew Greaves

In order to continually improve performance, we need first to understand what we mean by performance, what actually is performance, and what is public sector performance in particular? This chapter will review what Auditors-General have been saying about public sector performance, and in particular performance reporting over the last decade. Some lessons and consistent themes can be drawn from these reports. We will then apply those lessons to several case studies.

> At its core, 'performance' is about how well an entity or program is accomplishing what is intended, as measured against defined goals, standards or criteria. More broadly, performance may also relate to efforts, capabilities and intent (CCAF 2002).

In most jurisdictions, the performance management focus these days tends to be on outcomes and outputs. We need to appreciate and understand the importance of achieving our outcomes against the objectives that we set for ourselves as organisations. However, when trying to improve performance it is not only the outcome, quality, timeliness or cost of the outputs that need to improve—in many respects the activities and processes also need to improve so that the outcomes can actually be achieved.

Thus, we should not constrain ourselves to focusing solely on outcomes and to some extent outputs (the goods and services we produce)—we must have regard to our inputs and our processes as well.

What is public performance reporting?

> 'Public performance reporting' refers to the formal mechanisms that a government uses to communicate with the public and legislatures in accordance with agreed guidelines (CCAF 2002).

I see public performance reporting not as an end in itself. There are two dimensions. Certainly there is a key accountability dimension—asking where public sector monies are being used, and being accountable for the use of those public sector monies. Auditors-General are fond of saying that when you look at a set of public sector financial statements, they tell you how much, but they never tell you how well. We need to report non-financial information about our performance in order to discharge the accountability that we as public servants have for the expenditure of those monies.

But ultimately, reporting must help us improve our operational performance. The performance information we report publicly must be part of a suite of performance information we are generating internally to use and apply in our business, to understand how we are performing and how we can improve this performance.

In setting out what is good public performance reporting, the guide produced by the Canadian Comprehensive Auditing Foundation (CCAF 2002) endorses some core principles of best practice, including:

- Focus on the few critical aspects of performance—centre on core objectives and commitments.
- Look forward as well as back—track achievement against established expectations, and inform how short-term achievements affect longer-term prospects.

- Explain key risk considerations—identify key risks as viewed by management, explain the influence of risk on choices and directions and relate achievements to levels of risk accepted.

- Explain key capacity considerations—inform about capacity factors that affect, at a strategic level, the ability to sustain or improve results or meet expectations, and apprise of plans to bring expectations and capacity into alignment.

- Explain other factors critical to performance—help users to understand them and their impacts.

- Integrate financial and non-financial information—public reporting should address this relationship. It should explain how management views the link between activities and desired results, show how much is being spent on key strategies and explain how changes in spending affect results.

- Provide comparative information—when it would significantly help to understand or use the report, and when relevant, reliable and consistent information is or can be reasonably available.

- Present credible information, fairly interpreted—embody characteristics of consistency, fairness, relevance, reliability and, most especially, understandability.

- Disclose the basis for reporting—including the definition of the reporting unit; the selection of certain aspects of performance as critical; and decisions to change the way performance is measured or presented.

I consider the first one to be particularly important—focusing on a few critical aspects of performance. A trap we often fall into is to try to measure too much; we get overloaded and side-tracked from the main issues. We need to instead understand which things are the most important to measure.

Reviewing reports of public performance in the last decade—far from best practice

Many of the states and territories have publicly reviewed performance with varying degrees of effectiveness. In the late 1990s, the Victorian government introduced an output/outcomes framework and three tiers of performance reporting at a strategic level and at an organisational and output level. In 2001, a report by the Victorian Auditor-General was definitely not necessarily pleasant reading; things were still under development and there were key components missing, particularly outcomes that had not at that stage been thought through well enough. There was an absence of clear linkages between outcomes and performance indicators (Victorian Auditor-General's Office 2001).

The next report to discuss was produced by the NSW Audit Office (2006). It too was not very positive about performance reporting and provided an interesting critique of the limitations of not having verifiable sound information on which to base performance judgements. The NSW agencies that were examined in 2006 by the Auditor-General could not tell whether their services actually made a difference to their customers. They had no way of knowing and, as a result, they did not have information about the impact of their services.

What was the root cause of these examples of poor reporting? What was underlying some of the problems with performance information and performance reporting back in the early and mid-2000s in Victoria and New South Wales? Essentially there was a general lack of awareness about the importance of good informative information, and many agencies were merely collecting data on their activities rather than on outputs or outcomes. There were also associated systems limitations—that is, information systems were not in place to capture the data that were required to monitor performance. After years of experience, I still often wonder about the fact that public servants measure things that are easy to measure, rather than things that need to be measured. Much of that experience is driven by the systems that are in place—or perhaps, more accurately, by the systems that are not in place.

In 2008, the Tasmanian Auditor-General also released a report critical of poorly defined policy objectives (Tasmanian Audit Office 2008). He found again a recurring theme—that activity measures were counted rather than evidence of progress towards output/outcome measures. Remember that this is in the context of external public reporting, so the question is: does the public really want to know how busy you claim you are, or do they want to know what you are actually achieving for them? When auditors criticise plain activity measures produced by agencies, we are not criticising them for not being useful to the internal management of an organisation, but rather we are criticising from the perspective of external accountability to the public sector.

Nine years after the first report from the Victorian Auditor-General, there was still a lack of effective outcomes performance reporting in that state (Victorian Auditor-General's Office 2010). It was the same type of problem, and once again framed in the following way: Is what we're doing helping? How is it contributing to the achievement of targets? And are our clients satisfied?

Finally, at the Commonwealth level, Auditor-General Ian McPhee has been running some pilot programs on performance reporting, particularly outcomes/ outputs reporting (ANAO 2013). Interestingly, McPhee's most recent comments highlighted a most pertinent concern: namely, while we are still struggling to develop effectiveness indicators (which I equate to outcomes and the achievement of objectives), we have also lost sight of efficiency indicators.

McPhee also remarked on the paucity of the administrative frameworks used by departments, that is, the systems and processes for actually developing and auditing these performance indicators. Similarly, in the various *Reports on Government Services*, produced by the Productivity Commission, quite often there is a focus on 'effectiveness, equity and efficiency', but there are not many efficiency indicators obviously apparent in the policy sectors they evaluate, at least in the Commonwealth jurisdiction.

The lesson that I take from that quick survey of Auditors-General's reports is that if we are going to improve performance, we have to understand performance. In order to understand performance, we cannot afford to become lost in a morass of information—we need to identify the important qualitative and quantitative indicators. As the Auditors-General have commented over the last decade, there should be less focus on activities and more focus on outcomes and outputs, as well as a balance between effectiveness, efficiency and equity. But we cannot achieve that unless we have the necessary underlying systems. We need to start thinking about our enterprise architecture, and design our information systems with the performance information we need at the forefront of our minds. In Queensland, we still have many legacy systems that have a long way to go in generating effective performance information.

A study of performance gone awry—the right of private practice in Queensland public hospitals

A recent audit that we tabled in the Queensland parliament was an investigation into the right of private practice in Queensland public hospitals conducted by doctors, specialists and nursing staff (Queensland Audit Office 2013). On admission to a Queensland public hospital, one question patients may be asked is, 'Would you like to use your private health insurance?' This allows the hospital to bill the federal government for Medicare and get some unsourced revenue into the system. But we needed to ask why did hospitals in Queensland introduce private practice? What were the objectives? What were they trying to achieve? Certainly uppermost in their minds was being able to attract and retain the services of senior medical officers (SMOs) in the public health system. At the same time, the initial objective expressed was that this should be cost neutral and, of course, have no adverse health outcomes for public patients in the public health system.

So, what was the performance like against those three objectives? There was an improvement in the availability of SMOs, but it cost $800 million more than they thought it would. This is an important consideration, especially when a cost neutral target had been set by Queensland Health. There was also some indication that Category 2 (elective surgery patients) electing to be treated as public patients would suffer a disadvantage compared to those who elected to go private. Of the three scheme objectives, arguably two failed.

The first objective was arguably successful because there are now approximately 2,200 SMOs in the public hospital system—a significant increase. But crucially, Hospital and Health Services (HHS) had not set employment targets. We cannot be sure whether or not this initiative was actually successful, because HHS did not set a target number of SMOs. Good performance is not just about the outcome but also the target against which you can compare performance.

Why then did the system not work as intended? In Figure 6.1, the big red slice represents the proportion of all the SMOs in the public health system who generated no revenue under their right of private practice. In other words, SMOs were supposed to generate revenue under right of private practice, but almost half of them generated nothing. We found some of them cannot generate income, some because they do not have Medicare numbers to do so, some because they actually work in administration rather than in the hospitals.

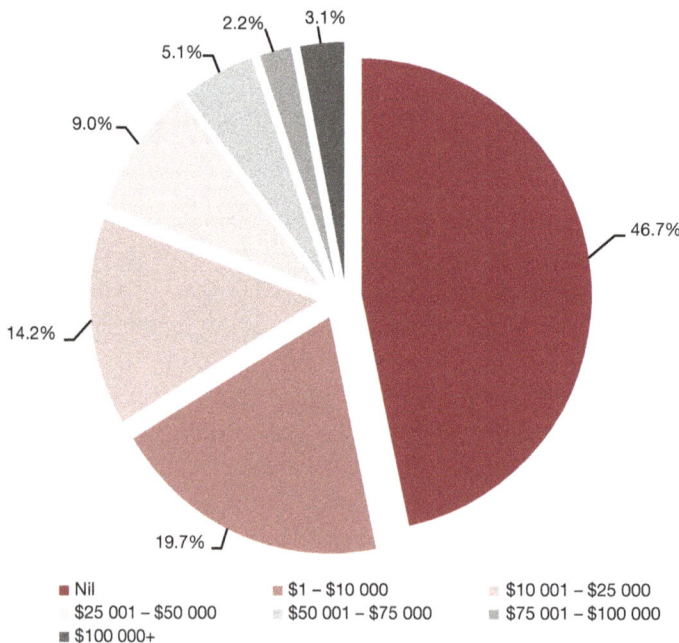

Figure 6.1. Distribution of amounts billed, Queensland public hospitals, 2011–12
Source: Queensland Audit Office using data extracted from Queensland Health billing and payroll systems.

It is possible, therefore, that there was some poor design in the implementation of the right of private practice arrangements. Looking at Category 2 elective surgery patients in Figure 6.2, it is apparent that there was a huge disparity between public and private in the five hospital and health services listed, and this was a statewide issue. This finding indicates some potentially adverse outcomes for public patients in the public health system.

Hospital and Health Service	Category 2 (within 90 days)			
	Public		Private	
	Per cent seen in time	Total patients	Per cent seen in time	Total patients
Children's Health Queensland	75%	1 127	92%	121
Metro North	71%	8 002	90%	933
Metro South	83%	7 872	91%	303
Sunshine Coast	67%	2 548	84%	207
Townsville	66%	3 131	81%	140
Listed HHS	74%	22 680	88%	1 704
Statewide patients (SMOs)[1]	72%	38 756	88%	2 210
Statewide patients (all)[2]	69%	78 547	97%	20 404

1. Statewide (SMOs) includes all category 2 elective surgery performed during 2010–11 and 2011–12 including HHSs not listed.
2. Statewide (all) includes all surgeries performed, including those by registrars and VMOs and in HHSs not listed.

Figure 6.2. Category 2 elective surgery, Queensland public hospitals
Source: Queensland Audit Office using data extracted from Queensland Health clinical and payroll systems.

Our analysis of the data we obtained during the audit uncovered other performance issues, especially in relation to administrative activity measures (note that this now focused on efficiency issues not our assessment of output/outcome performance). Figure 6.3 shows that across the health system it took some hospitals and HHS an inordinately long time to bill for the activity they undertake. In some cases it took HHS up to 650 days to eventually bill the Commonwealth for the activity that was undertaken, a delay that resulted in missing revenue opportunities. We found that through their existing administrative systems, there was an opportunity for HHS to generate more revenue simply by improving administrative practice. This is all part of performance, because one of the performance criteria was to be cost neutral and to maximise their source revenue. We calculated that they were failing to generate approximately $22 million additional revenue a year through inefficient administrative processes.

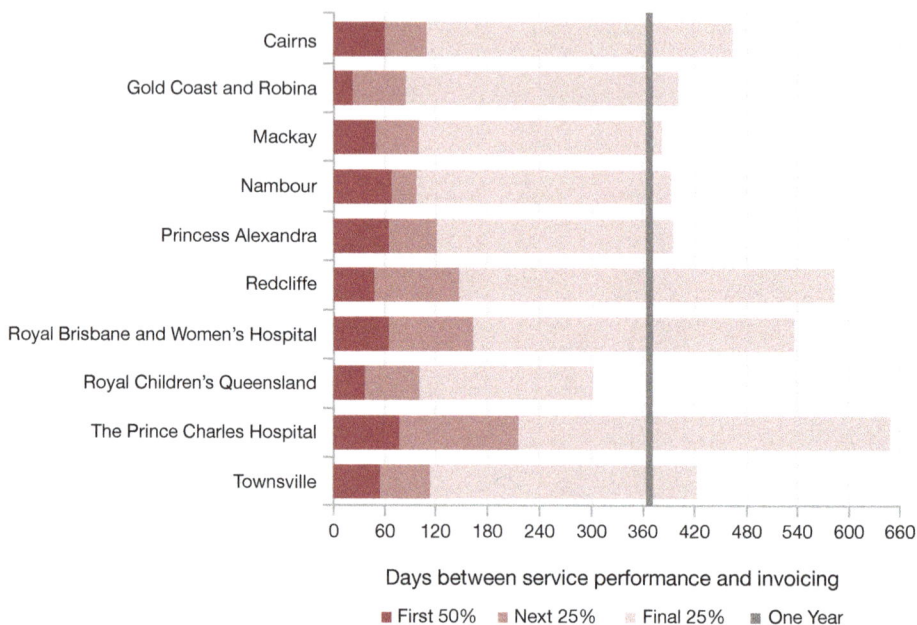

Figure 6.3. In-patient billing by system, Queensland public hospitals
Source: Queensland Audit Office using data extracted from Queensland Health billing system.

We also examined how much HHS was paying SMOs. With an increase in the number of available SMOs, overtime in theory should have gone down. Instead, as Figure 6.4 indicates, it went up. We started asking why—surely activity had also gone up? When we examined the records, activity per SMO had in fact dropped, and thus productivity was falling. In addition, we mapped the days of the week when SMO activity happened in the public health system; normal activities occurred mainly on Monday to Thursdays, but almost all the overtime was taken on Fridays. It was then we first encountered the concept of 'rostered overtime' on a Friday—SMOs regarded the entire last day of the week as incurring overtime payment.

Much of this was news to Queensland Health. They could not tell us how much SMOs were being paid, or how much overtime they were doing. Why did they not know this? It was partly because of their legacy systems. Queensland Health had not joined their computing and information systems together, they had not integrated their patient billing systems with their administration systems and their payroll systems. They were unable to generate meaningful information to produce the findings we generated as represented in Figures 6.3 and 6.4; they wanted to know the information, but they could not generate it. This goes back to my earlier point about having systems to support the performance information.

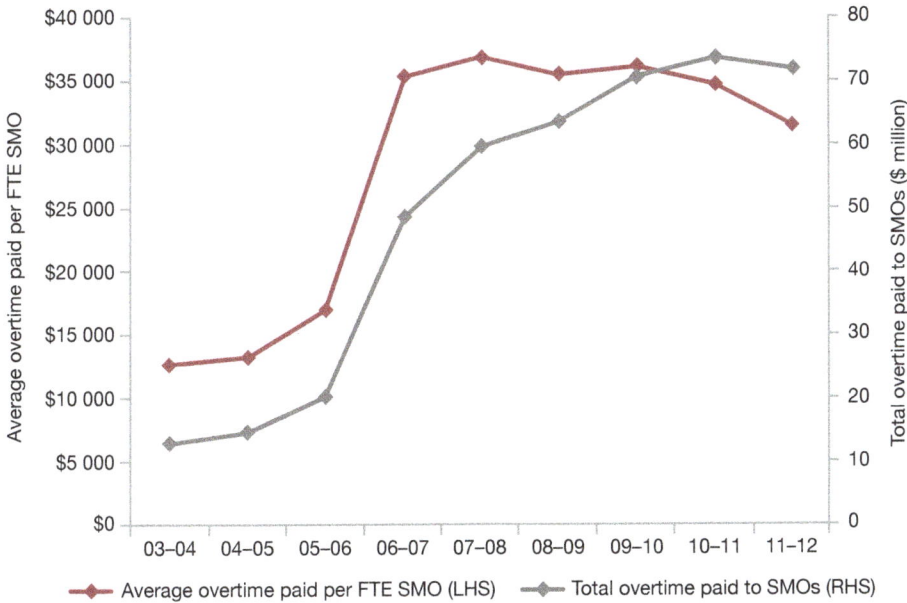

Figure 6.4. Total and average overtime paid to SMOs, Queensland public hospitals, 2003–12

Source: Queensland Audit Office using data extracted from Queensland Health payroll system.

So, to conclude, if governments want to improve their performance, they must set the right measures and collect meaningful data to chart progress. In this case, a health department wanted to increase the availability of SMOs, but they needed a target to work towards, and some measurement of levels of activity. They wanted to be cost neutral, but they could not adequately measure whether they were achieving this in a timely manner. And they wanted to improve patient outcomes but could not demonstrate that they had achieved this, and our reading of the situation tended to imply that at least some patients had been disadvantaged.

Peter Achterstraat

In this section of the chapter I will look, in particular, at case studies in the project sphere and in the operations sphere. I will then discuss the lessons we have learned from our audits and how we might improve delivery. For instance, there are tactical responses available to managers to improve performance, but there are also two key strategic responses which have been successful in New South Wales.

Problems with managing the project sphere

I will discuss problems we discovered with three projects: the Sydney Metro, the solar bonus scheme, and some IT projects. With the Sydney Metro, I unfortunately had to report that the government spent $500 million on this project, and when they cancelled it they had to write off $428 million—that is, $428 million was wasted. Why did that happen? How could a project be started and then written off a year later with losses of $428 million? What could have gone wrong?

Contributing factors included problems with scope, lack of a full understanding of risks and very poor project management. But the main problem was that there was fundamentally no effective business case to begin with. The people responsible thought it was a great idea and decided to jump into it without further consideration.

It was a similar story with the solar bonus scheme. The NSW government decided to pay participants 60c for every kilowatt of electricity they put into the grid, and at the same time allow them to buy it back from the government for approximately 20c. So everyone started selling into the grid for 60c and buying back for 20c. What was that going to cost the government? The original estimate was $362 million per annum—not too bad perhaps. Eleven months later, another estimate revised the total to $4 billion. How did such a miscalculation occur? Essentially, the same problems of poor thinking that occurred with the Sydney Metro project were also issues here with the solar bonus scheme. Fortunately, during the course of our audit and before we reported, government was aware of these issues, and they changed some of the parameters. In fact, that loss of $4 billion did not come to pass.

Turning to IT projects, we know from experience that very few are delivered on time, on budget and on specification. The message to people then is that they do not really have to try particularly hard, because expectations are already low. If specifications are on the web, people are held to account more and have to be more proactive. Yet time and again we are finding that IT projects run over time, go over budget and are affected by under specification. Why is that?

Problems in the operations sphere

Performance problems can and regularly do occur in the operations sphere. For instance, we conducted an audit on injured police, because we were losing far too many highly skilled, highly trained police on medical grounds and thus eroding our capabilities. New South Wales was losing five times more police officers on medical grounds than Victoria. Our audit suggested the poor results for NSW were largely down to operational matters and some neglect. In response to our findings, the government and the police force eventually made a number of important changes. They have changed some of the rules to reduce liability, and they have also increased the support available to police while they are working. They have made several positive changes.

We also conducted audits on public complaints against RailCorp and looked at efficiencies related to how much time train drivers actually spent at the wheel. Why were passenger complaints going up? Behavioural economics might say that people's expectations were rising too quickly and that RailCorp's performance was not meeting these expectations. When investigating driver performance we discovered that only 28 per cent of the drivers' time is spent actually driving a train. If we could increase that to 31 per cent (a 10 per cent increase), or even double it to 56 per cent, imagine what we could do with the savings.

Levers to improve performance

Why do we have these projects and operations that do not do as well as they should? There are many 'tactical issues' that auditors can uncover. By 'tactical issues', I mean the elements of best business practice such as better business cases, better gateway reviews, service level agreements (i.e. spelling out exactly what's expected from people), quality assurance processes, better contracts, HR and IT capacities, security of information and so on. If we could do all of those things a little better we might improve, for example, from 28 per cent to 31 per cent of drivers' time at the wheel.

We can undertake these changes incrementally. However, there are more effective options available to improve performance, particularly focusing on the strategic aspects of policymaking—and I would nominate governance and leadership as the two most important 'levers'. In recent times, there is evidence we have been able to use these to good effect in NSW.

Governance

Research from the Commonwealth Treasury shows that corporations which follow the Australian Securities Exchange (ASX) principles of corporate governance have higher earnings per share (EPS) and higher sales growth than corporations that have poorer governance (Brown and Gørgens 2009). The reasoning is that better governance means you know the checks and balances are there, and also that people will feel comfortable taking greater risks if they know there is an effective governance structure in place.

In New South Wales, we found that most public organisations have only part of a governance structure in place—for example, a risk management model, code of conduct, ethics, annual audit committees—but they were not always harmonised, and they were not integrated. So we began a project that brought all these pieces of corporate governance together into a best practice model. We assembled a corporate governance lighthouse of 17 components, adapting the ASX's governance principles for the public service. For example, the ASX emphasises a good ethical environment; we say as a bare minimum, agencies need to have a code of conduct, fraud and corruption control, compliance management and diversity policy. The organisations that use this model are more effective than those that do not.

In putting together the corporate governance lighthouse, the biggest issue we have encountered is that people think that having these 17 components, ticking all the boxes, is all they are required to do—end of story. The challenge is to show that this is a bare minimum—we need to have a much more effective culture at the top to achieve change.

Leadership

In speaking recently to the heads of the agencies whose projects had underperformed or failed in some way, I said, 'Something went wrong. How can we do it better? What can we do?' I spoke one-on-one with these people—28 leaders in total—and asked them their opinion on how we could do things better. It all boiled down to leadership and the leaderships skills we need in the public service.

In our 2011 survey of leadership in the NSW public sector, on a scale of 0 to 10 (0 meaning hopeless leaders and 10 meaning excellent), perception of the public sector leadership was at 5.2. In 2012, this rose slightly to 5.6, and in 2013 there was a further increase—but not a comforting result. What was the response from my survey of agency heads? They all said to me, 'Well, there's no definition of what is an effective leader', which dodges the issue. My basic criterion for an effective leader is one whose peers think they are an effective leader.

The CEOs and chairs I spoke to talked about the attributes of a leader, the skills of a leader, and the behaviours of a leader. Attributes of course are who we are. The skills are what we can do, and the behaviours are what we actually do. Each of my interviewees had a big list of what they thought were the necessary skills, behaviours and attributes of a leader and we were able to systematically analyse these to get an idea about what makes a good leader.

The commonalities my interviewees highlighted between the public and the private sector included being a good communicator; able to set a vision; and be people-focused. There is a list of many common things, but there is also a list of some differences. Differences include the reality that in the public sector you must be able to lead through ambiguity (this came out loud and clear), and the fact that you are responsible to ministers rather than a Board of Directors—a significant difference. Also the public sector has different stakeholders (and a wider range of stakeholders), different values, different scrutiny, a need for thicker skin (particularly in operational areas), the need to inspire and motivate staff, the tools rather than remuneration. Those are important differences.

Then there is the volatility, uncertainty, complexity and ambiguity of the environment, requiring new skills to be able to meet those changes in the public service. There is tension between the short-term and the long-term approach in the public sector—we need to focus on the long term, but we also need to meet short-term needs. Essentially, however, my interviewees said that what makes a good leader comes back to values. Whether we call it integrity or genuineness or authenticity, unless we develop these qualities in the public or the private sector, our leaders will not make it to square one and they will be unable to enthuse their staff and organisations.

References

Australian National Audit Office (ANAO). 2012–13. *Measurement and Reporting Framework: Pilot Project to Audit Key Performance Indicators*. The Auditor-General Report No. 28, April. Online: www.anao.gov.au/Publications/Audit-Reports/2012-2013/The-Australian-Government-Performance-Measurement-and-Reporting-Framework (accessed 18 May 2015).

ANAO. 2013. *The Australian Government Performance and Reporting Framework: Pilot Project to Audit Key Performance Indicators*. Commonwealth of Australia. Online: www.anao.gov.au/~/media/Files/Audit%20Reports/2012%202013/Audit%20Report%2028/2012-13%20Audit%20Report%20No%2028.pdf (accessed 22 May 2015).

Brown, Rebecca and Tue Gørgens. 2009. *Treasury Working Paper 2009–02*. The Treasury, March. Online: archive.treasury.gov.au/documents/1495/PDF/TWP_2009-02.pdf (accessed 18 May 2015).

CCAF. 2012. *Reporting Principles: Taking Public Performance Reporting to a New Level*. Ottawa: CCAF~FCVI Inc. Online: www.ccaf-fcvi.com/attachments/267_ReportingPrinciples-EN.pdf (accessed 18 May 2015).

NSW Audit Office. 2006. *Performance Audit: Agency Use of Performance Information to Manage Services*. Sydney. Online: www.audit.nsw.gov.au/ArticleDocuments/138/153_Agency_Use_Of_Performance.pdf.aspx?Embed=Y (accessed 18 May 2015).

Queensland Audit Office. 2013. *Right of Private Practice in Queensland Public Hospitals*. Report to Parliament 1: 2013–14, July. Brisbane.

Tasmanian Audit Office. 2008. *Public Sector Performance Information*. Auditor-General Special Report No. 72, April. Parliament of Tasmania. Online: digital.statelibrary.tas.gov.au/webclient/StreamGate?folder_id=0&dvs=1431928906549~935&usePid1=true&usePid2=true (accessed 18 May 2015).

Victorian Auditor-General's Office. 2001. *Departmental Performance Management and Reporting*. No. 126, Session 1999–2001. Parliament of Victoria. Online: www.parliament.vic.gov.au/papers/govpub/VPARL1999-2002No126.pdf (accessed 18 May 2015).

Victorian Auditor-General's Office. 2010. *Performance Reporting by Departments*. Report No. 20, 2009–10.

PART TWO: THE NEED FOR GOVERNMENTS TO INNOVATE

INNOVATION IN THE PUBLIC SECTOR: BEYOND THE RHETORIC TO A GENUINE 'LEARNING CULTURE'

Andrew Podger

The Australian National University

There are several key points I want to highlight in this chapter. First, that the word *innovation* has become very fashionable—you see it in the names of organisations, departments and public service values, and so on—but we need to be careful when using the term. This is not to say it is unimportant or irrelevant, but that we need to clarify what innovation means, test the suggestions that are made to promote it in the public sector and be conscious that there are downsides and risks involved.

Second, and in the same context, it is also important to remember that *stability* is in fact a core public sector role. Textbook public finance literature (Musgrave and Musgrave 1980) identifies three functions of government, one of which is stability. This refers mainly to handling the economic cycle and managing the risks of inflation and unemployment, but it is also more generally about setting the legal and economic framework within which individuals and private organisations can go about their lives and businesses with confidence.

Innovation in the public sector has to take account of public sector factors. Various Australian Public Service (APS) agencies have issued guidelines in recent years on how to foster innovation. Some of them have useful suggestions; others are more mixed, and in many respects do not square with the reality public servants work within today. Actions speak louder than words, and quite a few recent developments have worked *against*, not towards, innovation. Innovation requires a culture of trust and learning rather than a culture of control, and yet the culture of control has been a hallmark of recent history.

For this reason I am going to propose two strategies: one is what I call 'back to basics'—things that we ought to do that we seem to have lost sight of recently. We need more time and resources for policy research, regular statistical work, and so on; we need technical expertise, not just generalist skills; we need more permission and devolution—things that have been harder to find in recent times; and we need to revisit the idea of learning organisations. If we get these basics right, we can apply them equally in times of austerity as we can in times of plenty, to help governments meet prevailing challenges.

In addition to some 'back to basics', I suggest we try some new approaches. In particular, I suggest we explore the ideas of Charles Sabel about 'experimentalist democracy' and 'pragmatic governance' (Sabel 2004). These ideas are not entirely foreign to Australia—we have successfully taken a pragmatic approach to many of our reforms over the last 30 years—but I want to suggest we explore how to pursue the approach more systematically.

International interest in innovation in the public sector

Innovation in the public sector has become a popular topic around the world. Interest seems to have started in the UK some years ago (the Improvement and Development Agency (IDeA) established by the Local Government Association (LGA) in 1998 (LGA 2014; NAO 2000; Mulgan and Albury 2003; DIUS 2008)), then crossed the Atlantic to the Harvard Kennedy School (Eggers and Shalabh 2009). The Organisation for Economic Cooperation Development (OECD) also became interested (Box 2009) and established its Observatory of Public Sector Innovation in 2010. In Australia, we have had a series of reports starting with *Ahead of the Game* (DPMC 2010—Terry Moran's 2010 report on Australian government administration) promoting greater innovation in the APS, and an Australian National Audit Office (ANAO) guide (ANAO 2009), and an Australian Public Service Commission (APSC) Management Advisory Guide (MAC) guide (MAC 2010).

More recently, a few commentators have expressed caution. Wolfgang Drechsler was in Australia recently questioning aspects of the enthusiasm for innovation in the public sector (Drechsler 2012). He noted that the Schumpeter definition of innovation is fundamentally about the market—it is not simply about inventions, but is a phenomenon where a new product or service is successfully introduced and the innovator can exploit their short-term monopoly. That is what innovation in the economic literature refers to. But good public administration rarely, if ever, looks innovative in that sense. Yet it can—and has to—be supportive of Schumpeterian innovation. Understanding this matters, because some of the popular focus on innovation sounds like novelty for novelty's sake, and novelty for novelty's sake can be counterproductive in facilitating private sector innovation.[1]

As mentioned, another reason for caution is that stability is one of the three core functions of government in a market economy (along with allocation of resources and redistribution). The public sector sets the framework within which individuals and businesses can go about their lives and operate with confidence knowing society's rules. This provides an environment conducive to investment and innovation. So a degree of stability in government can actually enhance innovation in society.

None of this means that innovation is not important in the public sector: it *is* important and the popular interest in it is both understandable and appropriate.

Drivers and challenges

Some of the drivers for more innovation in the public sector are the same drivers behind new public management (NPM) 25 years ago. These include the need for agility and flexibility and the capacity to adjust to rapid change in society— whether it be from globalisation, technological change or something else. Efficiency in public administration is important—and it always will be. There is a need to improve our responsiveness to the needs and preferences of citizens, so we have to be able to adapt. Moreover, there are benefits from drawing on private sector experience, including risk management, strategic planning and performance measurement. This was the context for the new public management reforms and they are no less relevant today to the current interest in innovation.

Promoting innovation offers additional benefits beyond those of NPM (and its subsequent modifications and enhancements through network governance etc.). In particular, it looks to foster new ideas and to subject these to experimentation and practical evaluation. There is more emphasis on translating ideas into practice—so implementation receives more attention than it did in the early days of new public management. While it is consistent with continuous

---

1   Joseph Schumpeter argued that a fundamental force of capitalism is innovation and what he termed 'creative destruction' whereby entrepreneurs develop new products for which for some time they have a monopoly (Schumpeter 1942).

improvement, it also promotes testing of more radical change. This is perhaps particularly relevant in times of austerity and crisis. Such times often permit more radical change as well as require it.

In promoting innovation, however, we also need to learn from some of the mistakes made in the NPM reforms. One of the lessons from our experience was that private sector practice is not always the most appropriate model for the public sector. The public sector context nearly always involves multiple objectives which are not always able to be clearly articulated. Yet in new public management we tried to set specific goals and targets; to use organisational and programmatic stovepipes and principal-agent frameworks which could be tightly managed or monitored, applying private sector practices. But we did not always take sufficient account of the complexity of political accountability, and the challenges of identifying the broader public interest. There were also, at times, issues about the ethical application of public power, because in our focus on results we sometimes understated the importance of means and processes in the public sector.

When considering innovation in the public sector, we need to think about the public sector factors that may be particularly important. One of them is the importance of engaging with politics. Innovation is not just a matter for technical experts or administrators; engagement with politics is essential to making any major innovation work. That engagement will almost certainly identify multiple and competing objectives, and it also offers a process to allow these to be tested and weighed up. The other key public sector factor concerns the role and values of public service: having impartial, professional, consistent and stable management, notwithstanding the need to be innovative. The challenge, as I once put it some years ago, is to promote innovation with integrity (Podger 2004).

Australian guidelines for innovation

The two main guides issued in Australia came from the ANAO in 2009 and the MAC (published by the APSC) in 2010. The ANAO guidelines discuss the preconditions for innovation and the processes to foster and shape innovation. Both give a lot of emphasis to what might be referred to as the ideal 'policy cycle view' of the world of decision-making—you make a decision, you implement it, you review it, you then look at the problems with it, you come up with a new set of suggestions and make a new decision and repeat the cycle. I will return to this approach shortly, as I am not sure it represents the real world or necessarily the most desirable way to promote useful innovation.

The two sets of guidelines include many very sensible suggestions, particularly about the importance of organisational leadership (for example, fostering a permissive or empowering culture) and having a supportive corporate strategy. There is also quite a lot of emphasis on organisation capability: knowing your business, having the necessary information, having the right information flows and having capacity within the organisation to think outside the current paradigm. Moreover, the guidelines promote collaboration and external engagement, and rightly expound the importance of implementation.

But there seem to be several somewhat questionable elements. Firstly, the guidelines are presented rather like cookbooks—a list of things to do and to tick off—and I don't think that is the way innovation is ever going to work. There is also the suggestion that innovation is a core public sector value, when I would say firmly it is not. Public servants should be innovative, but innovation is not actually one of the core values that helps to define the public sector. It is a core value of the private sector, which must retain a competitive edge.

Most importantly, I contrast what is presented in these guidelines with what has actually been happening over the last five or six years. In that period—at least at the Commonwealth level, and I suspect in most of the states—there has been a reversal of devolution. There have been increased numbers of people at the top, fewer 'Indians', and a lot of authority down the line has been taken away. There has also been reduced tolerance of risk. The 'pink batts' story provides a telling illustration. What are the lessons so far taken from that? Essentially, they are: do not let such a thing ever happen again; put in place stronger central controls; have more senior managers. And yet, the pink batt story included some really innovative, clever ideas, such as the use of the vocational training sector, and the Centrelink processes for actually managing payments, which had never been thought about in the environmental field before. But the political and bureaucratic lessons in practice are exclusively about minimising risk—not managing risk and welcoming innovation. (This is not to suggest that risk was managed well—it evidently was not.)

We have also experienced ever-increasing political control of communications and policy debates. Consequently, departments are not engaging outside their organisations as much as they used to, and they are publishing less and speaking publicly less often. There are exceptions, but senior public servants are understandably cautious about being drawn into partisan public debates, particularly when they see colleagues get into political strife because of misrepresentations of what was said. But such caution is hardly conducive to the atmosphere and culture needed for innovation. There is also increasing emphasis on being able to answer a policy issue *immediately*—allowing no time to reflect, let alone to test different ideas and approaches. 'We need something now … it's in the press today … on the radio or in social media right now … 24/7 … the minister has got to respond to stop the speculation building further, so get the briefing with clear and firm points that are "on message" ….'

Even within *Ahead of the Game*, there is the disappointing suggestion that more mobility is necessarily a good thing. Well, mobility *can* be a good thing, but in many places much expertise has been lost in recent years and regaining it is now more important than increased mobility. Stability is also important to nurturing effective relationships with external stakeholders. Agencies need to balance mobility and stability, and generalist and specialist skills: innovation is often facilitated by bringing in different perspectives, but it also requires expert knowledge and deep ongoing partnerships, and there is often nothing more dangerous than generalists running off with what they think are clever ideas.

Two complementary strategies

This leads me to propose two strategies for promoting innovation in a way that is relevant to the public sector: 'back to basics' and exploring more systematically the 'experimentalist democracy' ideas from Charles Sabel.

The 'back to basics' strategy is about rebuilding our strategic policy capability. This was one of the priorities in Terry Moran's report *Empowering Change: Fostering innovation in the Australian Public Service* to the Department of Prime Minister and Cabinet 2010, one I strongly endorse. Steve Sedgwick (APSC 2013) and others have also referred to it publicly, including through the recent capability reviews. Associated with this is the need to reintroduce some learning organisation principles. This 'back to basics' strategy, however, is still within a framework that is policy-oriented and rather top-down. The experimentalist democracy idea is much more bottom-up and experiential. As such, it could usefully complement the first strategy.

'Back to basics' strategy

What would the 'back to basics' strategy involve? First, notwithstanding all the pressures on departmental budgets, we need to allocate resources to ongoing policy research and data analysis in every department. This would assist the ideal cycle of systematic policy development and informed decision-making that I referred to earlier. More importantly, it would assist in the rather different real world in which today's policy advisers live. Most of us know that the policy cycle is a normative way of looking at the world, but it is not actually how it works. In practice what happens is an event occurs and departments are pressed to give the minister immediate advice to respond to that event. So how do you make sure that advice is well informed? The key is for the department to have invested in ongoing policy research and development and in ongoing statistical data analysis, which can be drawn upon quickly as required. The dedicated resources involved need to be somewhat protected from the 24/7 media cycle, but able to be promptly accessed. They also, in turn, need to have close links with external expertise, whether in universities or think tanks or the more skilled advocacy organisations. Getting the most from external expertise requires considerable internal expertise, and internal experts are often in a unique position to understand administrative data. I am also not sure the policy cycle is necessarily an ideal approach; getting the most from external experts often requires an iterative process leading to shared understanding often outside the context of current policy debates.

Which brings me to the importance of retaining and nurturing expertise and not overemphasising the role of the generalist: a key part of the 'back to basics' strategy is to ensure there is a balance between generalists and specialists.

We also need to think, once again, about devolved authority. Particularly under the Rudd and Gillard governments, too many matters went to cabinet (or, worse, to a small kitchen cabinet), and not enough was left to portfolio ministers and their ministerial teams. Within portfolios and agencies, the idea of flatter structures has largely been lost and with this the ability to push things down the line giving people more management authority including in relation to policy advice. Of course to do this you do need to have a framework of performance management and risk-based quality assurance controls.

This strategy includes a renewed focus on leadership that promotes a culture of learning (learning will also receive close attention in the second strategy). Doing this requires activities such as regular forums for discussion of both program experience and policy research. This may be harder than in the past because of the greater separation of policy from administration (for example, where service provision is contracted out or administered in a different agency or portfolio or by a different jurisdiction), but it is essential to innovation that works.

It also encompasses engagement with external expertise and external stakeholders. Australia (and New Zealand) have done a lot of good work in this space in recent years, but a lot more needs to be done. Amongst other aspects, access to the data that departments hold is still not nearly good enough to promote effective interchange and dialogue, and there remains considerable reluctance to engage fully with academic experts.

Peter Senge's 'Learning Organisation' ideas (Senge 1990) are now more than 20 years old, but many aspects are still highly relevant. Indeed, some of the more recent writings about innovation apply very similar concepts to Senge's five 'disciplines', including in particular 'systems thinking'—the need to consciously consider connections and interactions between programs and organisations when addressing significant problems. 'Personal mastery' is also important, involving both expertise in the organisation's core business and skills with working with people. 'Mental models' are relevant to the appreciation of different perspectives, understanding where people are coming from and recognising the assumptions being made that may never have been stated. 'Shared vision' and 'team learning' are also relevant, going beyond learning by each individual to group learning towards a shared objective. These principles of learning organisations need to be taken on board again as part of the 'back to basics' strategy, as they are particularly relevant in the press for innovation.

The reason why this 'back to basics' agenda is important is that we know from past history that when we did these things well, we saw a lot of good policy changes supported and initiated by the public service, including in times of austerity. A number of prominent Australian public policy practitioners were involved in these. I was involved in the 1976 family allowances reform: the new Fraser government wanted budgetary savings, Treasury proposed means-testing child endowment; a good cross-agency system of reviewing this proposal came up with the alternative of family allowances—a much enhanced child endowment system that brought together tax rebates and welfare payments, a very different and innovative outcome compared to the one originally suggested. In 1983, the new Hawke government was looking for budgetary savings to redirect towards employment enhancing activities. One of many reforms that year was a total rethink of housing programs, replacing highly expensive tax assistance with enhanced support for public housing and other measures that both promoted employment and helped more needy people. First steps were also taken that year to remove distortions in our then very weak superannuation arrangements as part of a review of the retirement income system. The youth allowance reform was introduced over several years but it was in the context of the extremely tough 1987 budget that it was finally pushed through, realising savings in youth unemployment benefits in a package that aimed to promote continued education and training. It was also around this time that the original Higher Education Contributions Scheme (HECS) was introduced, involving not only the budgetary savings from requiring people to repay some university costs when their incomes later grew, but redirecting savings to greatly expand places, including for disadvantaged youth.

I raise each of these here as they are all areas ripe for further reform, now that we are in another period of austerity. The policy mechanisms and processes in those times were, I believe, factors in their success even if, undoubtedly, political leadership was the final essential ingredient.

Sabel's 'experimentalist democracy' strategy

The second strategy I propose is taken from Charles Sabel's work on experimentalist democracy (Sabel 2004). His focus is primarily on where ends and means cannot be easily distinguished and where issues cross agency and jurisdictional boundaries—'wicked problems'. He is concerned that a top-down approach using principal-agent mechanisms is often not appropriate in these cases and he suggests instead a bottom-up approach often using civil society actors who not only provide the services but have permission to both set many of the rules and to supervise themselves. This is nonetheless subject to public monitoring of that self-supervision and to the legislature setting and reviewing the broad policy intent.

Democratic accountability is firmly in place in this model, but it allows much more discretion than is currently the norm and relies on much more open, informed debate and review. It is directed as much to improving public political discourse as it is to improved public service management. Under the model, 'framework laws' would commit society to identified broad goals. The administrative infrastructure would help agents to set and revise standards in light of what they learn and from pooling their efforts to improve (typically these would include requirements for independent professional bodies to monitor performance and to disseminate lessons). Independent monitoring and evaluation in turn would contribute to regular reviews by parliament, including of the framework laws.

Sabel has written about a number of case studies in both Scandinavia and the US. The Finnish one is particularly interesting: it concerns special education for kids from particularly difficult backgrounds. The monitoring and evaluation process, and dissemination of lessons learned, was led by independent professional organisations, not the teachers' unions. His other case studies include food safety in the US and hospitals in Sweden.

There are limitations and risks associated with this model. The most obvious one relevant to Australia is whether Australian politicians or the media would ever allow this level of experimentation and discretion? This may suggest the model should first be explored in areas where there is more likely to be bipartisan agreement on the importance of the problem and of the uncertainty about the best policy response.

In these areas, there is still the challenge to articulate meaningful, broad society goals without detailed, specific objectives and program rules. For example, one of the problems we have seen in the Indigenous policy field has been the continued insistence at the top (whether it be the parliament, or the Council of Australian Governments) to set detailed measures of performance when perhaps what we really need is something broader which allows detailed measures and their objectives to be worked through at a more localised level subject to independent monitoring and dissemination of lessons learned.

A related challenge is to decide when this highly discretionary, bottom-up approach would be more likely to maximise public value, than our more developed top-down performance management approach. Other contributors to this volume have identified the advantages of principal-agent and provider competition arrangements. This is not the model here—which is much more about collaboration and learning. Which policy areas are most suited to competition and which ones to collaboration and learning? There is no simple answer, but relevant factors might include the complexity of the policy issue and the extent to which the culture and values of the charitable sector and other key external stakeholders have proven to be important.

Other challenges include containing provider self-interests, establishing financial controls, balancing the desirability of discretion and experimentation with concerns for equitable entitlements to services and treatment, and ensuring ethical standards in the experiment methodology and practice.

There are a number of current initiatives which bear some resemblance to Sabel's ideas. The National Disability Insurance Scheme and its pilot studies provide one example. To a lesser extent, the work done recently to give hospital boards more autonomy and professional independence (but with high-level performance metrics) fits the model. Regional primary healthcare organisations, or Medicare Locals, have certainly been the subject of experimentation in recent years. And there is scope to return to the agenda explored some years ago through the coordinated care trials for chronically ill patients.

Perhaps the area most suited to the experimentalist approach, at least for the Commonwealth, is Indigenous welfare. If we were to pursue this more systematically, the following action might be considered:

- Establishing a joint parliamentary committee to agree society goals and oversee developments (assisted by the National Congress of Australian First Peoples).

- Allowing considerable bottom-up experimentation including reporting to (not by) local communities.

- Having a lead Indigenous agency that can coordinate across government for each community/experiment, with sufficient expertise and on-the-ground experience to maintain close relations with communities.

- Various professions, researchers and independent Indigenous organisations to ensure independent monitoring and sharing of lessons.

A major state example would be child protection. The social benefit bonds initiative in New South Wales discussed in this book is a good example within this policy field. More generally, there may be scope for more carefully designed experimentation even involving randomised trials, within a framework that ensures findings are public and lessons disseminated. Other possibilities include prisons (perhaps drawing on New Zealand experience) and special education.

Conclusion

The current interest in innovation in the public sector runs the risk of being just another fad. We need to appreciate the public sector context and role.

This is not to deny the relevance and importance of innovation in the public sector but to promote a more nuanced understanding. If we are to promote innovation that contributes to public value, I suggest serious consideration be given to two strategies: the first is to return to some practices which seem to have been allowed to wither, and the second to explore a new approach that allows for more experimentation and learning from practice, particularly in complex policy areas.

References

Australian National Audit Office (ANAO). 2009. *Innovation in the Public Sector: Enabling Performance, Driving New Directions Better Practice Guide.* Canberra. Online: www.anao.gov.au/uploads/documents/Innovation_in%20 the_Public_Sector.pdf (accessed 19 May 2015).

Australian Public Service Commission (APSC). 2013. *State of the Service Report 2012–13.* Canberra. Online: apsc.gov.au/about-the-apsc/parliamentary-reports/state-of-the-service-series/state-of-the-service-2012-13.pdf (accessed 15 June 2015).

Box, Sarah. 2009. 'OECD work on innovation—a stocktaking of existing work.' Directorate for Science, Technology and Industry. STI Working Paper 2009/2. Paris. Online: www.oecd.org/sti/42095821.pdf (accessed 19 May 2015).

Department of Innovation, Universities and Skills (DIUS). 2008. *Innovation Nation.* March. Norwich: UK Government.

Department of Prime Minister and Cabinet (DPMC). 2010. *Ahead of the Game; Blueprint for the Reform of Australian Government Administration.* Report of the Advisory Group on Australian Government Administration. March, Canberra.

Drechsler, Wolfgang. 2012. 'Is public sector innovation overrated?' Institute of Public Administration Australia 2012 International Congress, Melbourne, 18–20 September.

Eggers, William D. and Kumar Singh Shalabh (Deloitte Research). 2009. *The Public Innovator's Playbook: Nurturing Bold Ideas in Government*. Boston: Harvard Kennedy School, Ash Institute for Democratic Governance and Innovation.

Local Government Association (LGA). 2013. *Improvement and Development Agency for Local Government (IDeA)*. London. Online: www.local.gov.uk (accessed on 15 June 2015).

Management Advisory Committee (MAC). 2010. *Empowering Change: Fostering Innovation in the Australian Public Service*. Canberra: Australian Public Service Commission.

Mulgan, Geoff and David Albury. 2003. *Innovation in the Public Sector*. London. Cabinet Office Strategy Unit. Online: www.childrencount.org/documents/ Mulgan%20on%20Innovation.pdf (accessed 19 May 2015).

Musgrave, Richard and Peggy Musgrave. 1980. *Public Finance in Theory and Practice*. 3rd edition. Tokyo: McGraw-Hill Kogakusha Ltd.

National Audit Office (NAO). 2000. *Supporting Innovation: Managing Risk in Government Departments*. London: Report by Comptroller and Auditor-General.

Podger, Andrew. 2004. 'Innovation with integrity – the public sector leadership imperative to 2020.' *Australian Journal of Public Administration* 63(1) (March): 11–21.

Sabel, Charles F. 2004. 'Beyond principal-agent governance: experimentalist organisations, learning and accountability'. In *De Staat van de Democratie voorbij de Staat*, ed. E.R. Engelen and M. Sie Dhian Ho. Amsterdam: Amsterdam University Press, 1–24.

Schumpeter, Joseph. 1942 (2014). *Capitalism, Socialism and Democracy* (2nd edn). Floyd, VI: Impact Books.

Senge, Peter. 1990. *The Fifth Discipline: The Art and Practice of the Learning Organization*. New York: Image Books.

8

UNLEASHING CHANGE IN GOVERNMENT

Steven J. Kelman
John F. Kennedy School of Government,
Harvard University

This chapter will explore organisational change in government with the aim of enhancing productivity or bringing about service delivery improvements. Specifically, in the context of government austerity and budget cutbacks, I will discuss how we can unleash change as a response to those conditions. In particular, I will focus on how we can initiate a change process and then how we can consolidate it to good effect. My perspective will be one of a manager at any level, from a Director-General or Minister right down to a frontline supervisor. The chapter is based on my book *Unleashing Change* (Kelman 2005).

Do public servants really resist change?

I start with the proposition that it is usually difficult to change ideas in government or in large organisations, because people in general resist change. If change is difficult precisely because people *resist* change, then I would argue what managers or leaders need to do is change the attitudes of those who resist.

Broadly speaking, there are two methods advocated by consultants, advocates and scholars about how to get people to overcome their resistance to change. One common view—a kinder, gentler approach—is to encourage employees to participate in the change process. This is an idea that extends back 60 years in the academic literature. The article 'Overcoming Resistance to Change' (Coch and French 1948) was first published in 1948, but is still widely read today. It involved a field experiment by two social psychologists at a pyjama factory, who were researching how to introduce changes in the production process. The control group of employees was told that there was a lot of competition, and as a result production processes had to be changed. The experimental group was told the same thing, but also asked for their ideas about how to design the new jobs. The control group resisted, and did not change their processes, whereas the experimental group did change, and their productivity increased. There is now a whole strand of literature about how to introduce change to improve performance.

There is also a harder approach, which is that those who resist change in organisations will do so until they confront the metaphorical 'burning platform'; the image evoked is of some oil workers operating out in the ocean who are so set in their ways that they will only change if the platform they are on is actually burning. The presumption here is that people will only change or respond when the circumstances are dire, even life-threatening.

But I want to query the underlying assumptions behind these arguments and beliefs. If, for instance, we hypothetically presume that government civil servants in general resist change, then that would suggest to me that those people in government must be very different from people in general. For in everyday life, it is obvious there are some people who resist change but also some who welcome it—for example, in fashion. There are people with conservative taste in clothes, but also trendsetting, 'fashion conscious' people who seek and embrace change. Think also of technology. There are some people who resist change in technology, but others who welcome change and are 'early adopters' of new technology. Similarly in politics, there are some who resist change, and others who welcome it. So, I would contend that in normal life we do not consider that people *in general* always resist change—that some people do, and some people do not.

This message is my starting point; that many civil servants do resist change— but similarly many do not. My argument grows from the empirical context of my own experience and research on trying to improve procurement systems in the US to assist the government. Now, most outsiders would have said that if you want to look at a prototypical activity of government where people will resist change, look at a procurement system, especially if you are trying to deregulate and free up the system. Most people would argue that this is precisely the source of their authority—telling people they cannot do this or that—so why would they ever want to change that? But, surprisingly, that is not what I found when I started working on this project within government.

Initiating a change process—the 'change vanguard'

In this paper, rather than begin with a purely academic argument, I will start by giving an illustration. As part of my work with the government, I visited a procurement office that was part of the Department of Defence responsible for buying field clothing. In the course of the trip, I met a career civil servant whose main job was to purchase uniforms for soldiers. He had been a civil servant for 30 years, having gradually moved up the chain until he became the senior uniform purchaser—the so-called 'czar' of uniform purchasing. What would be your image of this person and what kind of person do you think he would be? His business card that he showed me might surprise you. It included the usual basic contact details, but in addition, this unusual civil servant had listed his position title as 'Starship Captain' of the Field Clothing Branch of the Defense Logistics Agency of the Defense Supply Center. The business card also contained a photographic image of Doctor Spock from *Star Trek* giving his famous salute; this image was subtitled 'We Are The Force'.

My point is that not everyone fits our stereotype. What I discovered when I came to work in government was that even in the procurement system, there existed what I call a *change vanguard*. When using the term 'change vanguard' I am pointing to the reformers who advocate change before reform occurs. It can include people of all levels inside the organisation, who themselves support new ideas for change within the system. They support change not because external consultants or clients are pushing them to make changes, but because they believe it worthwhile themselves. In my case, when we began this research project we in no way had to coax or persuade these change agents, they were there before we arrived, and had good ideas. From my research, I estimated that about 15 per cent of frontline employees, and about one third of frontline managers in the system, make up the 'change vanguard'. This group is far from everyone in a large organisation, and it is usually not even a majority—but equally it is not nobody.

So, why would a person be in this 'change vanguard'? My research found that the most obvious reason was that they did not like the way the organisation was working at the time. These people often felt they wanted to be able to use their minds and not be so passive in just applying the rules. There were also people who believed in the mission of the organisation for which they worked, but felt that the system was not helping this mission.

In a survey of frontline and supervising procurement professionals, I asked some questions that were not only unrelated to procurement, they were also unrelated to government. I asked them to state whether they agreed or disagreed with the following statements:

> I can't understand people who like to climb mountains.
>
> When I go to a city, I like to explore the city without a map.

When I did the data analysis, the single strongest predictor associated with whether or not a person was in the *change vanguard* was their response to the questions above. These people had an individual personality trait of being more open and adventurous. Similarly, their response to the following question was further indicative of whether they would be in the *change vanguard* or not:

> I consider myself to be an idealist more than a practical person.

Idealists were more likely to be in the *change vanguard*. These were not people who were charged with running the present system, they were a little on the outside of the system, but had been ground down by it. These were the kinds of people who were ready to change even before we arrived.

The key here is that it is very easy for us to operate under the assumption that we, as managers, are the ones with the vision, trying to introduce change, and everyone is against us; and that we do not have any allies. Before anyone in an organisation makes the assumption that everyone will resist change and therefore we must get them to participate or scare them, remember that a 'change vanguard' exists. It is not that we will have to persuade them to change, they are already open to these kinds of reforms. The first question then as managers we need to ask as we begin a change process is: Who are the people in our organisation who can act as the 'change vanguard'? And the second question is: How do we use them to bring about a change process?

The additional message I want to emphasise when an organisation is initiating a change process is that a 'change vanguard' cannot institute a change purely on their own—perhaps because they are too few in number, or because they are not senior enough. In my research I found that some of these managers actually did try to do things on their own but were silently hoping for change from above. Nor can the leaders do anything on their own—they rely on the people at the coalface, the ones who actually do the work. Both groups need to work together to get the change process to happen. The way a change process gets started is that the 'change vanguard', when a change effort is announced by leaders, sees this initiative as the opportunity for change that they wanted but could not effect themselves. So when the leaders announce the change, the 'change vanguard', on its own, gets going.

As a university professor, I believe in the power of words. I think managers fixate too much on the word 'resistance'. So, instead of talking about 'overcoming resistance', I prefer to talk about 'unleashing change'. Instead of worrying about how to convince those who do not agree with the intended changes, I prefer to focus on the change vanguard that doesn't need to be convinced. If we can encourage them to translate their verbal agreement with the changes into action, that will produce a huge change by itself. This is a lesson on priorities for leaders.

Consolidating a change process

Turning to consolidating a change process, how can managers transform a new idea into a part of the way the organisation does ordinary business? If a change effort does not actually eventually improve productivity or service delivery, it will not be consolidated—and, indeed, I would argue it should not be consolidated. There are many change efforts that seem like a good idea worth trying, but they do not work in practice. Sometimes they are bad ideas in the first place. But there is a lot of evidence showing that the initial effect on productivity of a change effort is almost always negative, because there is a learning curve effect. There will be an initial decline in productivity even if it eventually becomes a more efficient way of doing things. However, if productivity keeps falling, perhaps there is cause for concern.

Beyond the obvious that changes that don't improve things won't become consolidated is the interesting idea that change can feed on itself. That is, the very action of initiating an effort and persisting with it can set forces in motion that encourage the effort to consolidate itself and keep expanding. A number of years ago, some social psychologists from Stanford University did an experiment where, in stage one, they went to a random sample of houses in a neighbourhood and showed the residents a petition that said 'we support safe driving'. Everybody signed up. In the second stage they sent a different group of researchers to the neighbourhood—half went to the houses from stage one, the other half went to a different group of houses. This time the researchers went with large, sloppily-made signs for people to place in their front gardens that read 'drive safely'. Of the people who had not been approached earlier, only 20 per cent agreed to place the sign in their yard. Of those who had signed previously, 62 per cent agreed to put the sign outside their house (Freedman and Fraser 1966). This phenomenon is known as the 'foot-in-the-door' technique— if you can earlier get someone to undertake a small change, it becomes easier later to get them to agree to a big change. The take-home message is that if you can get people to commit to the simplest, most uncontroversial part of your change program, it then becomes easier to get them to make more significant changes later on.

So the lesson for managers is: don't get bored as the change process unfolds. This is simple to say, but hard to do. I believe that most change efforts fail because the leaders of the effort abandon the campaign too early, and thus lose the opportunity.

Change in the context of austerity

Let me conclude with a bit about change in the context of austerity. The 'burning platform' concept contains an underlying argument—it starts with the idea that those in government have it too easy, because government is a monopoly with no competition, and that people cannot be easily fired. So how do we remedy this and bring about change in government? One way is to introduce more competition—there is a lot of evidence that suggests that competition spurs better performance, at least in reference to innovation in the private sector—or we could frighten people through job layoffs and budget cuts, with the hope that they will be scared into improvement under this pressure. To what extent and under what circumstances is either of these methods a plausible mechanism for producing change?

The answer in short is not always clear cut. We often do not know enough to be definitive about which types of pressure work most effectively, and I for one hope to do more academic research in the future on the impacts of different kinds of pressure. However, there is some relevant research in this area.

The first finding, from over a century ago, is the 'Reverse-U' impact of stress (see Yerkes and Dodson 1908). When stress levels are low, increasing them improves performance, but only up to a point; at very high levels of stress, performance starts going down. It is hard to know in advance where you are on that U. This is a well-established finding in social psychology.

Moving to competition in government, it is important to note that competition in the private sector has both upsides and downsides. There are upsides if you do well in the competition. But research shows that among companies that are doing badly in competition, downsizing has a negative impact on productivity. So in a government context, if the only benefit is avoiding being fired, it is unclear whether this will have the same positive effect on performance as it would in the private sector.

There is a lot of other research showing that high stress over a long period has negative health impacts. There is also evidence that threats may get people to work harder on existing tasks, but reduce their creativity. They will concentrate their efforts and lose their peripheral vision. It makes them narrowly focused. So there is substantial evidence to say that productivity goes down in a threat situation.

Accordingly, how managers 'frame' a crisis is crucial, because the performance impact of stress depends on the extent to which people who are subject to stress can conceive of it as a threat or a challenge. Framing stress as a challenge leads to better performance. Managers should think about what they and the organisation do to frame the stress. The bad budget environment in the US has demoralised a lot of civil servants. A person who allows this to get to them, to discourage and annoy them, is only hurting themselves—they will not make the austere budget environment go away by feeling depressed about it. Instead, they should think about how they can respond to it creatively, how they can fight back and improve the situation.

These kinds of austerity crises may provide a window of opportunity, not so much in relation to changing people's attitudes, but by encouraging them to focus more on the fact that their organisation has a tough financial situation and they may want to do something about it.

References

Coch, Lester and John R.P. French. 1948. 'Overcoming resistance to change.' *Human Relations* 1: 512–32.

Freedman, Jonathan L. and Scott C. Fraser. 1966. 'Compliance without pressure: The foot-in-the-door technique.' *Journal of Personality and Social Psychology* 4(2): 195–202.

Kelman, Steven J. 2005. *Unleashing Change: A Study of Organizational Renewal in Government*. Washington, DC: Brookings Institution Press.

Yerkes, Robert M. and John D. Dodson. 1908. 'The relation of strength of stimulus to rapidity of habit-formation.' *Journal of Comparative Neurology and Psychology* 18: 459–82.

EIGHT-AND-A-HALF PROPOSITIONS TO STIMULATE FRUGAL INNOVATION IN PUBLIC SERVICES

Jean Hartley
Open University Business School

Introduction

In this chapter I aim to distil some of the key ideas and practices that research has revealed can stimulate or support the processes and outcomes of innovation in public service organisations. Some of the propositions may be surprising to readers, given the conventional wisdom about innovation, which sometimes includes frankly wishful thinking. There has also been an over-reliance (still) on the private sector for the understanding of innovation, and more written about manufacturing than about service innovation.

I intend to set out how innovation can be fostered, in a way that recognises the distinctive features of public services (Osborne et al. 2013; Benington and Moore 2011) and that draws on but is not blinded by the private sector. My hope is that these propositions will act as provocations to policymakers, public managers and academic researchers, challenging current thinking and creating new ways to approach innovation, drawing on evidence and the latest research. The chapter originally consisted of 10 propositions, but following the global financial crisis, many public services have been cut, and this includes academic writing! However, hopefully I have been able to do 'more with less' in this chapter.

This is an opportune time to revisit the processes and practices of innovation, for at least two reasons. First, the cutbacks in public spending following the global financial crisis have led policymakers and public managers to think more closely about innovation—instead of 'salami-slicing'—as a way to cope (Kiefer et al. 2014).

Second, a new phenomenon of *frugal innovation* has been observed in emerging markets such as India (e.g. Immelt et al. 2009; Prahalad and Mashelkar 2010), and the concept is being picked up and applied to cash-strapped post-industrial economies. Frugal innovation provides a different way to go about innovation: instead of costly Research and Development (R&D) laboratories and top-down strategies, innovation can also occur at the bottom of the corporate pyramid, and can be undertaken with the careful use of resources and the avoidance of waste. In public services, some innovation has always been of this type, created by employees close to where services are delivered. The concept of frugal innovation now perhaps gives this approach a greater respectability. The Oxford Dictionary defines frugal as 'simple and plain and costing little'. As we shall see, a newer approach to innovation means that frugal innovation involves borrowing and not just inventing, which entails an outward focus beyond the organisation.

These two trends in thinking about innovation mean that public services innovation has to operate effectively on very limited resources, given the financial context of public services around the world. One of the most obvious ways to stimulate frugal innovation is to reduce the costs of creating, developing and trialling innovations, and the propositions here will offer some opportunities in this respect.

Before presenting the propositions, it is worth addressing one myth about the public sector—that it is not very innovative. Innovation is something often seen as reserved for the private sector—this is an ill-founded view (Hartley et al. 2013). We are surrounded by innovations created by the public sector, not least the origins of the internet, but also a range of information technologies such as the Global Positioning System (GPS), the touchscreen and Siri, as noted by Mariana Mazzucato (2013). There are also many innovations in human services including social innovations, such as microcredit, or the use of iPads for pharmacists to check on the medicine-taking of elderly patients. We may wish for more innovation by public organisations, or that it is done in different ways, but there is already a great deal happening (Hartley et al. 2013; Osborne and Brown 2013).

To set the scene, we need to define what is meant by innovation. First, innovation is more than ideas or invention—rather, it is about new ideas and new practices that are actually *implemented* (Bessant 2005). Second, innovation is not the same as change; it is a particular form of change. Many scholars argue that it is disruptive change, or 'step-change' (Lynn 1997). So innovation is different from continuous improvement, because it is not about gradually increasing efficiency and making things better—rather, it is about doing things *differently*. This may involve a different mindset, a different set of practices; something that is quite disruptive for the organisation. Third, innovation should not be conflated with improvement, or better performance, or success. It is quite possible to have very interesting innovations that, for whatever reason, are not successful at that particular time and place (or at all). Fourth, innovation is not necessarily an entirely new idea never seen before—it is innovative if it is new to the organisation or group adopting the innovation. Thus, innovation is about newness to the organisation—it doesn't matter that it is something that has already happened somewhere else.

In order to examine the propositions carefully, it will help to draw on three analytical phases of innovation: invention, implementation and diffusion. *Invention* relates to the processes of finding or creating the ideas that will be worked up into an innovation. It includes creativity and experimenting with new ways of doing things. *Implementation* is about turning an idea into an actual product or service. It might include piloting, trialling, and going larger scale in the organisation or partnership; so it is about embedding the innovation. *Diffusion* refers to the spreading of a particular innovation outwards across different organisations.

This is, admittedly, a simplified view of innovation, as there are many different models of the stages or phases (Hartley 2013). In addition, the phases may be more emergent than planned. Christian Bason (2010) describes innovation as more like a half-wound ball of yarn than a fixed set of phases. However, while simplified, the three phases are useful for the analysis in this chapter because they suggest different processes at different phases. Some of the propositions will relate to some phases and not others, or have different effects according to the phase. Having briefly outlined the characteristics of innovation, I now turn to consider the propositions.

Proposition 1: Market competition does not necessarily stimulate innovation

Market competition can, but does not inevitably, stimulate innovation. Indeed, sometimes it can hamper innovation. This sounds a little counter-intuitive, especially in an era when there have been strong policy reforms designed to make public organisations more competitive and/or create quasi-markets, and therefore (so the logic goes) increase pressures to be more innovative.

The market competition linked to innovation argument has a long pedigree, going back to Joseph Schumpeter (1950) and echoed since then in economic arguments about 'creative destruction'—the idea that firms are under continual pressure to innovate or else they die. This notion has often been imported into public services with attempts to bring about or simulate market competition. But does market change really help to bring about innovation?

Analysis by Jean Hartley, Eva Sørensen and Jacob Torfing (2013) shows, from a review of the literature, that private sector markets can produce both too much and too little innovation (e.g. Teece 1992). Markets produce too much innovation in the sense that competition often encourages firms to innovate at the invention stage—they put a lot of effort into creativity and into protecting their innovation prototypes through patents and design rights. However, many firms deplete their resources at that stage and so are not able to capitalise on the benefits to be gained at the implementation stage. So, there is less innovation than one might expect. Markets also produce too little innovation where the level and scale of competition leads firms to believe that they will not be able to corral the benefits of the innovation to their own firm, but rather that other firms are going to snatch the benefits. This degree of competition reduces innovation. For the public sector, Richard M. Walker (2008) found that competition was associated with marketisation as a form of innovation but did not affect other aspects of innovation.

It is also known that market competition reduces the diffusion phase of innovation, which involves spreading good (or promising) practices, because it reduces or blocks the sharing of knowledge and ideas across competitor boundaries (Nelson and Winter 1977). I will argue later in this chapter that diffusion is a key element of innovation for public services. So, in increasing competition between public services, is there a risk of damaging the willingness to share and spread innovations?

From this first proposition comes the need to think carefully about the role of market competition or quasi-markets in public services. Market competition may increase innovation, or it may hamper it depending on the conditions—

and this may also vary over time. There is a need for a more contingent view of markets in public services—when do they stimulate and when do they hamper innovation?

Proposition 2: Bureaucracy can be both a help and a hindrance to innovation

Whether an organisation is in the private, public or voluntary sector, bureaucracy can have contradictory effects (rather like competition but for different reasons). I mean 'bureaucracy' as a particular form of organising characterised by job descriptions, tasks, offices and division of labour (Weber 1947; du Gay 2000) rather than a pejorative term.

Research suggests that bureaucracy (whether in the private or public sector) generally makes it more difficult for employees to be creative and for organisations to foster the early stages of innovation, which require imagination, experimentation and risk (Thompson 1965; Damanpour 1991). Bureaucratic organisational processes exist to reduce uncertainty, and enhance predictability and efficiencies in mass production, stability and routine. So it is not really surprising that the more organisational processes and cultures are ordered, routinised and standardised, the harder it is to experiment with innovation in the invention stage. Research shows that the private sector can be just as bureaucratic as the public sector (Rainey and Chun 2005), so government institutions are not particularly afflicted in that sense. One of the key challenges for many organisations wanting to foster innovation is how to become ambidextrous (e.g. Levinthal and March 1993; Utterback 1996). This means being able to run business as usual—serving clients and citizens and so on—but also being able to foster creativity and innovation at the same time. There are different strategies to try to achieve this, not always successful because it is a tough ask. However, some organisations illustrate that it can be done, and there is a lot to learn from ambidextrous organisations.

So far, so conventional: bureaucracies make innovation more difficult. However, research also shows that bureaucracy can *aid* innovation (Hartley et al. 2013). This is perhaps surprising, but bureaucratic organisations sometimes find it easier to *implement* innovation (Hage and Aiken 1967; Zmud 1982). Although the invention stage is more difficult, once ideas have been trialled, developed and accepted, then bureaucracy helps in embedding innovations. For example, the processes of order and routinisation mean that new procedures and standards get written down, and line management can be used to help implement the changes. By contrast, less bureaucratic organisations can be creative at the trial stage, but find it harder to ensure that new procedures or practices are followed.

Fariborz Damanpour and Marguerite Schneider (2006) found that size (which is often related to being bureaucratic) was helpful in all phases of innovation. Finally, there is some evidence that larger organisations are better at diffusing the innovations they have implemented, as was found in a study of UK local government (Rashman et al. 2005). Overall, the concepts of 'innovation' and 'bureaucracy' are not as inimical to each other as is sometimes supposed.

Proposition 3: The key resource in organisations isn't primarily finance but human energy

In a period of substantial fiscal constraint, discussion about change and innovation in public service organisations is often dominated by finance. As a result, innovation is discussed in one of two ways: as either the quick-fix technique to do more with less, or as an attractive but expensive luxury that cannot be undertaken for the time being because there are insufficient funds.

However, while the focus is on finance and budgets, it can be argued that the key resource is people. Emerging research suggests that the energy that they have as individuals, as groups, as teams, as departments, is important. Nurturing a positive climate for innovation can really help in the creation and development of new ideas and new practices, and in their implementation (West et al. 2003).

The NHS Institute of Innovation and Quality (Land et al. 2013) has been exploring five types of energy relevant to organisational performance:

- social energy (the energy that happens in teams, *esprit de corps*, energy created through working with others)
- spiritual energy (a sense of a higher purpose and direction that people have about the organisation; it is not defined as faith-based)
- psychological energy (courage, trust in other people, a sense of psychological safety in taking risk)
- physical energy (to do things and make things happen), and
- intellectual energy (curiosity, horizon scanning, strategic analysis, planning).

This is a promising approach to thinking about how organisations are less or more effective. Some of the types of energy have counterparts in existing organisational concepts (morale, commitment, trust), but the originality lies in thinking of the organisation in energy terms. Energy can spread or fizzle out. The metaphor has intuitive appeal in that any manager can recognise a team or department that has energy, buzz, initiative, proactivity, compared with one that is flat, demoralised, lacking in energy. This initial research deserves further attention.

It is worth considering which of these energies are particularly present in our organisations, and which ones are much weaker or absent. The NHS study found considerable intellectual and physical energy (very bright people engaged in strategic planning and healthcare analysis; as well as people doing things, performing operations and caring for people). However, social, spiritual and psychological energy levels were much lower.

Neuroscience provides valuable metaphors for conceptualising human energy in organisations, and could provide an interesting research agenda (Butler and Senior 2007). Chemical and electrical energy are constantly flowing and moving between synapses in the neural system, continually creating new pathways and neural networks. The network is dynamic as it responds to stimuli. Transferring these ideas into an organisational or partnership context raises some interesting diagnostic questions. Where does the energy move around in organisations and partnerships? What are the conduits for it? Who are the people that act like synapses, helping to translate energy from one neuron to another?

This provides a very different picture of innovation to one derived from a static organisational chart. Energy concepts lie not far below the surface of some accounts of organisational change and innovation. Consider this statement about innovation:

> A leader/entrepreneur is more effective if a bit of charisma is combined with a lot of good judgment, tolerance of ambiguity and a love of argument, passion, risks and action. Leave your door, and your mind, open (Lynn 2013, 41).

In the quotation, a number of words are about energy: *charisma, argument, passion, action*. Innovation is something that alters the status quo, and supplants or modifies existing ways of planning or providing public services. Arguably therefore, human energy is at the heart of the process.

Proposition 4: Harvesting ideas and practices from others can save time and money

The stereotype of innovation is that it starts with lots of people encouraged to be creative within the organisation, perhaps working in an R&D department or policy unit, or perhaps in a workshop or 'sandpit' event. In other words, the assumption has been that invention happens within the organisation.

This was a dominant model of innovation in the private sector for a number of years, but interestingly that model is radically changing across all sectors. It is not always necessary to invent and create things from scratch, because a number of promising products and practices already exist somewhere and may be ripe for use in a different organisation or in a different context. This represents a shift from creating ideas to harvesting ideas as an approach to innovation.

Sometimes this can be 'recombinant' innovation—taking an idea, a product or a practice from somewhere else, and using it in a different way (Hargadon 2003). An illustration of this process comes from Great Ormond Street Hospital's use of ideas and practices from Formula 1 racing. Doctors were concerned about the transfer of sick children from surgery to intensive care, which involves a change of team and potential loss of key information in the transfer. Watching Formula 1 on television one day, some doctors were struck that a pit stop represented an important concept that could be modified and applied in the hospital. The transferable concepts were: a team-based approach, with each team member having a clear and specific role; the clear communication of the current state of the car through a set procedure; rehearsal of the pit stop so that everyone is clear about the tasks and has had practice in what to do; and, having one person in charge who makes the decision about whether the car is ready and safe to go back out on the track. As a team, they used these basic practices, modifying and adapting them for the different context and task. This is frugal innovation because the team with the need for innovation harvested ideas from elsewhere, and it was not a costly invention procedure. There are many opportunities to use ideas from different (or similar) contexts, with careful thought about how to apply or adapt those ideas in a different setting.

Another approach to harvesting ideas comes from open innovation (Chesbrough 2003). This is innovation that draws on the ideas and suggestions of users, clients, members of the public, and citizens. Some of these groups are interested and knowledgeable about public services. They may be experts in particular public services, either as users or as professionals who come into contact with that service. For example, children are helping to design hospital environments to make them child-friendly, and former drug addicts are helping to design and develop addiction services in Denmark. Dennis Hilgers and Christoph Ihl (2010) call this 'citizensourcing' (the public counterpart to crowdsourcing), and argue that it is an important source of ideas and practices for public organisations. It is different from public consultation (where a course of action has often already been decided). However, unlike open innovation in the private sector—where a firm can harvest ideas from anyone—public service organisations need to carefully think through who contributes and on what basis so that certain groups in society are not disadvantaged through the innovation process.

Harvesting ideas rather than (or as well as) inventing them in-house is a radically different model of innovation. It requires looking outwards, not inwards, because the innovation may be a novel application of a product or practice in an entirely different setting. It still depends on a positive innovation climate—energy and curiosity to engage with ideas from the external world beyond the service or organisation.

Proposition 5: Diffusion of innovation is the public sector's secret weapon

Not enough attention is paid to diffusion as a phase of innovation in public service organisations. This may occur for a number of reasons. The public services innovation literature has, until quite recently, been over-reliant on the understanding of innovation derived from the private sector (Hartley 2013), in part because of the assumption that innovation comes through competition, but also due to the lack of research from public management researchers. In the private sector, diffusion is often the last thing that firms wish to engage in, especially where there is stiff market competition enabling value capture by other firms. Consequently, the literature on diffusion is still somewhat sparse compared with the other phases of innovation.

Yet, for public services, diffusion can be a very effective way of undertaking innovation. It reduces the costs of invention—instead of reinventing the wheel, the existing wheel can be used, avoiding the development costs and mistakes made by another organisation. Diffusion reduces the operational and political risks of the innovation, because it has been tried and tested in another context. Snags have hopefully been smoothed out, improvements in design or operation can be made, and the political risk of working with an unknown product or service reduced. The argument that risk is a problem for public service innovation is thus mitigated by drawing on others' experience. Furthermore, in public services, those who have innovated are sometimes keen to share their experience (Rashman et al. 2005). Finally, many public organisations have a moral imperative to share their innovations, because society needs innovation to be spread beyond the initial innovator. There is little value in having an effective innovation in (for example) cancer care if it is limited to a single hospital. Despite these arguments about the value of innovation, how much do public managers allocate in the way of resources and organisational procedures towards sharing good and promising practices, compared with inventing and implementing innovation?

There are some important examples of diffusion, for example in health and in local government. Diffusion is not simply replication or 'copy and paste' from the innovator. In a large study of sharing innovation in UK local government (Hartley and Benington 2006; Rashman et al. 2005), diffusion was found to be widespread but also to involve critical processes of adaptation to local context and conditions. The UK's Beacon Scheme was a national program operating for over a decade in the early twenty-first century. It aimed to celebrate high performance and innovation, and spread good practice from the 'innovators' to the 'learner' organisations. Among the learner organisations in 2004 that had used ideas from the innovator, there were varying patterns in the way that diffusion was implemented. Sixty-three per cent reported that they had adapted the idea from the innovator. This shows that adjustment takes place as the innovation moves from one organisation to another. *Adaptation* happened more than *adoption*. In addition, 29 per cent reported that they *accelerated* an idea which they already had. From interviews, it was possible to ascertain that this gave the learner greater confidence in using the innovation, and also that it reduced risk and built political (both small and big 'p') support. Finally, only a small percentage—8 per cent—said they based their change *closely* on the innovator.

Diffusion does not need to cost much. The innovations are already there, being used, and with some known properties. Why is diffusion not more widespread? And why is there not more research on diffusion as a critical stage of innovation for public services?

Proposition 6: Knowledge creation and learning is central to innovation

It is easy to get fascinated by innovative technologies—the information and communications technology (ICT), the new equipment, and so on—and treat them as though they are the innovation. But this is rarely the case; the innovation is likely to be not just the technology but also the practicalities of making it work—and that requires new knowledge being created and transferred between human beings (Nonaka 1994; Hargadon 2003). Learning is partly undertaken by individuals in relation to their own job, but it also involves learning in teams and sections, and indeed learning across the organisation and between organisations (Rashman et al. 2009). Knowledge and learning may be particularly critical for service innovations, where the key elements of the innovation consist of the new or substantially altered relationships in service creation (whether those relationships are between service user and professional, between professionals, or between managers and subcontractors).

Learning may involve new concepts and procedures, and also involve working out how the innovation fits with existing practices and procedures (Behn 2008). Adjustments may be necessary as plans are altered after 'teething problems', or there is recognition of fine-tuning. Sometimes an innovation will create unanticipated problems (and benefits) in areas not directly connected with the innovation (Hartley 2005). So observation, reflection, discussion and learning are advisable as the innovation develops from invention to implementation to diffusion. It is generally not possible to innovate without people (whether managers, staff, clients, or politicians) having to learn new ways of doing things, making mistakes, giving up particular ways of doing things, and adopting new ways. This is essential, but often goes unremarked.

Innovation is rarely a primrose path—it is full of all sorts of obstacles, cul-de-sacs and frustrations, and people need time to learn from that, and time to put this learning into practice. Learners generally want to learn as much about the frustrations, barriers and problems in innovation as they do about the successes (Rashman et al. 2005).

Proposition 7: Public innovation can benefit from the contributions of politicians

This might sound like an obvious proposition, but whether explicitly or under their breath, some managers tend to feel that they could innovate much better without politicians. In addition, relatively few academics have studied the role of politicians in innovation. This may be a legacy of over-reliance on private sector thinking about innovation.

Some research shows that elected politicians, whether national, state/devolved or local, are important in all sorts of ways (Rashman and Hartley 2002; Hartley and Rashman 2007). They can build public support for innovation before it occurs, help to deal with sceptics, listen to the views of doubters and bring them round to support, and mobilise various stakeholders, including collaborators across sectors and services. They can provide the right climate to enable managers and staff to experiment, and they can challenge technical thinking, combining it with political nous. They can help unblock problems and build coalitions to support the innovation. In short, they can be a key part of the leadership of innovation (Hartley 2013). Not all politicians play these roles or play them effectively, but they are active in case studies of significant innovations in public services.

Proposition 8: 'Innovation and improvement' is not a single concept

'Innovation and improvement' is often used as a single policy phrase, as though innovation were so naturally and inevitably beneficial that it always leads to improvements (e.g. in service scope or quality, in efficiency, in value for money). However, not all innovations lead to improvement, and not all improvements require innovation.

An innovation, by virtue of its newness to the organisation or partnership, inevitably carries some risk of failure or partial failure. Joe Tidd, John Bessant and Keith Pavitt (2001) estimate that in the private sector approximately a third of innovations fail, or are inappropriate for the particular time or context. In the public sector the percentage may well be higher, because there is a more critical and transparent environment within which innovations occur.

Some organisations in any sector suffer from having too much innovation. Michael Moran (2003) argues that the UK state is characterised by 'hyper-innovation', with too many innovations being initiated. He questions the extent to which this has had a beneficial impact. From a different perspective, Marianne Jennings (2006) argues that hyper-innovation within an organisation can be a sign of ethical collapse, where managers use innovation as an argument to take unjustified ethical risk.

Conversely, not all improvement involves innovation. Improvement can occur through continuous improvement methodologies, which are based on doing things *better*, rather than innovation, which is based on doing things *differently* (Hartley 2011). These different approaches to improvement have different implications for managing change, leadership, motivating staff and the extent to which one might anticipate the outcomes being planned or partly emergent. Working out what magnitude and kind of change is desirable, in what context, and over what timescale, may help to shape whether an organisation should embark on continuous improvement or innovation.

Buy eight, get one free: Building a robust evidence base

The final (half) proposition concerns the creation of a robust evidence base about public innovation. I have noted several times in this chapter that policymakers, public managers and academics are still overly reliant on concepts, frameworks and theories about innovation derived from the private sector. It is important to construct and use a systematic evidence base about what works for innovation in public services, and for collaborative innovation across sectors and services.

There is unlikely to be 'one best way' to innovate—it depends on the context, the political climate, the purpose of the innovation. But what works, for whom, in what circumstances, and why still needs addressing in detail. There is a need to learn from failures as well as successes, rather than quietly sidelining innovations that do not work. This is not easy of course, given the glare of the media, particularly in relation to the more spectacular innovation failures in the public sector. There can also be a 'blame game' in politicised environments such as public services. However, public managers and others can gain from understanding what went wrong, or what failed to thrive in particular contexts, and use that to craft modified or alternative innovations. It is valuable to monitor and evaluate both successful and unsuccessful innovation initiatives, across all phases, including implementation and diffusion—not just the early buzzy invention phase. Bringing together learning from academics, policymakers and practitioners will create rich data about innovation for public service organisations, and build better understanding of innovation for the future.

Conclusions

I have presented eight-and-a-half propositions about innovation to stimulate debate, reflection and action. These derive from research findings, and create a picture of implications for action that are different from conventional thinking about innovation. For too long, innovation for governance and public services has been in the shadow of concepts and research derived from the private sector, and often a manufacturing perspective has been prioritised over a service perspective. There is a lot to learn from aspects of private sector innovation processes and outcomes, but like innovation itself, diffusion of ideas from one sector to another needs adaptation not adoption. There is a need to think carefully about the specific elements of the public innovation context, processes, stakeholders and outcomes, so that approaches to innovation are appropriate to context and purpose. So, quasi-markets or market competition may be problematic as well as helpful, just as bureaucracy can help as well as hinder. In public innovation, diffusion takes a much more prominent place than has previously been recognised.

I hope that taking account of these eight-and-a-half propositions will help public organisations, either alone or in partnership with the private and voluntary sectors, to create frugal innovation. It is the right time to create and deploy a more informed understanding of public innovation, given the current interest in innovation as a means to avoid 'salami-slicing' public services, and given new developments in frugal innovation. I do hope these propositions have provoked the readers of this chapter.

Acknowledgements

Thanks to John Benington for alerting me to the idea of human energy, and to Richard Blundel for reading an earlier draft of this chapter. An earlier version of this chapter was published as 'New development: Eight and a half propositions to stimulate frugal innovation', *Public Money and Management* (May 2014): 227–32.

References

Bason, Christian. 2010. *Leading Public Sector Innovation: Co-Creating for a Better Society*. Bristol: Policy Press.

Behn, Robert. 2008. 'The adoption of innovation: Learning to adapt tacit knowledge.' In *Innovations in Government: Research, Recognition and Replication*, ed. Sandford Borins. Washington, DC: Brookings, 138–58.

Benington, John and Mark H. Moore. 2011. *Public Value: Theory and Practice*. Basingstoke: Macmillan.

Bessant, John. 2005. 'Enabling continuous and discontinuous innovation: Learning from the private sector.' *Public Money and Management* 25: 35–42.

Butler, Michael and Carl Senior. 2007. 'Research possibilities for organizational cognitive neuroscience.' *Annals of the New York Academy of Sciences* 1118: ix–xii, 1–211. Online: onlinelibrary.wiley.com/doi/10.1111/nyas.2007.1118. issue-1/issuetoc (accessed 13 May 2015).

Chesbrough, Henry. 2003. *Open Innovation*. Boston: Harvard Business School Press.

Damanpour, Fariborz. 1991. 'Organizational innovation: A meta-analysis of effects of determinants and moderators.' *Academy of Management Journal* 34(3): 555–90.

Damanpour, Fariborz and Marguerite Schneider. 2006. 'Phases of the adoption of innovation in organizations: Effects of environment, organization and top managers.' *British Journal of Management* 17: 215–36.

du Gay, Paul. 2000. *In Praise of Bureaucracy*. London: Sage.

Hage, Jerald and Michael Aiken. 1967. 'Program change and organizational properties.' *American Journal of Sociology* 72(2): 503–19.

Hargadon, Andrew. 2003. *How Breakthroughs Happen: The Surprising Truth about how Companies Innovate.* Boston: Harvard Business School Press.

Hartley, Jean. 2005. 'Innovation in governance and public services: Past and present.' *Public Money and Management* 25 (January): 27–34.

Hartley, Jean. 2011. 'Public value through innovation and improvement.' In *Public Value: Theory and Practice*, ed. John Benington and Mark H. Moore. Basingstoke: Palgrave, 171–84.

Hartley, Jean. 2013. 'Public and private features of innovation.' In *Sage Handbook of Innovation in Public Services*, ed. Stephen P. Osborne and Louise Brown. London: Sage, 44–59.

Hartley, Jean and John Benington. 2006. 'Copy and paste, or graft and transplant? Knowledge sharing through inter-organizational networks.' *Public Money and Management* 26(2): 101–08.

Hartley, Jean and Lyndsay Rashman. 2007. 'How is knowledge transferred between organizations involved in change?' In *Managing Change in the Public Services*, ed. Mike Wallace, Michael Fertig and Eugene Schneller. Oxford: Blackwell, 173–92.

Hartley, Jean, Eva Sørensen and Jacob Torfing. 2013. 'Collaborative innovation: A viable alternative to market competition and organizational entrepreneurship.' *Public Administration Review* 73(6): 821–30.

Hilgers, Dennis and Christoph Ihl. 2010. 'Citizensourcing: Applying the concept of open innovation to the public sector.' *International Journal of Public Participation* 4: 67–88.

Immelt, Jeffrey R., Vijay Govindarajan and Chris Trimble. 2009. 'How GE is disrupting itself.' *Harvard Business Review* (October): 56–65.

Jennings, Marianne. 2006. *The Seven Signs of Ethical Collapse.* New York: St Martin's Press.

Kiefer, Tina, Jean Hartley, Neil Conway and Rob B. Briner. 2014. 'Doing more with less? Employee reactions to psychological contract breach via target similarity or spillover during public sector organizational change.' *British Journal of Management* 25(4): 737–54.

Kelman, Steven. 2005. *Unleashing Change.* Washington, DC: Brookings.

Land, Martin, Nick Hex and Chris Bartlett. 2013. *Building and Aligning Energy for Change*. London: National Health Service.

Levinthal, Daniel A. and James G. March. 1993. 'The myopia of learning.' *Strategic Management Journal* 14 (Winter): 95–112.

Lynn, Laurence E. 1997. 'Innovation and the public interest: Insights from the private sector.' In *Innovation in American Government*, ed. Alan Altchuler and Robert Behn. Washington, DC: Brookings Institution, 84–103.

Lynn, Laurence E. 2013. 'Innovation and reform in public administration: One subject or two?' In *Handbook of Innovation in Public Services*, ed. Stephen P. Osborne and Louise Brown. Cheltenham: Edward Elgar, 29–43.

Mazzucato, Mariana. 2013. *The Entrepreneurial State*. London: Anthem Press.

Moran, Michael. 2003. The British Regulatory State: High Modernism and Hyper-innovation, Oxford: Oxford University Press.

Nelson, Richard R. and Sidney G. Winter. 1977. 'In search of a useful theory of innovation.' *Research Policy* 6: 36–76.

Nonaka, Ikujiro. 1994. 'A dynamic theory of organizational knowledge creation.' *Organization Science* 5: 14–37.

Osborne, Stephen P. and Louise Brown. 2013. *Handbook of Innovation in Public Services*. London: Sage.

Osborne Stephen P., Zoe Radnor and Greta Nasi. 2013. 'A new theory for public service management? Toward a (public) service-dominant approach.' *The American Review of Public Administration* 43(2): 135–58.

Prahalad, C.K. and R.A. Mashelkar. 2010. 'Innovation's holy grail.' *Harvard Business Review* 88(7/8): 132–41.

Rainey, Hal G. and Young Han Chun. 2005. 'Public and private management compared.' In *The Oxford Handbook of Public Management*, ed. Ewan Ferlie, Laurence E. Lynn and Christopher Pollitt. Oxford: Oxford University Press, 72–102.

Rashman, Lyndsay and Jean Hartley. 2002. 'Leading and learning? Knowledge transfer in the Beacon Council Scheme.' *Public Administration* 80: 523–42.

Rashman, Lydnsay, Erin Withers and Jean Hartley. 2009. 'Organizational learning and knowledge in public service organizations: A systematic review of the literature.' *International Journal of Management Reviews* 10(3): 463–94.

Rashman, Lyndsay, James Downe and Jean Hartley. 2005. 'Knowledge creation and transfer in the Beacon Scheme: Improving services through sharing good practice.' *Local Government Studies* 31(5): 683–700.

Schumpeter, Joseph. 1950. *Capitalism, Socialism and Democracy*. New York: Harper and Row.

Sørensen, Eva and Jacob Torfing. 2011. 'Enhancing collaborative innovation in the public sector.' *Administration and Society* 43(8): 842–68.

Teece, David J. 1992. 'Competition, cooperation and innovation: Organizational arrangements for regimes of rapid technological progress.' *Journal of Economic Behavior and Organization* 18(1): 1–25.

Thompson, Victor. 1965. 'Bureaucracy and innovation.' *Administrative Science Quarterly* 10(1): 1–20.

Tidd, Joe, John Bessant and Keith Pavitt. 2001. *Managing Innovation*. 2nd edn. Chichester: Wiley.

Utterback, James M. 1996. *Mastering the Dynamics of Innovation*. Cambridge, MA: Harvard Business School Press.

Walker, Richard M. 2008. 'An empirical evaluation of innovation types and organizational and environmental characteristics: towards a configuration framework.' *Journal of Public Administration Research and Theory* 18: 591–615.

Weber, Max. 1947. *The Theory of Social and Economic Organization*. Trans. A.M. Henderson and Talcott Parsons. London: Collier Macmillan.

West, Michael, Carol S. Borrill, Jeremy F. Dawson, Felix Brodbeck, David A. Shapiro and Robert Haward. 2003. 'Leadership clarity and team innovation in health care.' *Leadership Quarterly* 14: 393–410.

Wilson, James. 1989. Bureaucracy: What Government Agencies Do and Why They Do It. New York: Basic Books.

Zmud, Robert W. 1982. 'Diffusion of modern software practices: influence of centralization and formalization.' *Management Science* 28: 1421–31.

STRATEGIC ADVICE TO THE PUBLIC SERVICE FACING AUSTERITY

Paul McClintock
New South Wales Public Service
Commission Advisory Board

This book is about doing things with less or improving productivity. In business this is linked with competitive advantage, given the role of outputs in the equation. Business has a long history of reducing costs and driving and measuring productivity, and most would agree that it is well ahead of the public sector in this task. This is not surprising, as measuring productivity in the public sector is difficult—the inputs are often reasonably easy, but the outputs and outcomes are not. For some time, productivity in government has been seen more as a reaction to 'efficiency dividends' than as a real analysis of the value of what is produced for what cost.

I welcome the broader focus that is apparent in this book's theme and structure, set out particularly in John Wanna's introductory background chapter. Yet I still feel there is a real danger that we leap into the details of service delivery— important as they are—and skip over the broader issue of the value of the output we are measuring. To use a business analogy, we would be surprised if the productivity of a car plant were measured purely by how long the workforce took to screw a bolt on a car, as we all know that the greater productivity benefits are likely to come from designing a car with fewer bolts. Equally in the public sector, a focus on how to deliver more of the same with lower costs may miss the greater question of whether we are producing the right outcomes. The best example of this mismatch is the shuddering reaction of business when the government tells us a measure of its success is the number of pieces of legislation it has managed to pass!

Difficulty in measurement should not prevent a broad view of the factors to be considered when looking at public sector productivity. I consider it vital to see the sector as part of the whole national economy, not just because of its size but also for its impact on the rest of us. If there are opportunities from austerity (as suggested by my former COAG Reform Council (CRC) colleague Doug McTaggart in Chapter 2 of this volume) they must include a rethink of what the public sector value-add really is, and is it delivering it at the best possible price for the community?

Let me expand that question by looking at the regulatory burden impacting on the costs of major infrastructure works in Australia, both public and private. This topic has been analysed at length, with the suggestion that delays alone caused by government in many projects add millions to the cost of those works. Every dollar added unnecessarily to spending reduces Australia's national productivity and its international competitiveness.

Every politician and commentator in the country says this is the main game, so one might think that there would be intense scrutiny of whether such costs were justified, or whether the national goals sought, such as proper environmental protection, could be achieved for less. This wider impact on productivity is likely to be far greater than the question of excessive costs within the public sector itself, yet the two are rarely added together to try to assess whether the gains sought are worth the national cost. I very much hope that this book will help us see the larger picture as being the real mountain worth climbing.

Lifting the productivity of policy work or administrative work is particularly challenging. I once attended a lecture presented by the notable Canadian Professor Roger Martin of Integrated Thinking and Design Thinking fame. His talk was on white-collar productivity growth, which he argued from his US studies was around 0 per cent. He went on to state that productivity elsewhere, such as in the factory, remained at its historical average of about 4 per cent, so in terms of the national economy the white-collar workers were seen as the problem. Yet, it seemed to me that the challenge he was throwing out to private business to drive productivity in what he called the 'decision factory' applied even more so to the public service, where white-collar work is disproportionately located. So the challenge here is not one only for the private sector but for the public sector too, and perhaps the sectors have more to learn from each other than they perceive. Interestingly, Professor Martin's thesis for greater white-collar productivity in the private sector involved dramatic workplace flexibility, which is a huge challenge for the current way we appoint public sector officials and give them considerable ownership of the static job position they have won through a competitive process.

Let me propose five pieces of strategic advice for public servants and the public service in general.

Be positive—austerity is an opportunity

First, try to look happy with austerity; it is your chance to get rid of boring jobs you only did because the old minister was paranoid about something happening on his or her watch—or perhaps anything happening at all. Your success is not linked to the people in the department doing menial tasks, like auditors in the old days checking the travel dockets. Spend some time developing really good ideas on what could and should be axed, and take your minister firmly to the issue of function before you get caught up with efficiency.

I tried this idea on a senior officer in the Defence Materiel Organisation, which most readers will know is a large part of our Defence establishment. I suggested that the organisation could not only shed the usual 5 per cent, but could be half as big and much more fun to work in. It would need a different approach to contracting, more discipline in what was bought, and an acceptance by all— including the Auditor-General and the Senate Estimates committees—that while leaving some discretion does sometimes lead to mistakes, the cost of second guessing everything that is done may not be worth the price.

They are not 'your dollars'

Second, and this is very relevant to the operation of the Australian federation, give up the concept of a 'Commonwealth' or 'state' dollar—as if the jurisdiction owns these resources. This applies more to the Commonwealth, as they have more dollars to dispense. Efficiency dictates that the Commonwealth is the logical national tax collector, but the Constitution assumes the states deliver most of the services. If we continue to live with this level of vertical fiscal imbalance, and jurisdictions still cling to the concept of 'their dollars', then we will condemn the system to significant overlap between jurisdictions and the consequential waste that goes with it.

I was impressed with at least the theoretical insight of the UK Public Accounts Committee (PAC), which grappled with this dilemma when the Cameron government was elected and was committed to devolve responsibility away from Whitehall and into local communities. The PAC is the House of Commons watchdog, with centuries of lively history behind it, and they had come to the view that they would not stop the oversight of a pound unless and until it was handed over to another body with real political accountability for its final destination. They were struggling, as the money was being spent by local authorities that were not seen to have political structures strong enough to ensure real accountability. What joy, I thought, that we have a federation with a national government created by the states, where that level of accountability is clear and well established.

During my six years at the CRC I am not sure I met many politicians or officers who shared this joy and this insight, but it is the essential prerequisite for a productive federation. The perennial round of arguments over school funding is a good example. More money from the federal government always warms the hearts of state politicians and their bureaucrats, but the difficulty in providing such largesse was created by other levels of argument about the appropriate level of Commonwealth involvement in school education. I hope that this debate was conducted thoughtfully in private, concentrating on the many benefits that Commonwealth involvement would bring to the quality of our children's education nationally. In public, however, we rarely got past the 'Commonwealth dollar' point, and most of us watching on got no sense of the value-add of the Commonwealth's arrival—apart from their money. Given that it is difficult to think of an area more in the heartland of state government than school education, it is understandable that the benefits of federal wisdom did not seem self-evident.

Convince the Australian public about long-term sustainability

Third, try arguing that long-term sustainability can be sold to the Australian public as a worthwhile goal. I know this goes against all the accepted wisdom that expediency triumphs, but perhaps politicians have not tried hard enough. Certainly austerity is a great companion for this view. A pertinent example here is 'generational health reform', and before anyone thinks that we had done that already under the Rudd–Gillard governments, let me tell you we did not get far. We were offered generational change, but instead of asking the difficult question of how to identify and implement a long-term sustainable health system, the reform went straight to telling the states how to fix their public hospitals. The old joke that you wouldn't start from here is apt, as it is hard to conceive a worse place to begin. The Bennett Commission inquiry had given some leads to the question, suggesting that the 20-year development and roll-out of the health system in the Netherlands was the best attempt at new thinking on how to build long-term sustainability into our system—an option for Australia called 'Medicare Select' by the Commission. That recommendation was largely ignored, and yet I felt it was the most important insight in the entire report.

Distinguishing our jurisdictions: We can tell the difference between state and federal responsibilities

Fourth, we must keep challenging the view that the Australian public is incapable of distinguishing between the roles of different governments. This is a new view largely but not solely held in Canberra, and fed by the growing confusion about the roles of the different levels of government. But it is wrong to accuse the public of driving this confusion—they managed for a century to understand that if hospitals, police, schools and urban infrastructure (including public transport) were inadequate, you blamed the state government. Equally, when issues of the economy, national defence or immigration arose, you looked to the Commonwealth. Now, with a tendency to create blurred accountabilities, we end up in situations where no one is really accountable, or prepared to accept accountability. But this does not need to be the case.

As the head of the CRC, I put it to the prime minister of the day that the Commonwealth government could not give adequate political accountability for an individual hospital, but a state minister could—and did. Accepting that the Commonwealth was by now the dominant funder (and recognising that that was an important development) was bound to move responsibility to the Commonwealth. But, I argued, the responsible Commonwealth minister (whether the Treasurer or the Health minister) could not deliver real accountability for delivery and day-to-day operations. There seemed little acceptance of that view in Canberra. I also could not work out why a Commonwealth minister wanted to have responsibility for each public hospital, given the difficulties inherent in that task.

Attempt tasks that are 'too hard'

Fifth and finally, I would urge our public officials to push the boundaries on issues that they know are right but which common wisdom suggests are too hard. Austerity affords us a window where conventional wisdom can be challenged. I am conscious that many officials work closely with the political executive, and therefore are constrained in what they can argue for in public, but I wonder whether the boundaries are really being pushed in the comparative secrecy of government offices and away from the public arena because we have lowered our expectations of what can be attempted.

In my own personal journey over the past few years I have entered the public arena on four 'too hard' issues: federalism (on behalf of the CRC); medical insurance regulation (on behalf of Medibank); proper process in the Australian Human Rights Commission; and a level playing field for GST tax on imports (both on behalf of Myer). In each case, cautious or wise advisors could have said I was wasting my time or I was taking on vested interests best left alone, but I felt strongly on all four and I thought my arguments should be made with conviction and in public. I was satisfied with the hearing I got in all cases, and although none of them seem as yet to be fully completed I did feel my decision to enter the debate at least enhanced the quality of the discussion. I hope it also improves the final result in each of them.

In my experience, there is nothing more dispiriting than being told by a national leader, politician or official that the points you are making about where Australia could go are both accepted and important, but too hard. This defeatism needs to be fiercely opposed.

Not so long ago I delivered the Sir Roland Wilson Lecture at The Australian National University, and in it I argued the logic for a review of how our federal system is working. In particular, I argued that a change of culture was needed, as I had consistently since I took up the CRC job six years earlier:

> Do the players really understand each other? Have they got to know each other and understand their respective talents, experiences and perspectives? Do they train together, think strategically together, spend time together beyond what is required to do today's tasks? Or is the great collective effort of leading Australia— which is shared by all our governments—a hostage to the electoral cycle, marked with cynicism, suspicion and lack of respect? (McClintock 2012).

This is a challenge for us all. The federation needs a great deal more investment, and our think tanks and executive development agencies such as the Australia and New Zealand School of Government (ANZSOG) should be a key part of the solution. I then went on to argue that both major political parties should have an approach to the federation to put to the electorate, so that they can 'read any policies that are impacted by the federal system—including health and education, disability and indigenous disadvantage, housing and training— in light of that federalism policy. If they are not in harmony, put a serious discount on the lot!' (McClintock 2012).

After that speech I was pleased to see the Coalition's commitment, given in the Leader's Budget Reply speech of 2013, to conduct a review of the federal system with the states, leading to a White Paper within a couple of years of their election to government (Abbott 2013). This exercise is perhaps a real opportunity to give these issues the attention they crave, and a new philosophical base will give us real guidance on how the whole system should run. I also welcome the growing prominence given to this issue by my business colleagues, particularly by the Business Council of Australia. So maybe we will have another chance at major reform and produce tangible benefits and lift national productivity—I know many are waiting for it.

Conclusion

To sum up, I urge all those who seek to influence government to try out my principles:

1. Embrace austerity and be creative on function.
2. Give up the ownership of a tax dollar—it belongs to the community and not to any government—and let responsibility flow to the party who controls the outcomes.
3. Long-term sustainability must be championed in the community and its support will be secured.
4. The community is capable of holding different levels of government accountable if they stay out of each other's business.
5. Challenge the 'too hard' assumptions—get a bit ambitious, or least get us free from mediocre aspirations that will leave us in the austerity zone for a long time.

This may sound simple, although I do accept that it is not. But let me end with a view of what is at stake. Australia has a wealth-generating sector that has been successful enough to fund generously a government sector empowered to control the use of that wealth, and to encourage its further generation. I have observed the Australian political scene closely for nearly half of the life of the federation—I started as the young son of a senior Canberra official—and the confidence and respect between the public and private sectors is profoundly low. It affects not only the political class, but also the public service. This gulf will do great damage to the nation if it is not addressed, and we all have a part to play.

References

Abbott, Tony. 2013. 'Budget reply speech.' Parliament House, Canberra, 17 May. Online: www.liberal.org.au/latest-news/2013/05/16/tony-abbott-budget-reply-parliament-house-canberra (accessed 14 April 2014).

McClintock, Paul. 2012. 'Harnessing federalism—the missing key to successful reform.' Sir Roland Wilson Foundation Lecture at the Crawford School of Public Policy, The Australian National University, Canberra, 19 November. Online: www.coagreformcouncil.gov.au/media/speeches/2012-11-19 (accessed 14 April 2014).

CAN 'NUDGING' CHANGE BEHAVIOUR? USING 'BEHAVIOURAL INSIGHTS' TO IMPROVE PROGRAM REDESIGN

David Halpern and Rory Gallagher
UK Behavioural Insights Team Cabinet Office

David Halpern

Observations from the UK's No. 10 Cabinet Office Behavioural Insights Team

Behavioural insights is, in essence, quite a simple idea: if we adopt more sophisticated models of what it is that drives human behaviour—including judgements of risk and what people actually do—we might make better policy which is easier, more effective, and more cost effective too. It is important to note from the outset that we use *behavioural insights* (rather than behavioural economics) to refer to that range of literature about human behaviour from behavioural economics, social psychology, neuroscience and sociology. We prefer the term 'behavioural insights' mainly because it is less doctrinal, and I know that there are many psychologists out there who feel that 'behavioural economics' has been appropriated by economists to the exclusion of psychologists. The UK Cabinet Office team feel that 'behavioural insights' is a broader, more encompassing term.

The Conservative–Liberal Democrat coalition government in Britain, particularly in 2010, brought this idea forward—that we could support and help people make better choices for themselves. It has been our brief for almost four years now, and we have had some fantastic results.

Nuts and bolts changes

There are two kinds of projects we do. One is 'nuts and bolts' changes, some of which have been quite long in the design and making. An example is a 2012 change to the defaults on employer-funded pensions (superannuation). We moved from an opt-in system to an opt-out system for employer pensions, leading to about 90 per cent of people staying in the system. It is a remarkable result. For decades, people have struggled to get the savings rate up of workers, and simply by changing the default we have achieved this remarkable effect. We are by no means the only ones in the world to do this, but it is still powerful and gratifying to see it working.

There are other examples I can mention. We have run many randomised control trials to test the effects of small 'nudges' across a number of areas of domestic policy. One great success has been our initiative to change the letters issued by our tax office, Inland Revenue. Our tax authorities write millions of tax letters every year. We found that small changes in the wording—for example, telling people something that is true: 'most people pay their tax on time'—can be a very effective way of encouraging people to pay their tax. Even a small variation on that—saying 'most people in your area have paid their tax and you are one of the few that are yet to pay'—turns out to be a very effective way of increasing compliance and tax rates. Interestingly, it also reduces the number of complaints. The marginal cost of these changes is almost zero, and they are now bringing in hundreds of millions of pounds in forward payment on tax in the UK.

Figure 11.1 reports our findings graphically. We identified a control group of people who needed to pay their self-assessment tax, and 34 per cent responded to a standard control letter. When we included a statement about the UK norm (e.g. '9 out of 10 people pay their tax on time'), the response rate went up to 35 per cent. When we added the local norm ('9 out of 10 people in Exeter pay their tax on time'), it went up yet again, to 36 per cent. When we included the debt norm (highlighting that the person receiving the letter is in the minority of those that have not paid), the response rate increased further still. When the local and debt norm were put together (e.g. '9 out of 10 people in Exeter pay their tax on time; this puts you in a minority of 3,000 people'), this resulted in a more than 5 percentage points increase in payment compared to the control group. This was a huge result simply generated by changing a few lines on a letter.

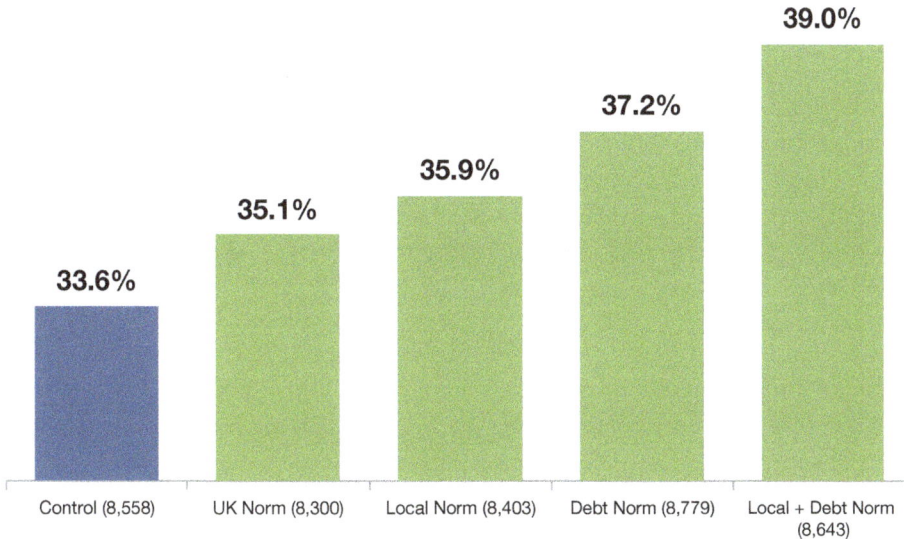

Figure 11.1. Percentage of taxpayers paying outstanding taxes after 23 days, by type of tax letter received
Source: UK Behavioural Insights Team Cabinet Office.

Another example relates to employment and changing what happens in job centres. We made substantial changes to the way the job-seeking contract operates. Instead of asking people to prove retrospectively that they have looked for at least three jobs in the previous two weeks, we asked them, 'What are you going to do in the next two weeks?' And prompted them as specifically as possible to tell us 'When? How?' and so on. An example a client might give could be: 'After I've taken my kid to school on Wednesday, I'm going to get on such and such a website and I'm going to look for retail jobs in Essex'. This small change was surprisingly effective, leading to a significant increase in the number of people who were off benefits at 13 weeks. After the success of this trial we are now seeking to replicate through a much larger trial across a wide chunk of the UK.

Many of these reforms though are 'nuts and bolts' changes; they are very practical and it is the kind of demonstrable results I have mentioned that have persuaded often quite sceptical public servants.

Structural and fundamental changes

Sometimes in relation to specific issues, we can use the same insights to change policy more fundamentally or structurally. In many areas, we find that markets do not work perfectly even if they are competitive in a formal sense. In such cases, there can be difficulties and friction in working out the right thing to do.

Mobile phones are a good example. In the UK there are millions of alternative phone network combinations. Customers want to know whether they are on the best phone plan. But in the marketplace that is hard to know. However, if consumers had access to their own transaction data, it would be a game changer. When we look at another area—energy markets—most people do not care all that much about where their energy comes from, but the basic question remains: Do they know what tariff they are on? Do people know whether they use more electricity at night compared to other people? Imagine if someone's electricity bill had a Quick Response code with their data and information, and they could hold their mobile phone up against it and it would tell them 'the best tariff for you is the following. Would you like to change?' and they could click and it would happen in a few moments. You can see straight away why that is also a game changer in the way markets operate.

These two structural examples change the way the system works. Rather than investing resources simply in tariff control, we might just be able to make things much easier so that people are able to be economically literate ('econs') when it comes to making decisions, as we read in the textbook models, rather than the normal human beings with other preoccupations that we are most of the time. In the UK we have found that these kinds of approaches have been incredibly promising across a wide range of domestic policy areas.

Rory Gallagher

Applying 'behavioural insights' in Australia

Behaviour change has a long history in public service around the world. However, the systematic application—and robust evaluation—of insights from the behavioural sciences is a more recent phenomenon. In 2009, the Australian Public Service Commission stated that 'behavioural insights can help us to better analyse problems and provide more effective and efficient ways of achieving particular goals'. This recognition was heavily influenced by the publication of *Nudge* (Thaler and Sunstein 2008), which significantly helped bring these ideas into the heart of the government in both the UK and the US, and now increasingly also in Australia.

Australia has some world-leading examples of behaviour change, perhaps most notably in cancer prevention. For example the pioneering 'Slip! Slop! Slap!' campaigns around the use of sunscreen were enormously effective in changing the behaviour of a wide population. More recently, plain packaging of cigarettes is another good example, while innovative new approaches to helping smokers quit have been developed here. For example, the *My QuitBuddy* app, funded by the Australian government, is an excellent example of the use of behavioural insights. It allows users to create their own commitment devices involving their family and friends. Consequently, when they start to feel a craving, they can email or call them, or they can play and record sounds to create a panic button alarm. For example, when a *My QuitBuddy* user feels the need for a cigarette, they can hear the voice of their kids saying 'Daddy, please don't smoke'. These seemingly minor prompts can have a profound effect on personal behaviour. Another strategy is the use of *mutual* pledges: for instance, if I give up smoking, what will my friend give up—they can try and give up something as well. These are innovative methods compared to the standard warning slogan of 'smoking kills'. Smokers already know that smoking kills, but there are other tools and techniques available to help people achieve behaviour change.

In service delivery, the federal Department of Human Services has a fantastic app to help students track their working hours. The problem in this case is that students were getting into trouble for not letting Centrelink know when they were working. If we look at the behavioural literature and try to understand the problem, two traditional hypotheses might be: 1) students are lazy; and 2) they will not want to tell us how much they work because they do not want to be taxed. But quite often it is simply because we do not make it easy for them to do what we want—because of the numerous forms they have to fill out, and the fact that it is difficult to find the relevant information. The department realised this and developed a hugely popular app, which has helped many more students log their working hours, simply by making it easier for them to do so.

The methodology used by the Behavioural Insights Team

There are four basic stages for most projects that we undertake (see Figure 11.2).

1 Define the outcome	2 Understand the context	3 Build your intervention	4 Test, learn & adapt

Figure 11.2. Four basic stages for most projects undertaken by the Behavioural Insights Team

Source: UK Behavioural Insights Team Cabinet Office.

The first is to *define* the *outcome*. Anyone involved in government will know that this is a crucial stage, but that it is also an iterative process. We begin by trying to work out what is sitting underneath the overarching concern— what is the actual problem we are trying to solve? When we run a trial, we try to quantify the outcomes we are trying to change, as well as the order of magnitude by which we are trying to change them. The second stage is to *understand the context of the problem*, which often involves doing qualitative, in-depth fieldwork. For example, the fieldwork we did in job centres in the UK involved spending weeks speaking with and observing frontline workers and services users. It's this combination of fieldwork with a deep understanding of the behavioural science literature that helps us *build the intervention*.

Wherever possible we co-design our interventions with frontline staff. The extent of this participation varies from issue to issue. When we were working with the tax office, for example, it was very difficult to engage users—we did not go out to find people who should be paying their tax, but we did talk to the call centre staff and to those writing the letters. We asked them, 'What do you think? How would you change the form? What are the sorts of complaints you get? What are people asking? What are they not understanding? What do you think about this?' Wherever possible, co-design is the best way to go, because if there is no ownership within the organisation of the eventual solution, it will never be scaled up. The staff themselves are usually far better messengers or champions of the intervention. They can spread it within their agency much more effectively than those of us at the central agency by saying, 'Well, that trial worked, so let's go to the head centre now and say everyone should do this'.

The final stage is to *test, learn and adapt*. We have made heavy use of randomised control trials, which until relatively recently were very rare in government. The basic idea is to randomly allocate people to either a control group or a treatment group, and then test the outcome. Because they are randomly allocated, we do not get the usual selection biases and we *can* identify causation. So we attempt to run randomised control trials wherever possible, and try to use that data to build our evidence base for what works. It is not always possible, but we are trying to increase this evidence base and embed a more empirical approach to government.

Those are the four stages. However, note that they are *not* linear—we will often move back and forth between those various stages.

The underpinning themes and principles

Context matters

These stages are underpinned by a set of themes and principles. The first is that context matters. If behavioural insights teach us anything, it is that government should be more humble in looking at what works, because often we actually do not know. There is around 40 years' worth of evidence in behavioural economics and related fields, but its application to government has only been investigated in recent years. When we first attempted changes in tax letters, we had some intuition from the evidence base that social norms would work, but we had no idea to what extent. Even now, when we are applying similar principles in NSW, we have to be open to the fact that just because it worked in the UK does not mean it will work in NSW. So we need to continually trial interventions.

Quite often techniques that have worked in the laboratory do not work as we expect in the field. That was one of our problems early on in the UK, when we visited various departments talking about the ideas in *Nudge*. Quite understandably—and correctly, I think—a lot of Permanent Secretaries thought, 'Sure, that's quite interesting but it doesn't relate to my justice system, or my education system'. It was only when we had put together an empirical base of randomised controlled trials that people started to take notice, because we were then able to say, 'This is the effect we had, and these are the savings'.

Details matter

A second thing to note is that details matter. Even if you create the most perfect policy and get all the conditions right, if the way that it is implemented on the ground or communicated to citizens is not right, it won't have the impact that you intend.

One of the most interesting and helpful things in *Nudge* is the concept of *choice architecture*. The argument is that in government we are all choice architects: when we design a process or a communication, we are influencing someone's behaviour. In government, we often strive to maintain a purely neutral tone and make sure everyone's got all the information they could possibly need. However, the truth is that people do not want to wade through five pages of information; if they really want more detail they will look into it themselves. What we must do instead is capture the most important information and use that information to persuade someone to achieve the outcome that you want. Often it is just a matter of making it easier and simpler. We have found that relatively small changes (for example, to tax letters) can have a profound impact.

Government often focuses too much on the big structural elements and does not give enough attention to the small micro changes that can create large savings and have significant implications.

People matter

The third one is that people matter. I have already mentioned the benefits of co-design—but none of this will work unless the people on the frontline want it to. We spend a lot of time and energy working with the people who are delivering the service, to make sure that they get the chance to provide feedback on anything that we design—that *they* have had a chance to design. The success we have had is largely due to those people then becoming champions within their own organisations; they take it and run with it.

Evidence matters

Too often we see policy-based evidence making as opposed to evidence-based policy making. Government can often commission research to tell us what we want to hear. But if we are spending taxpayers' money on an intervention, we really need to know whether it works or not. Evidence really matters.

Agile implementation

Agile implementation is the final principle. We ran a successful experiment about sending text messages including people's first names. The automatic reaction from the agency was: 'Fantastic, we'll just send personalised text messages to all our services and that's it—all of our problems solved'. But in fact, it worked in one trial, in that particular circumstance—that did not mean that we had found the universal answer. We should keep varying those text messages even with that group, rather than thinking that this will be the answer for all the other problems we want to solve. One of the questions I get asked most is about the sustainability of behavioural techniques, and I think that is something we genuinely need to consider. The effect of some of these techniques—changing the wording of communications, for example—may well wear off over time. But for me that does not undermine the overall principle; I think our approach should be to continue to change and adapt.

We often hear in government the words 'change management' and we think of that as a negative thing. In actual fact, change should be a great thing; we should embrace it. Most private sector companies are changing all the time. You want to keep your core values and your core services while changing things about how you engage consumers and the sorts of services you deliver. Change is often a good thing, and in government we should embrace it more readily.

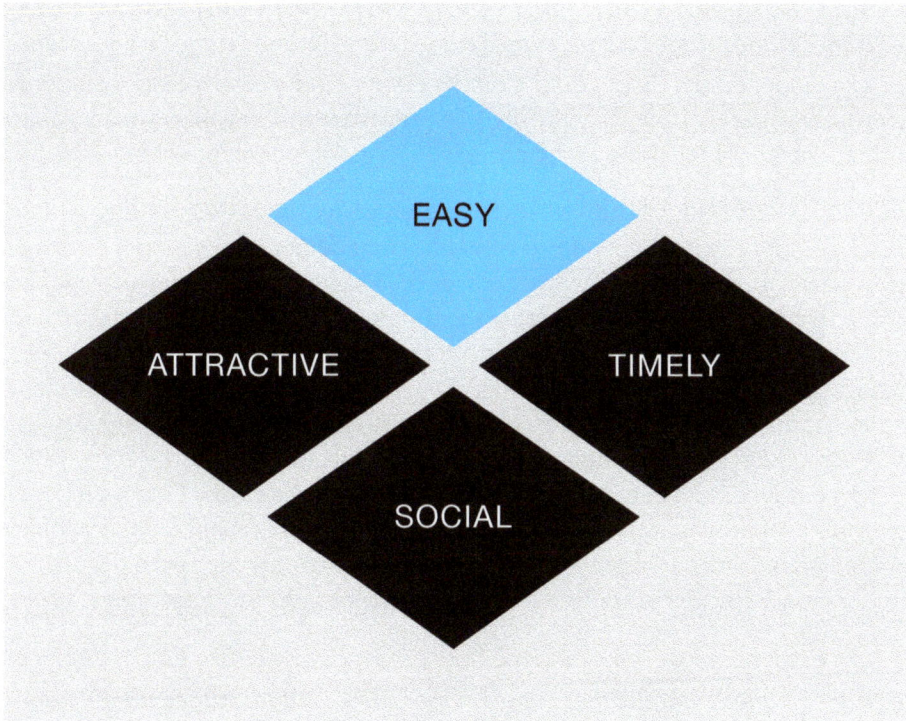

Figure 11.3. The four EAST principles for policy development
Source: UK Behavioural Insights Team Cabinet Office.

The four EAST principles for policy development

There is now a vast behavioural science literature out there—over 40 years' worth of studies—so we have attempted to make this more accessible to policymakers by simplifying it to a simple checklist: EAST. If you want to make your policy more grounded in human behaviour make it easy, make it attractive, make it social and make it timely.

Easy

There are always ways to make something easier, but we do not necessarily do that in government; we think about it quite coldly and rationally. So the first tenet is: make it easy. This is Richard Thaler's mantra, and in government we often do not make it easy for people to do the right thing. We send out very long, wordy letters written by policy teams and then pored over by the lawyers; or we create other little frictions that are enough to stop people undertaking the behaviour that we want to achieve.

We have mentioned earlier some 'macro' changes—changes to defaults on pensions, for example—opt-out rather than opt-in for pensions. A lot of what we have done has just been about simplification. A lot of our quick, early wins were in that space. How do you simplify processes and language, and how do you take out little frictions in the process?

Another experiment we ran with the tax office letters is illustrative. In one letter, we informed people in a control group about the generic webpage appropriate for the particular tax they had to pay; in the other, we sent the same letter, but this time we sent them to the exact webpage form that they had to fill out. So the only difference between the two letters was two clicks to one click. That is all people had to do extra from the control group to the treatment group. We found that for people who were sent to the general webpage details, 19.2 per cent responded; but when we sent them directly to the form page, 23 per cent did. That is roughly a 4 percentage point increase. This result does not sound world changing, but when it is scaled up across millions of people, that is a significant saving of administrative costs in following those people up. It is a saving achieved literally by sending them straight to a tax form.

That is what we mean about details. There are many little frictions in the way of people doing things like paying their tax, going to the gym, and so on—and because of these tiny barriers we can lose people. So it is worth thinking about ways in which we can reduce those barriers for citizens.

Attractive

The second rule is to make it attractive. How do we make it salient? How do we personalise it? How do we make it fun and appealing? Think about who the messenger is. Often in government we talk very abstractly—messages come from 'the department' rather than real individuals, and citizens generally want to know who they are dealing with and see who is the face of the government. Communications should come from a person that people can actually call and get in touch with, for example.

There was a trial run with an investment bank in London, encouraging investment bankers to pay a day of their salary (a decent amount of money, considering the average salary of a London investment banker). We had five treatment conditions. The control group received a general email from the chief executive officer (CEO) outlining the scheme and saying: 'Please donate a day's salary'. Five per cent of people responded. That is not a bad result; it is still a decent number of people and a significant amount of money that they are donating. But when we sent them the same email, but personalised at the beginning (for example, 'Dear Rory'), the response rate rose to 12 per cent. The effect was doubled just by adding someone's name. And when we gave people a small box of sweets—worth around 50 pence—as they entered the building, the result was more than double that of the control group: it went up to 11 per cent. This technique draws on feelings of reciprocity—charities will often send you something and then you feel good about it and want to donate. That is the feeling of reciprocity.

When we combined the personalised email with the sweets, it became three times more effective—so for the cost of a small bag of sweets we were getting a tripling of donations. This led to about £600,000 worth of donations on this particular day. If everyone had been given the most effective treatment, it would have been well in excess of £1 million in donations. This is an example of how we can achieve very significant results by paying attention to relatively small details.

Social

Make it social. Some of our work with the tax office is a good example of our effective use of social norms. As we indicated in the example shown in Figure 11.1, when we used social pressure to get people to pay their taxes the response rates of timely compliance went up. Our baseline control group only managed a compliance rate of 34 per cent, but when we invoked social norms telling our treatment groups about who pays their tax on time in their local area and which minority are still in debt, the response rate jumped to 39 per cent. The message is: people might not volunteer readily to pay taxes to 'the government' but they do not want to let down their local community or stand out from the herd. And better compliance rates saves the government millions simply from how socially a letter is worded.

Timely

Finally, make it timely. How do we engage people when they are most likely to change their behaviour? If you want someone to install energy efficiency measures around the home, or to change their commuting habits, a good time to do this may be when they have just moved house. They have just moved in, but have not got all their belongings in yet, and importantly they have not established their new routines—so that is a great time to intervene. When people have been driving to work every day for 14 years and can do that route with their eyes closed, and then someone comes to introduce them to a great new scheme (e.g. a free bike or a bus pass), they are unlikely to listen to it because they have an ingrained behaviour. In contrast, when people have just moved and are not sure about their routine yet, and someone gives them bike and public transport options, they are much more likely to consider it.

The private sector is good at this. They know that we are all pretty brand loyal, but there are certain times when this is challenged—for example, when you move in with someone or when you have a baby, your life is turned upside down. At these points in your life you are more susceptible to change in your shopping choices, and many private sector firms are very good at targeting that. Similarly, there are many touch points that government should consider, involving the best time to give these messages. But also the messages do not even need to come directly from government—there is a great example from our paper *Applying Behavioural Insights to Charitable Giving* (BI Team 2013) of using lawyers to ask people about charitable giving when they are writing their wills. We achieved some very good results simply by asking people at the right moment. Government could spend millions on advertising campaigns encouraging people to donate, but it may not be *timely*: the most effective time is when people are sitting down with their lawyer drawing up their will. We can work with third parties to harness those key moments.

Behavioural insights in New South Wales

We are implementing three projects in New South Wales: one each in the areas of tax, private health insurance, and return to work for rehabilitated workers.

Tax enforcement letters

The first intervention we introduced was on a tax form that the Office of State Revenue (OSR) sends out concerning speeding offences or vehicle infringements. It is an enforcement order (that is they have gone into debt with OSR), which is the third letter issued when a person has not responded to either an initial reminder notice or a penalty notice. We worked with OSR staff to co-design a new, different looking enforcement letter as well as a new reminder notice. Using theory and evidence from the literature, and looking at techniques that were used successfully in the UK, we engaged with OSR staff to get their feedback on different options. As with anything, there are always practical barriers. For instance, initially we could not point people to a specific webpage, we had to send them a generic one. And there are some elements that we had to retain in the letter for legislative reasons.

The new letter has a clear call to action, includes much clearer consequences, and we spell out our preferred payment options on the front page. The layout and the language have been simplified. We personalised the letters on a sliding scale, beginning with the amount owed and gradually getting to the point of saying 'You owe', so we escalated the tone and the language throughout the enforcement process. And where appropriate we used social norms (things like '9 out of 10 firms nominate a speeding driver') and highlighted factors like what the likelihood of success is if people decide to appeal.

The NSW Behavioural Insights Unit published the trial results to date in *Understanding People, Better Outcomes: Behavioural Insights in NSW* (June 2014). We were pleased to report that this trial led to 8,800 fewer vehicle registration cancellations and driving licence suspensions, as well as an estimated $1.02 million in additional payments over the year. All told, our trials with OSR combined have been projected to result in 60,000 late fees being avoided each year—thus saving NSW people $4 million a year in late fees. It also equates to an additional projected $10 million in fines being paid by their due date, not to mention a saving of $80,000 just in printing costs!

Private health insurance

The second case was about encouraging citizens to use their private health insurance in public hospitals. Our intervention here made it easier for patients to use their insurance and for staff to process this. We also explored the benefits for patients and staff. At present there is supposedly a focus on choice of doctor, but many people do not know what that means in practice. So we looked at introducing small but tangible rewards, such as overnight gift bags with toiletries for those selecting a doctor and using their insurance. But equally, it is not always clear what the benefits are for hospital staff for encouraging people to use their private health insurance, and there are no immediate rewards for individual wards or hospitals, because anything that comes in from health insurance funds is directed back into the overall health budget. We are looking at how we might feed some of the benefits of private healthcare back to a ward level. We could give them clear targets that they work to, and allow them to think about and choose what life-saving equipment to purchase if they hit those targets.

The results of this trial as of July 2014 have been overwhelmingly positive. One Emergency Department at Westmead Hospital generated a 2 percentage point increase in the use of private health insurance. This may not seem like much, but it equates to an additional $1.7 million dollars in revenue and cost savings just during the trial period. Importantly, there was very positive feedback from both patients and staff about the changes we had introduced, and it saved staff time and effort. This money is now being reinvested into the hospital, with staff themselves having chosen to allocate a proportion to purchasing more life-saving equipment. Replicating the trial at Auburn Hospital has seen even greater increases, jumping from an average of around 2 per cent of patients using private health insurance over the five-month period, to an average of 5.4 per cent.

Return to work

The final example is about helping injured workers return to work. We collaborated with an insurance company and a government department to improve and speed up their progress rates for injured or rehabilitated workers returning to work. As in the case of the hospital, the first step was streamlining the process. We found there were up to 20 pieces of paperwork for an injured worker to read through in the first 21 days after they reported their injury. As noted earlier, government tends to swamp people with large amounts of information, some of which is about complex legislation. By about the third letter, it is not difficult to imagine that people switch off and don't even bother opening the material, let alone engaging with it.

We also used commitments to elicit a return-to-work goal. The original process was very passive for the injured person—the government took the lead and the initiative, saying to the injured worker: 'This is when we think you should be back at work'. What we wanted to do is ask *them* to say when they thought they would be able to go back to work, and ask what they would do to help achieve that goal. And there would be reciprocal commitments from the support team as well, so it would be a much more active process for all parties.

The trial ran from September 2013 until July 2014, with encouraging results. Injured employees returned to full capacity 27 per cent faster in the first 90 days of the trial compared to the control group. Also, workers in the trial were nearly three times more likely to have completed their claims within 30 days. And again, we checked with staff and injured workers to get their qualitative feedback on what they thought about the new process. Both found the new approach more engaging, with one case manager saying: 'I'm noticing from my conversations with injured workers that they actually give us some great information that we can use as goals and actions without even asking for them, we just need to listen more. The new process has really opened my mind and ears up to what these workers say and how we can work with them.'

Conclusions

Behavioural insight is having a major impact in the UK, and increasingly now in Australia too. It provides new tools, frameworks and approaches for policy and process improvement. Most policy areas can be at least informed (if not driven) by the application of behavioural insight, but it is by no means a silver bullet.

In essence, we argue for a more experimental approach to government. When we roll out policies, how do we acknowledge that we need to vary it for the particular context rather than having a 'one-size-fits-all' model? The context, detail, people and evidence all matter—more so than we in government may have appreciated before.

There is a long way to go before these approaches become embedded. We have made a lot of 'nuts and bolts' changes such as changing letters, because they are easier to implement and measure, and we needed to prove the effectiveness of our unit. The challenge now is to move upstream to policy design.

There is also a question around sustainability: do those interventions continue to work year after year? What about segmentation? This chapter has looked at population or aggregate response levels, but drilling deeper, how do commitments, for instance, work with young people as opposed to older people? How do they work with young people who have already been through the system before? These are the specific data we still need to gather and analyse.

Finally, there are some enablers in the system that will help sustain this approach. Having more data will assist the process of segmentation, while the increasing move to digital services will allow us to do some of this testing in a new and more efficient way. The theme of this book is 'delivering under pressure' and under reduced budgets. And we believe that the application of behavioural insights can provide cost-effective new approaches for governments around the world.

References

Behavioural Insights Team (BI Team). 2013. *Applying Behavioural Insights to Charitable Giving*. London: Cabinet Office.

NSW Behavioural Insights Unit. 2014. *Understanding People, Better Outcomes: Behavioural Insights in NSW*. NSW Government. June. Online: bi.dpc.nsw. gov.au/assets/Behavioural-Insights/Library/Understanding-People-Better-Outcomes.pdf (accessed 22 May 2015).

Thaler, Richard and Cass Sunstein. 2008. *Nudge: Improving Decisions about Health, Wealth and Happiness*. New Haven: Yale University Press.

PART THREE: COLLABORATION WITH THE PRIVATE AND THIRD SECTORS

12

FRUGAL INNOVATION: BEYOND THE CONCEPTS OF 'PUBLIC' AND 'PRIVATE'

Gary Sturgess
University of New South Wales

Mixing public and private provision

In Denmark, around 85 per cent of ambulance services and 60 per cent of fire services are delivered by a private company—Falck. This has been the case since the 1920s, when a socialist government allowed local councils to contract with external providers. Unlike its public sector counterparts in Denmark, and most other places in the world, Falck offers an integrated rescue capability that brings together all manner of emergency and non-emergency services. The company's slogan, 'Always There', captures rather neatly this vision of an integrated service.

In addition to the traditional emergency services, which are provided free of charge, Falck offers a wide range of subscription services: patient transportation, an ocean salvage corps, auto assistance at home and abroad, animal rescue, trauma counselling, chiropractic treatment, and even care of chronic illness through telemedicine. They have agreements with the police to tow illegally parked cars, provide divers for searches, and remove bodies from crime scenes. The Animal Protection Foundation contracted with them to transport sick and injured

183

animals. As a Chief Executive explained to me some years ago: 'We've acquired this role. If you need help, call Falck, irrespective of the problem you might have.' No one else provides such a broad service. If you were to contact your local municipality, you would not know which department to call. But if you needed help, you only needed to contact Falck. If a horse fell in a ditch, it was always Falck. If a storm removed the roof from your house or you needed to pump water from your basement, you phoned Falck.

The cartoon (see Figure 12.1) was published more than 100 years ago in Denmark, and neatly depicts this idea of an integrated rescue service. As you'll see, Falck is everywhere, rescuing portly gentlemen who have fallen into fountains, recovering hats on the street corner, holding screens to provide some privacy for couples who are canoodling in the street.

Figure 12.1. Danish cartoon about Falck

Source: 'Blæksprutten' (Octopus), an annual Christmas cartoon about the year's events.

Among the Danes, Falck is seen as a public service. In local directories, the company is listed after the emergency services number 112 and ahead of the police. At Legoland, the fire engines bear Falck's name.

I first became aware of Falck in 1995, when the ABC interviewed British academic Norman Flynn about the denationalisation of public services in Europe. Flynn was clearly uncomfortable with the whole idea of privatisation and outsourcing, but he struggled to categorise Falck. He said:

Falck's an anomaly in Europe, it's a complete aberration. Everyone trusts Falck like they trust the state, it's a quasi-state thing. It just happens to be privately owned. But it is a national monopoly for these emergency services, but it's interesting because the Danes trust Falck as they trust the state (ABC's *Life Matters*).

To a much greater extent than those of us in the English-speaking world recognise, the social democratic countries of Western Europe rely on a mixed economy for the delivery of their public services.

I was reminded of this while facilitating a seminar on behalf of the Forum of Federations in Melbourne in mid-2013. There had been a series of front-page articles in the Melbourne press about some scandal in the state's hospitals, and a British academic, Clive Grace, held up a newspaper and observed that it could just as easily have been the headline of a paper in the UK. I could not find any of those exact headlines again, which probably indicates it was one of those passing crises that the media discovers and quickly moves on from. But here is a random list about crises in Australian public hospitals:

> Nurses to strike at 160 public hospitals (*Sky News*, 21 July 2013).
>
> Only one SA hospital meets emergency department patients target
> (*Advertiser* (Adelaide), 25 July 2013).
>
> Hospital target waiting times down, fewer surgeries performed (*ABC News*,
> 6 June 2013).

The speaker after Grace was German academic Wolfgang Renzsch from the University of Magdeburg. He commented that such an issue would not make a headline in Germany, because with the exception of some veterans' facilities, German hospitals are owned and managed by private, not-for-profit, and municipal providers. The management of hospital services is not the responsibility of state and national governments, and therefore politicians would not be caught up in these stories. In examining, from here, the role of public services in the social democratic countries of northwest Europe, we overlook the extent to which they are mixed economies. In part this is because the Europeans do not draw the same crisp distinctions between public and private that we do in the English-speaking world, and as a result, the privatisation debate resonates in a different way.

My proposition is that we would have a better chance of pursuing innovative, new approaches to public service delivery if we were to bridge the deep and largely ideological gulf that we have constructed between public and private. If we were to reframe the debate, to move beyond simple concepts of public and private, we might be able to advance this discussion about new models and new approaches in an age of austerity. In fact, over the past decade there has been a discernible softening of this strict divide, particularly in the UK and Australia.

On both sides of the political fence, governments have increasingly turned to external providers for the delivery of public services, and we have begun to see the emergence of public–private hybrids that defy simple classification.

In truth, the boundaries between public and private were never as severe as the ideologues would have us believe. There was certainly a preference for large, industrial institutions over the first half of the twentieth century, but the public sector was always a mixed economy with hybrids that did not easily fit in any camp. Private and not-for-profit schools have always been part of the education sector in Australia, and the debate over state aid that has raged since the 1960s is not about whether we will proscribe non-government schooling, but whether taxpayers will subsidise them with partial vouchers. Britain had grant-maintained schools as early as 1902.

Much the same applied when it came to the health sector; in NSW we have a number of privately owned and operated public hospitals, established in the early twentieth century, and known in the relevant part of the *Health Services Act 1997* as 'affiliated health organisations' or 'Schedule 3 hospitals'. The most prominent of those is St Vincent's Hospital in Darlinghurst, Sydney. It is an iconic part of the public hospital system, but is in fact a not-for-profit private hospital operating as a public hospital. The vast majority of what we now call community services were conceived and created—and to this day are still operated—by the not-for-profit sector. I grew up in a little country town in southeast Queensland, and I can remember watching the cars from the 'Blue Nurses' come and go in the street as we played cricket in the front yard. It was just one of those community services that were a continual presence in the background as one grew up.

The voluntary sector has always been the great innovator when it comes to the development of new public services. Indeed, it is difficult to think of a public service—apart from those which required some element of coercion—which was not invented by the voluntary sector. These include hospitals, schools, fire brigades, ambulances, ocean rescue, social insurance, home care for the sick and disabled, the concept of a probation service, and even professionally designed and maintained highways.

I have often challenged audiences to name a non-coercive public service that was developed by government, and over three to four years of putting that challenge to my audiences, nobody's been able to identify one. Somebody once suggested urban planning (which is a regulatory service, but could also be regarded as a public service), but in fact the garden city was conceived by a private individual, Ebenezer Howard, and the first garden cities in England— Letchworth and Welwyn—were constructed by not-for-profit organisations that he created (Parsons and Schuyler 2002). Indeed, England has a history of privately developed towns which date back to the Middle Ages. In the UK, someone suggested the National Health Service (NHS). But the principles of integrated healthcare, which was supposed to be one of the unique offerings of the NHS, were drawn from the Great Western Railway (GWR) Medical Fund. This was established by the GWR at Swindon in 1847—a very innovative model that influenced the early design of the NHS a century later.

The Australian Public Service sector is, and always has been, a mixed economy with a diverse range of public, private and not-for-profit providers. My rough calculations indicate that approximately one third of public sector services in this country are provided by independent proprietors. In some community services, it is as high as 90 to 95 per cent: in health and education it is around one in three; whereas an average of one in five prisoners are held in privately managed prisons. In some other public services such as policing, of course, the role of external providers is negligible.

There is bipartisan agreement in this country on the desirability of having a mixed economy—nobody is suggesting that the aforementioned ratios should be wound back. Indeed in the last few years, we've seen Labor governments as well as Coalition governments substantially expand the role of private and not-for-profit provision. In arguing that in its search for solutions to the austerity challenge, the Australian government should move beyond simple notions of public and private, I maintain that it needs to look at the *full* range of public service providers, not merely those that are directly controlled by public officials. Among the 30 per cent of public services that is provided by public and not-for-profit organisations, there are monopolies that need to be opened up to contestability. There are services delivered under programs that are decades out of date, and are in urgent need of being recommissioned. If we reframe the debate so that we are scrutinising the performance of, and drawing upon the capabilities of, the full range of public service providers, we substantially expand the scope for reform.

Benefits from contestability

Let me suggest another way in which we can reframe the debate about reform. Many of those who advocate privatisation or outsourcing as a means of transforming public services base their argument on an assumption that the private and not-for-profit sectors are inherently superior to the public sector—'private good, public bad'. With limited exceptions, that proposition is not borne out by the evidence, and to maintain such a proposition is offensive to the hundreds of thousands of men and women who have dedicated themselves to a career in the public service.

The evidence suggests that it is *contestability*, rather than privatisation, that delivers the benefits. While the concept of contestability is deeply challenging to policymakers engaged in frontline delivery, and while there are some public services where an uncontested government monopoly is unavoidable (and indeed desirable), there is nothing inherently offensive in the slogan 'competition good, monopoly bad'. The public at large is generally sceptical about privatisation or outsourcing of public services, but it has little sympathy with monopolists in either sector. The public likes the idea of user choice—just witness the overnight popularity of Australia's National Disability Insurance Scheme (NDIS)—and it warms to the idea of competitive tendering, as long as it can be reassured that the tender is conducted openly and fairly.

One of the significant breakthroughs over the past decade in thinking about public service reform has been the discovery of contestability. Contestability is not just outsourcing, and it does not necessarily involve competition—it is the credible *threat* of competition, or 'benchmarking with teeth'. Where there is already a monopoly in the private sector, simple outsourcing will result in a less contestable outcome than robust benchmarking or other innovative models that involve public sector provision. Contestability is limited by contracts that have a longer term than is necessary or justified by the nature of the contract. Traditional outsourcing is often inappropriate where public services are inherently monopolistic, where the services in question are unique or so closely integrated that they can't be broken down into parts, or where there is a problem with physical or human asset specificity.

To my knowledge, the first person to explore the application of contestability to public services was Chris Ham, then Professor of Health Policy and Management at the University of Birmingham, who published a brief note on the matter in the *British Medical Journal* in 1996. Ham was seconded to the Department of Health from 2000 to 2004, where he served as Director of the Strategy Unit. He is now CEO of the King's Fund, which is probably the most influential think tank in the UK health sector. In that 1996 note, following the collapse of the first experiment with the NHS internal market, Ham wrote:

> While competition as a reforming strategy may have had its day, there are nevertheless elements of this strategy that are worth preserving, not least the stimulus to improve performance which arises from the threat that contracts may be moved to an alternative provider should not be lost. The middle way between planning and competition is a path called contestability. This recognises that healthcare requires collaboration between purchasers and providers and the capacity to plan developments on a long-term basis. At the same time, it's based on the premise that the performance may stagnate unless there are sufficient incentives to bring about continuous improvement. Some of these incentives may be achieved through management action or professional pressure, and some may derive from political imperatives.

In addition, there is the stimulus to improve performance that exists when providers know that purchasers have alternative options. The essence of contestability is that planning and competition should be used together, with contracts moving only when other means of improving performance have failed. Put another way, in a contestable health service, it is the possibility that contracts may move that creates an incentive within the system, rather than the actual movement of contracts. Of course for this to be a real incentive, it must be said, contracts must shift from time to time (Ham 1996, 71).

In some situations, outsourcing is still the most appropriate course of action. There is now a well-developed market in this country for warehousing and logistics, and the onus of proof must now rest on those who would argue that warehousing and logistics should be done in-house. This is the so-called '*Yellow Pages* test', which was described by California Governor Pete Wilson as follows: 'If a service provided by government is advertised by private companies in the *Yellow Pages*, it's a good candidate for privatization' (Wilson 1996, 29). Put another way, if you can find somebody in the *Yellow Pages* that's doing this, you really ought to be asking the question: Why are you doing it in-house? Note that he uses the term 'privatisation' here rather than 'contracting'.

In some cases, the technological capabilities of private sector firms have outstripped those of the public sector, and in those cases governments might decide outsourcing is the most suitable course. The innovative new road maintenance contracts tendered by the NSW Road and Maritime Services (RMS) are an example of this. Each of the shortlisted consortia has one or more international companies involved in their bid, because the RMS is drawing heavily on models that have been developed in New Zealand and the UK. The NSW government has elected *not* to develop its capabilities in-house or form joint ventures with international corporations, and this is an understandable decision.

There are also situations where, in order to create a credible threat of competition in the rest of the system, governments may elect to outsource a proportion of their services. It was for this reason that the NSW Labor government did not permit an in-house bid when it conducted a competitive tender for the management of Parklea Prison in 2009. Throughout the rest of its term in office, Labor employed a policy of contestability in the reform of its prisons. Contestability drives robust benchmarking, and it motivates public service managers to undertake serious reform. It recognises that private sector monopolies are no better than public sector monopolies and, in many cases, worse. It is a good example of an approach to public sector reform that goes beyond the traditional debate of public versus private.

Performance contracting

I spent 10 years in the UK running a corporate think tank for a large public service company. The first research project we undertook after my arrival was to interview contract managers who had previously managed the same service in the public sector—the same people who were doing the same job, but in a different model. It was a very insightful piece of work, and we found that many of the benefits of competitive tendering come not from competition but from contracting.

Competition is by no means unimportant; the process of winning a competitive tender bestows on management a powerful mandate for reform, which enables them to renegotiate custom and practice. But a great deal of work is done by the contract itself. A performance contract provides much greater clarity to frontline managers about the government's priorities. When they are written into a contract, performance targets provide predictability, so that management and staff know how they will be judged and are able to adapt their behaviour accordingly. A term contract provides frontline managers with stability so that over a period of five to seven years, for example, they are isolated to some extent from the policy churn that has become a feature of modern politics.

It is unsurprising, then, that contract managers who used to work in the public sector reported that the contractual shield provided them with a great deal more authority and autonomy in managing their team. However, they also reported feeling personally much more accountable. Since the boundaries of the organisation were more clearly defined, and since performance targets were more predictable and stable, they knew that they would not be able to shift responsibility to someone else. Service level agreements between the commissioners of public services and public sector agencies have made little impact because they have failed to comprehend the essence of what makes a contract work. Again, if we reframe the question so that we focus on the contract rather than just competition or contestability, we can open up a whole new range of tools to use in addressing the challenge of austerity.

Recognising diversity

The concept of diversity offers us another way of doing this. Some of the examples and themes that I am about to refer to have been woven into the fabric of this book. Traditionally, public service commissioners have drawn on a very limited range of tools in the design of solutions to policy problems. That has begun to change, but there are still not enough tools in the policymaker's toolkit. As psychologist Abraham Maslow observed: 'I suppose it is tempting, if the only tool you have is a hammer, to treat everything as if it were a nail' (Maslow 1996, 15).

Our capacity to understand the problem in front of us is constrained by the range of possible solutions at our command. If the only tools you have available to you are a hammer and a monkey wrench and someone gives you a watch and asks, 'What's the problem and can you fix it?', you are going to struggle because you have got two tools that are not particularly appropriate for the task at hand. Privatisation and outsourcing have certainly introduced diversity into the range of models from which policymakers can draw—but not very much. There are many public services where privatisation and outsourcing would be decidedly inappropriate. Much the same applies to 'digital government'. It is a useful addition to the toolkit, but it is only one instrument in a range of alternatives we should be exploring.

Over the past few years, we have seen the emergence of new models that are not easily slotted into the old categories of public, private and not-for-profit. Simone Walker's chapter in this book relates to social impact bonds. While we have not really moved beyond the pilot phase even in the UK, and certainly not in the US or in NSW (where the first two pilots are underway), there is significant interest in this radical new approach. What is interesting, given the subject of this chapter, is that in the UK some of the providers in these consortia of social impact bonds are public entities, local governments and similar institutions.

We are also seeking public–private hybrids that provide scope for contestability where traditional outsourcing would not. In the UK, one of the most interesting is GSTS Pathology—a public–private joint venture between two leading NHS hospital trusts and a large public service company. The NHS trusts bring to the joint venture their expertise in pathology, while the private company brings its expertise in management. NHS staff are seconded rather than transferred, so that the trusts have retained their negotiating power within the joint venture. This is not soft and woolly—rather, it is a grown-up, very commercial joint venture. Now we have seen the emergence of some hybrids here in Australia, for example the Chris O'Brien Lifehouse, a new oncology facility at the Royal Prince Alfred Hospital (RPA) in Sydney.

In the UK's welfare to work and rehabilitation sectors—the probation sectors— we have seen the emergence of a new service model, generally referred to by public officials as the 'integrator model'. Table 12.1 shows Serco's model; G4S have adopted this approach as well. In this particular case, the company assumed significant financial and operational risk for delivering service outcomes, but the integrators deliver none of the actual services themselves. Rather, they assemble and then closely manage a diverse supply chain on behalf of government. There is then an interesting argument that the integrator is acting as manager of the government's supply chain, rather than being the head of a virtual organisation selling into government.

There is widespread criticism of 'public service mutuals' in the UK. Private corporations dismiss them as nostalgia for the cooperative movement of the nineteenth century. Union leaders insist they are just another form of privatisation. In fact, employee-owned enterprises are relatively common in one part of the private economy—the professional services sector. Lawyers, accountants, consultants, and some healthcare professionals usually operate under a partnership model, which is essentially employee-owned. Structural features explain why employee ownership is common in professional services, and in my view, those features occur in many parts of the public service economy. Other than lack of imagination, I find it difficult to understand why public service mutuals could not succeed as an alternative business model (see the later chapter by Hems in this volume for greater discussion on mutuals).

Table 12.1. Serco Welfare to Work model

	Coventry	Staffordshire	Herefordshire	Shropshire
Engage	Sarina Russo	Shaw Trust	Beacon Employment	Shropshire County Council
Enable	Trainbrains	Stoke on Trent Council	Beacon Employment	Shrewsbury College
Empower	Shaw Trust	Inspire 2 Independence	JHP Group Ltd	Shaw Trust
Specialists	Birmingham Chamber Training; Royal National College for the Blind			

Note: Each provider listed in the table above is indicative of each of those elements of the model; in the full model, there are two to three providers in each category.

Source: From Serco Group plc, 'Work Programme West Midlands & South Yorkshire', presentation to the author, 20 April 2012.

Some of the greatest innovation is taking place in India, where social entrepreneurs are developing profoundly different models of public service delivery in circumstances where governments, because of inadequate tax revenues, cannot hope to meet the needs of a population demanding basic services such as health and education. In fact, the term 'frugal innovation' comes out of these social entrepreneurs developing these new models in India ('First break all the rules: The charms of frugal innovation'). Examples include high volume, high quality heart surgery performed at a fraction of the cost of comparable services in the West. In large part this is possible because these industries are lightly regulated in India; the professional guilds do not have the same capacity to prevent experimentation with innovative new approaches.

While the Australian public will not want their governments to directly adopt those models, I think it is highly likely that they will be deeply influenced by the lessons that have been learned out of the 'frugal innovation' period in India.

In the exploration of alternative service models, it is vital that government ensures appropriate transparency and accountability; issues of competitive neutrality inevitably arise, but these issues are by no means insuperable. I was intimately involved in the development of the competitive neutrality principles in this country, when we were designing a framework for the corporatisation of government business enterprises in the late 1980s. Contrary to what some analysts now maintain, corporatisation was not developed as a staging post on the way to privatisation, but as a means of enabling government business enterprises to behave in a more commercial way and to compete fairly in the wider economy. Corporatisation was intended as a reform to carry the debate beyond public and private, and a succession of reports by the Productivity Commission and the NSW Independent Pricing and Regulatory Tribunal bear witness to the massive productivity gains produced by that process.

Stopping budgetary elephants in a time of austerity

Surveying the recent debates over the parlous state of the Commonwealth budget, there is little doubt that Australian governments are in for a period of sustained austerity. Scope for further tax increases will be limited, and both state and federal governments must look to the effectiveness with which they deliver public services. The fiscal gap is now so large that it cannot be closed just through staff freezes, efficiency dividends and waste-watch committees.

In looking at plausible reform tools, I have been deeply influenced by Aaron Wildavsky's assessment of zero-based budgeting in the US government in the 1960s. In his writings on the matter, he quoted a public servant he interviewed: 'Some butterflies were caught, no elephants stopped' (Wildavsky and Hammond 1965, 336). Governments have to start looking for the elephant-stoppers and, done well, contracting and contestability offer that potential. But governments must also offer solutions that are capable of commanding bipartisan support. They must find a framework that unleashes the energy of the *change vanguard* (see Kelman, in this volume). They must find a narrative that will generate a broadly based reform coalition within government, well beyond that vanguard.

To use a metaphor taken from Steve Kelman's book, having made the effort to get the flywheels spinning, they must find a way of maintaining the momentum of reform over time, through successive changes of government (Kelman 2005).

It must outlast any electoral cycle. There are a variety of ways in which this might be done, but none of them will be possible, in my view, if we do not find a way of moving beyond traditional concepts of public and private.

References

Capps, Steven A. 1996. 'Wilson unveils plan to shrink government.' *SFGate*, 11 April. Online: www.sfgate.com/news/article/Wilson-unveils-plan-to-shrink-government-3147391.php (accessed 3 January 2014).

'First break all the rules: The charms of frugal innovation.' 2010. *Economist*, 15 April.

Ham, Chris. 1996. 'Contestability: A middle path for healthcare.' *British Medical Journal* 312: 70–71.

Kelman, Steven. 2005. *Unleashing Change: A Study of Organizational Renewal in Government*. Washington, DC: Brookings Institution Press.

Life Matters. 1995. Radio National, 23 October, 9.30 a.m.

Maslow, Abraham H. 1996. *The Psychology of Science: A Reconnaissance*. HarperCollins.

Parsons, Kermit C. and David Schuyler (eds). 2002. *From Garden City to Green City: The Legacy of Ebenezer Howard*. Baltimore: Johns Hopkins University Press.

Wildavsky, Aaron and Arthur Hammond. 1965. 'Comprehensive versus incremental budgeting in the department of agriculture.' *Administrative Science Quarterly* 10(3) (December): 321–46.

Wilson, Peter. 1996. *Competitive Government: A Plan for Less Bureaucracy, More Results*. Sacramento: Office of the Governor.

13

THE ROAD TO GENUINE PARTNERSHIPS WITH THE THIRD SECTOR: ARE WE THERE YET?

Peter Shergold
University of Western Sydney

Liberation

I am a 'liberated' public servant—I retired from the Australian Public Service (APS) six years ago. Nevertheless, I continue to serve on a range of government boards, councils and committees. Indeed I sometimes feel that I am more engaged with a wider range of public policy issues today than when I was a public servant. Living now in a world of 'care without responsibility', it's easy to think boldly about the future. It's easier to preach if you don't practise: the burden of administrative routine and political crises tend to overwhelm one's strategic impulse.

I hope I am not simply a blowhard. I strive to ensure that the enjoyment I get from being an *agent provocateur* on public administration is matched by active engagement in new approaches. I chair, for example, the NSW Social Investment Expert Advisory Group, overseeing one of the most interesting innovations in policy. Social Benefit Bonds involve the harnessing of private sector social finance for the creation of public good through a not-for-profit intermediary. It is a particular form of 'social impact investing'. The state's purpose is to attract private investors to fund early intervention by community providers. The original goal was to reduce the need to place at-risk children in out-of-home care, and to lower the rate and cost of prisoner recidivism, but the NSW government has now announced a significant widening of its ambition. If successful, the result will be significant budgetary savings and a more civil society. This represents a quite different way for a government to undertake its business.

Until taking a position as Chair of Opal Aged Care, I also headed the Commonwealth's Aged Care Reform Implementation Council and its successor, the Aged Care Sector Committee. In my recent address at the Leading Age Services Australia convention, I talked about the potential transformation of aged care delivery, focused in particular on the value of 'consumer-directed care' (CDC) approaches. This, too, represents an unorthodox approach to implementing publicly funded services. I envisage the possibility that as citizens become used to tailored, individualised, self-managed and 'self-directed' funding (not only in aged care but in the provision of disability services and mental illness support), they will become empowered. Instead of learning to be helpless recipients, they will be encouraged to take control of the government assistance they require. They will refuse to accept the constraints imposed upon their autonomy both by public service agency 'purchasers' and the third-party service 'providers' that presently deliver standardised services through block grant funding.

The main focus of this chapter, however, is on 'the road to genuine partnerships in the third sector'. This is another matter that arouses my passion. I served on the Western Australian Economic Audit Committee and, in particular, contributed to a volume that emphasised *Putting the Public First* (Economic Audit Committee 2009). For more than three years I then chaired the Partnership Forum that the report had recommended. This body brings together the key directors-general and not-for-profit CEOs in Western Australia. Together they negotiate more equitable financial arrangements for providers, simplify and streamline the administration of outsourced service delivery, and 'co-produce' program design. It was an energising experience because it was an initiative that actually walked the talk of collaboration. The strong support of the Premier, Colin Barnett, and the leadership of the Department of the Premier and Cabinet provided the necessary authorising environment.

More recently, I have worked with community organisations (particularly the Victorian Council of Social Services) and the Victorian government on new ways of improving collaboration in the development, as well as the delivery, of publicly funded human services (Shergold 2013). In response to my recommendations, which were based on extensive consultation with the state's not-for-profit sector, Minister Mary Wooldridge announced the establishment of a Community Sector Reform Council. Like WA's Partnership Forum, the Council's goal is to bring together senior representatives from across the government and non-government sectors to plan the implementation of reforms in the delivery of human services.

I also bring my interest in cross-sectoral collaboration to the NSW Public Service Commission Advisory Board, which I chair, and the Queensland Public Service Renewal Board, of which I am a member. Unfortunately, it was recently abolished by Annastacia Palaszczuk MP. In NSW, the board released a public report on collaborative partnership (NSW PSC Advisory Board 2014). Make no mistake: changes are afoot.

I still believe major reform in the public sector is an imperative, and new approaches are needed to improve performance. It is true that some of today's administrative creativity is partly driven by financial austerity or the buzz words going around—'frugal innovation'. To be honest, however, I see the new approaches much more as 'disruptive innovation'—and my sympathies are very much on the side of the disruptors. Partnership approaches can reinvigorate the participatory nature of Australian democracy. They can build networked forms of governance. They can increase trust in the state and its institutions; create more flexible structures of public administration; and, in the process, help us to re-envision and revitalise the significant role of public servants.

That is what I hope for. Sometimes I think we might actually make it happen. Others, who are more cautious and less optimistic than I am, counter that public organisations tend to become trapped by their past. I do not think that organisational sclerosis is inevitable. Certainly I am doing my level best to try and make sure that public administration is not resistant or impervious to change. The desire of governments to deliver services more effectively, driven in part by budgetary pressures, will ensure that the status quo is challenged. Opportunities beckon.

Embrace contractualism

I want to tell a tale. This story may have begun before your time as a public administrator, or it may be a narrative in which you have been an active participant. Its beginning coincides with when I entered the public service a generation ago. It was a period when public services started to talk seriously about 'contestability' and 'outsourcing'. Often that discourse was associated, usually critically, with the so-called new public management. The focus was on 'managing for results'. One key element of that change process was the willingness to pay organisations outside the public service to deliver a government's programs and services.

Some of you will remember what now seems a rather dated language: the organisational distinction between 'purchaser' and 'provider', and between 'steerer' and 'rower'. The terms, contractual or metaphorical, implied profound change in the nature of delivering government. Public servants would be required to benchmark their cost-effectiveness and evaluate their performance, and if there was 'value for money' in it, they would fund third parties to implement government policy under service agreements.

Part of the reform process was marked by the privatisation and corporatisation of government enterprise activities that had traditionally operated in the public domain. In the construction of public infrastructure it often took the form of public–private partnerships. In the area of human services it was epitomised by the contracting out of the delivery of support programs.

Perhaps delivery of services through third parties seemed newer than it was. Gary Sturgess (see his chapter in this volume) is quite right: the popular notion that Australian governments had traditionally delivered public services only through public servants is ahistorical. If you are a student of colonial Australia, you will be aware that so much of what we now consider the role of the public service was initially provided by the business or community sector—whether it was Australia's first charity, the Sydney Benevolent Society, which supplied health, nursing and a range of essential social services; or the Australian Mutual Provident Society, which wrote its first policies in 1849, one of a number of mutual and friendly societies which provided funeral benefits and life insurance; or the range of agricultural and retail cooperatives, which redistributed their profits back to members. Contracting out government was commonplace. It was, to revert to my earlier work as an economic historian, the primary means of transporting convicts to NSW. Nevertheless, to many public servants in the early 1990s, the contracting of not-for-profits to deliver government programs appeared as the shock of the new.

It was, I remember, a matter of fierce political debate. I found the process quite exciting. What most interested me at the time was the development and delivery of family and community support, disability care, employment and training, Aboriginal affairs, education, health services, and aged care. In those areas implementation was predominantly, although by no means exclusively, outsourced to community-based organisations.

As Secretary of the Department of Employment, I had particular responsibility for the early days of the Job Network (now Job Services Australia). I supervised the second tender process, at the conclusion of which the delivery of employment services was divided more or less evenly between the private and not-for-profit sectors. It was apparent that public sector organisations such as Employment National found it hard to compete. For 50 years, labour market brokerage had been largely a government monopoly, provided by a network of Commonwealth Employment Service offices. Now, in the mid-1990s, the delivery of services was moved out of the APS.

Similar developments occurred in many other areas of public policy. Today, at both the state and Commonwealth levels, a wide range of human services is delivered not by public servants but by contracted providers, predominantly in the community sector. Critics, usually in academia, sometimes characterise this development as the emergence of the 'contract state' or the 'hollow crown'. I see it differently. I was a naïve enthusiast in the 1990s, and I remain a wiser (more chastened) supporter today. My major frustration is that the potential of commissioning service delivery has too often been undermined by administrative red tape.

The scale of outsourcing is enormous. The 2010 Productivity Commission research report on the contribution of the not-for-profit sector found that each year about $26 billion of government services was delivered directly through the sector. This is a profound transformation. The amazing thing is that most Australians do not really understand it, nor are they even fully aware of it. It has happened largely beneath the radar of public opinion. Not-for-profit organisations that traditionally saw themselves as charities, and often as advocacy organisations, are now regarded by public services as 'government service providers'. I emphasise that this is not how most of them see themselves.

I witnessed this change take place at first hand. When I entered the public service, my task was to set up the Office of Multicultural Affairs (OMA). Together with the Department of Immigration, OMA made many grants to ethnic groups and migrant centres that provided settlement services. Most of those grants were intended to subsidise what community organisations were already doing of their own accord. In other words, government assessed that their activities were beneficial and in the public interest, and so provided small grants of public money to assist them. Accountability was based on acquittal. This is a very different approach to the typical relationship today. Most of the direct government funding now takes the form of contracts: they are intended not to supplement community-developed public services but to deliver the government's programs.

The implications of this change are often inadequately comprehended. Neither side of the contractual equation—public service purchasers on the one hand and not-for-profit providers on the other—has clearly appreciated the substantive difference between a grant subsidy and a payment-for-service agreement. Too many of the contracts that are being written remain ambiguous in their nature. This is unfortunate. Trust depends on both sides entering into a relationship with eyes wide open.

Experimental transformation through cooperative partnerships

I continue to believe that outsourcing the delivery of government human services to 'third sector' community organisations is a good thing. Scores of evaluations leave me in little doubt that in most cases the provision of programs through the not-for-profit sector has resulted in better quality services being delivered to clients at a lower cost. This is not unequivocally a good outcome. Many community organisations that tender for contracts may end up effectively cross-subsidising government for the delivery of services. In other words, community organisations—which raise funds from donors for charitable purposes, employ workers at lower wage rates than public servants, and make extensive use of volunteers—may find themselves delivering services at below their real cost. Their mission (to help those in need) persuades them to do it. PricewaterhouseCoopers estimated that in WA, community organisations were generally being paid about 30 per cent less than the true cost of service delivery. I suspect that situation would not be different in other jurisdictions. It is to the great credit of Premier Colin Barnett that he addressed that underpayment in his state's 2011 budget. He saw it as the first essential down payment on partnership.

So whilst I am still supportive of contracting the community sector, I believe that the relationship needs to be made over. In my view the potential revolution in public administration has only been half-fulfilled. The aim of outsourcing should be to create a wider diversity of providers, greater choice for users, and more experimentation in delivery. Instead, there is a bureaucratic impulse to standardise programs, to control delivery processes, to micromanage the service agreements and to avoid risk. It is time to pause, reassess and rethink where we have arrived, and consider where we should go from here.

We have the capacity to create a 'public economy' that is delivered by a cross-sectoral collaboration between public, private and not-for-profit organisations. Governments need to set, tender and pay deliverers on the basis of agreed outcomes. The ambition should be to provide citizens in need with flexible options. The arrangements should encourage social entrepreneurship. We need to stop perceiving contractual relationships, built over a quarter of a century, as merely transactional. Let us instead ask the question: How can we do things differently so that the process can become transformational? The answer, I believe, is to build collaborative relationships which allow public servants and community workers to design in a cooperative fashion the best ways to maximise value for the expenditure of public funds.

Let us stop thinking about how to build 'mind labs' and 'design centres' at the periphery of public administration. Let us instead seek to change the core. Let us harness the power of partnership to develop and deliver government services on behalf of government in ways that empower the citizens that access them.

Promoting a collaborative environment

There are four distinct aspects to the creation of a public economy.

First, we need to do more to appreciate and embrace the experience of community organisations. Many of them have been in this game for a long time, and their workers have considerable frontline experience. Imagine how it must appear for many of these not-for-profits: a government decides on policy and announces it; a public service department, either through legislative or administrative means, translates that policy into particular services and programs; the contracts and guidelines are written to protect the government from risk; and only at that final stage is the delivery of the policy tendered out. Consider how it would feel to be at this low-value end of the development chain—especially if you believe that if your organisation had been consulted at an earlier stage, the programs and services could have been better formulated. 'Co-production' and 'co-design' are the keys to maximising public value and beneficial social impact.

Second, we need to encourage the latent entrepreneurship of community organisations. Of course things are tough—governments face an environment of shrinking revenues and soaring demand. But which businesses in Australia typically live in an austerity environment, often not knowing from year to year how they are going to survive? Answer: those in the community sector. Their constant struggle to pursue their mission whilst ensuring financial sustainability drives a willingness to embrace considered risk-taking. Unfortunately, when governments contract those enterprises, they often constrain organisational creativity by imposing an unnecessary burden of regulatory controls. Outsourcing should present an opportunity for diversity: it should be a means to challenge a variety of organisations—whether private or community-based—to come up with new and exciting ways of delivering the public interest.

Third, we should learn from 'the wisdom of the crowd'. Here I am talking as much about frontline public servants as community organisation employees. If you monitor the work of public servants at the most junior levels, you will often observe a remarkable degree of innovation. Unfortunately, it is to a significant extent diverted into developing the day-to-day 'workarounds' that enable staff to subvert the inflexible administrative guidelines under which they operate. We should learn from people at the grassroots level, and provide them with greater autonomy in the ways in which they deliver the outcomes sought by government. Bureaucratic hierarchy may provide an effective basis for quality control, but it can also diminish the capacity of policy to be informed by experience. We need to get more serious about devolving responsibility down the line. We need to value experience more highly.

Finally, we should seek to attract social finance from the private sector. Social Benefit Bonds (see Walker's chapter in this volume) are an exciting new financial instrument, but they represent only one small part of 'impact investing'. Governments can provide capital loans on a low-interest basis to 'social enterprises', allowing them to start up or to scale their growth. Social enterprises are not-for-profit organisations that raise revenue through engaging in trade, including through the delivery of government services, and then invest any surplus in their social mission. Governments would do well to help those enterprises to grow. Governments can make social investment more financially attractive. They can support financial intermediaries to provide capital (equity or debt) to social enterprises.

Facilitating genuine relationships—there is hope

Governments can act to promote a more collaborative environment. They can encourage public sector leaders to themselves become 'intrapreneurs', pushing change from the inside. We know public servants are good at this: in the last 25 years of public administration, most of the key reforms have been driven from within. Many public servants have the capacity and the will to do this; they just need the government authority and encouragement to act.

There exists an opportunity to push public sector innovation from the central point of the Venn axis at which public/private/not-for-profit engagement cross over. In the area of human services, in particular, contracted organisations should be afforded a genuine opportunity to contribute to policy. They should be enabled to participate actively in the design of more integrated and holistic wraparound services. Of course they should be paid and held publicly accountable on the basis of outcomes—but outcomes delivered in their own way, without unnecessary interference. That will make it possible for governments to move away from the delivery of templated programs. To my mind, it does not make sense to move delivery from the public service to a range of businesses and not-for-profit organisations, and then dictate that the service they provide must be implemented and managed in one particular way. It is possible to release the transformational potential of outsourcing by accepting that different organisations will have different ways of delivering outcomes and, by doing so, they will enable citizens to have a real choice in the services available. This, above all, should be the motive driving governments to commission the execution of their political goals.

That objective will be enhanced by an extension of local solutions—and by that I do not simply mean the regional demarcations that public servants construct for administrative convenience. I am talking about 'place-based approaches' that can be implemented at the level of urban neighbourhoods, remote townships, or Aboriginal settlements. I am also talking about devolving decision-making to schools, hospitals and social housing estates. These 'communities' should be afforded more opportunity to make their own choices and be given greater responsibility to use the government funds at their disposal.

The value of outsourcing will be enhanced by putting citizens in control of the services they need to live a full life. That means giving them the opportunity to manage their own budgets, to select their own services and to choose their own providers. This is not intended to diminish the responsibility or the status of public administration, but it does require the role and situational authority of public servants to be redefined.

The public service leaders of the future will be facilitators. They will be empathetic listeners, skilled negotiators, team-based designers and effective coordinators. In other words, public servants will play a crucial role as partners in the delivery of 'network governance'. They will be the stewards of public value and accountability, bringing together diverse actors that collectively give effect to the will of the state. This, then, will place them at the centre of a public economy, in which 'private-for-purpose' businesses, 'surplus-for-mission' social enterprises and the 'public-qua-public' agencies collaborate in the delivery of public value in the most effective manner.

The good news is that all of this can be done. The future is already with us—it is just not evenly distributed yet. When we talk about the potential of consumer-directed care, local-based solutions, cross-sectoral collaboration or social impact investing, we know that examples already exist. The innovative pilots, demonstrations and trials that are already underway need to be evaluated and, if successful, to take their place at the centre of mainstream public administration. That is the horizon at the end of the road to genuine partnership. We are not there yet but we are on our way.

References

Economic Audit Committee. 2009. 'Putting the Public First: Partnering with the Community and Business to Deliver Outcomes.' Perth: Government of Western Australia.

New South Wales Public Service Commission Advisory Board (NSW PSC Advisory Board). 2014. *Doing Things Differently: Raising Productivity, Improving Service and Enhancing Collaboration across the NSW Public Sec*tor. Sydney: New South Wales Public Service Commission. Online: http://www. psc.nsw.gov.au (accessed 30 March 2015).

Productivity Commission. 2010. 'Contribution of the Not-for-Profit Sector.' Research Report, January. Online: www.pc.gov.au/inquiries/completed/not-for-profit/report/not-for-profit-report.pdf (accessed 11 June 2015).

Shergold, Peter. 2013. *Service Sector Reform: A Roadmap for Community and Human Services Reform*. Melbourne: Department of Human Services. Online: vcoss.org.au/documents/2013/11/FINAL-Report-Service-Sector-Reform.pdf (accessed 11 June 2015).

Shergold, Peter. 2013. 'Risk-ready: It's time for innovation.' *Insight* 7: 28–30. Online: www.vcoss.org.au/documents/VCOSS%20docs/insight/07/ Insight_07_Risk-ready.pdf (accessed 4 February 2014).

Shergold, Peter. 2014. 'Community services without the red tape.' *Australian*, 16 January.

14

DEVELOPING SOCIAL BENEFIT BONDS IN AUSTRALIA: THE NSW FAMILY AND COMMUNITY SERVICES EXPERIENCE

Simone Walker
NSW Department of Family
and Community Services

In the Department of Families and Community Services (FACS), New South Wales, we have been working on a Social Benefit Bonds (SBB) pilot for two years, and it is now starting to come to fruition.[1] The benefit that I am most proud of is that it really is about combining a new financial tool with—in our case—better outcomes for children and young people.

When this process first started, my role in FACS was Executive Director for the Service System Delivery area, which relates to funding and contracting. I was involved in the pilot because it was a very new and different way to contract. Subsequently, I have become the Executive Director for Out-of-Home Care; it has been a good marriage of roles and positions. This is a bold direction, and one which we are very proud of in NSW. It is groundbreaking because it centres

---

1   This paper is based on a talk delivered in 2013. The bonds and outcomes it discusses have been progressing since this time.

on the ability to bring together new money (from investors), with outcomes for children and young people, in a better and safer way. That sort of alignment is something we do not get to work with very often.

Children in out-of-home care

In 2002 there were over 9,000 children in out-of-home care (Figure 14.1). These were children the NSW Children's Court had decided were not safe if they remained with their families. In June 2013, that number had more than doubled, rising to 18,400. This is a significant population increase, requiring urgent action to find better and safer alternatives for this population. We have a strong reformist government at the moment (2015), and we have a number of reforms currently sitting in this space. Simultaneously, FACS is moving out of the business of direct service provision; we are transitioning all of our statutory out-of-home care to the non-government organisation (NGO) sector. This is the context in which we began to explore the introduction of SBBs.

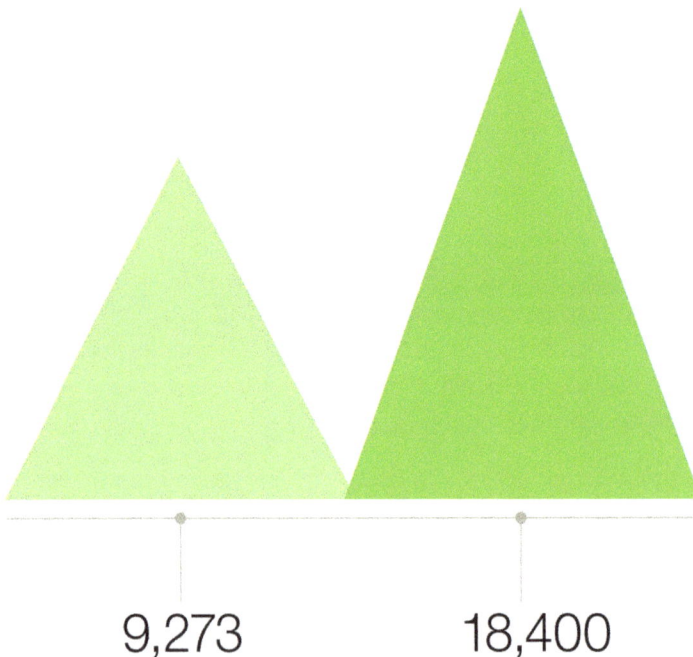

9,273   18,400

Figure 14.1. Number of children in out-of-home care in NSW, 2002 and 2013
Source: Family and Community Services, 2013, Transition Dashboard.

This transition to the NGO sector probably will not have a dramatic effect on the population, but we anticipate that it will produce much better *outcomes* for children, partly because caseloads in NGOs are currently around 1:13, compared to 1:28 in Community Services. In order to reduce the population, we turned to SBBs, and especially a pilot investment scheme known as the Newpin bond on which we have worked closely with UnitingCare Burnside—a leading child and family support organisation in NSW. This bond is strongly focused on the restoration of children to their families. Because this is all about restoration and aligning the outcomes with the financial tool, an upfront assumption that we needed to make with this bond is that children are better off with their birth families when it is safe. We know that most children in out-of-home care have poor outcomes, especially when compared to children in similar circumstances who stay at home with their families of origin. When that is your underlying assumption, you are extremely motivated to make this work, and I think that has been a driving force in the partnership between UnitingCare Burnside and Community Services. Where it is suitable to return these children to their birth families, with the right support, the right energy and the right service provider, that is what we will try to do.

How the bond works

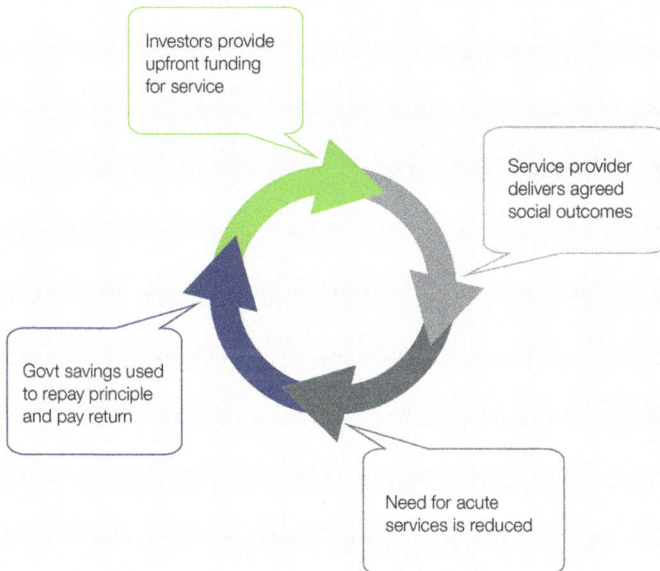

Figure 14.2. What is a social benefit bond?
Source: Cowling and Walker 2013.

Figure 14.2 is a very simple diagram, and it might oversimplify the concepts and processes underlying SBBs, but it is a good basic starting point. First, beginning with the green arrow, investors interested in social outcomes provide the upfront funding for a given service or outcome. The Newpin bond through UnitingCare Burnside is a $7 million bond; and we have an additional $10 million bond with the Benevolent Society, which was extremely successful in the subscriptions (see below). The government's aim here was to tap into the development of the social finance sector to support additional or better out-of-home programs.

Second, the NGO service provider delivers an *agreed social outcome*. For this initial pilot, what we were looking for was a known provider, an organisation that had a proven track record—and that was UnitingCare Burnside. We needed to be able to say to them, 'We want to put the responsibility and a substantial part of the risk with you as the provider for doing this work'. The desired outcome we agreed is about returning children to their birth families. The principal benefit in this outcome, from a measurement point of view, is that it is binary: children are either in out-of-home care, or they are not. This is very important for the measurement of performance in relation to the bond, especially when taking into account a return to investors. Ultimately, returning children to their birth families in a safe and considered way will result in an improvement in clients' lives, reducing the need for acute services. Consider that for each child in out-of-home care, even those with the simplest needs, an NGO receives $37,000 a year. If a child comes into out-of-home care aged two and stays until they are 18 (as many do), the figures mount up exceeding half a million dollars per child—and become especially high when you consider how many children NSW has in statutory care. Despite the additional support required by some birth families to keep the children at home with them safely, this is still a much better option for the NSW government (from both a financial and an outcomes perspective).

Third, it is the savings to government associated with these outcomes that are what really make the social bond work; some of the savings are returned to investors (as illustrated by the blue arrow in Figure 14.2). It is important to note that the returns are capped, because the idea of this bond is not for people to make extraordinary returns. This gives assurance to government, as well as to other people scrutinising the purpose of the bond, that this is not just a money creation scheme.

The key difference operating with the UnitingCare Burnside Newpin SBB is the availability of funding levels to which we had previously not had access. We are starting to see the untold potential of being able to tap into private funding sources as a way to get better social outcomes. We are very focused on performance outcomes and performance accountability, which goes to some of the comments made in John Wanna's introduction to this book. However, given the incredible energy it has taken to get the social bonds up, we are not able to consider any new bonds in the immediate future, but there is enormous potential here for other government agencies.

The Newpin process—three different bonds, three different models

The Newpin SBB was a twinkle in the eye of the previous government, but the O'Farrell–Baird governments in NSW have really taken it on; they are 100 per cent committed to this social bond innovation. A request for proposals was approved by Treasury in September 2011; after an evaluation process, proponents were selected in March 2012.

We currently have two bonds. The first is the UnitingCare Burnside SBB, called the Newpin bond, which has raised a $7 million bond over seven years. The main focus is restoration, but it also includes family preservation services. The response from the market was an unknown in early days, although there was a considerable amount of market testing. We originally thought that philanthropists would be very interested in the bond process, but what we have discovered over time is that it has actually been more popular with 'real' investors who are looking for a return on their dollars, and for a whole range of reasons has been less attractive to philanthropic investors.

A second social bond is with the Benevolent Society, which is focused mainly on family preservation (i.e. preventing children from going into out-of-home care). Because there was an overwhelmingly positive response to the Newpin SBB, that has given us great confidence that the Benevolent Society SBB will also be well-received. It is a $10 million bond over five years, and the Benevolent Society have partnered with Westpac and the Commonwealth Bank. It is a completely different financial model from Newpin, and there is a clear message here for us: there is massive opportunity in this space, but it needs to be something where people are passionate about the outcomes, because of the sheer amount of work that goes into making it happen.

It took two years to work out the financial models and other details. These were fit-for-purpose models, so it was very difficult to make the transition from one model to the other. In the Newpin bond, there will be annual payments for successful restorations. In contrast, the Benevolent Society will receive a large upfront payment, and then no further payment until five years later; at that point, we will measure how many of the children they worked with have ended up in out-of-home care. So there is a significant degree of risk to the agency at the five-year mark, but on the other hand there is a very large upfront payment, which represents a substantial risk to government.

As a result, we consider it crucial that we work with known substantial providers who are prepared to fully commit their staff, resources and reputation, but who are also big enough to sustain themselves throughout the process. This is not something that we could do with a small provider, or a niche innovative organisation.

A third bond related to recidivism, with Mission Australia, is still in the early stages of development. It is still on track, but there are some definite differences in relation to quantifying the savings for government. This is because of the nature of jail infrastructure—in out-of-home care we do not have to factor solid buildings infrastructure into the program, but jail infrastructure is an extra element that they are grappling with in the development of the recidivism bond.

The negotiation phase

Besides a lot of time and energy, a diverse set of skills was required to get this off the ground. We needed skilled project managers. We had significant input from people with expertise in specialist financial modelling, just to help us model what the potential savings to government were. Our economists and statisticians had to pull a vast amount of data to formulate a projection for children and young people. This was made more difficult by the questionable veracity of some of our data in FACS—it is not consistent, and timeliness and accuracy are not always high. This has certainly given us reasons to do a lot more work on our data systems.

We also worked closely with Crown solicitors. This is a commercial contract, something very different for us. Elements like the guarantee of referrals put a degree of requirement on FACS that we do not experience in our normal service agreements. In addition, we worked closely with representatives from Treasury. This process has been fantastic for the relationship between Community Services and Treasury, and there are clear benefits to knowing each other's business, understanding it and working so closely together on the financial modelling. Out-of-home care is the third biggest risk to the NSW government; our budget for 2013–14 is $799 million—not an insignificant sum. We should engage Treasury more about why we are the biggest risk, but also why we are thinking of different ways to tackle the issues, and why we want their support and backing to find innovation.

The other important thing was to have negotiators and executives meet frequently face-to-face. We met weekly for the last six to nine months, and we had to be able to make decisions in real time as the communication went forward—this feature of the process makes it very different from the way we work in most other circumstances. I needed to be able to say, 'I have the imprimatur in the room to make the decisions so that we can move these negotiations forward'. My role was to ensure that the Steering Committee and the Executive were aware of the direction, and their role back to me was to give me the imprimatur to push this forward. Knowing that our minister is 100 per cent committed was also important. Her message to us was: 'Find a way to make this happen', and our role in the room was to do just that.

Counterfactuals and controls

A significant part of the work has been building the outcomes and measurement framework, so this is where much of the resources were required. As I mentioned previously, a referral guarantee is something very new and different for FACS. We had to commit to delivering a certain number of families to the program, and the risk then transferred over to UnitingCare Burnside in their work with the families. FACS has had a chequered history with referral for some of our family programs, but it is something that we are working on consistently. This highlighted a need for quality data collection systems, and we have found that the Executive now wants to commit to more of that.

We also had to develop a counterfactual rolling control group, which became the basis of the measurement. We needed to work out how many children return home from out-of-home care, *regardless of intervention*. This process took many months, and ultimately, the figure we settled on was carefully negotiated. We as a government needed to be sure that we were not paying for outcomes that were going to occur even with no intervention, and UnitingCare Burnside needed to know that there was veracity in our figure so that they were achieving at a level where they would get a return for the investors. The weaknesses in our data systems were crucial here, because every time we felt our data let us down, it put us from a negotiated position to a worse place. What we determined, to the best of our ability, is that 25 per cent of children going into care will go home, regardless of the intervention that they receive. They are what we call our 'business as usual' group. Thus for any payment to be made, UnitingCare Burnside needs to achieve a restoration rate higher than that 25 per cent—that is a big ask for an agency, but one that they have absolutely committed to.

Another positive outcome of this program is the rolling control group. We will have a control group of 300 children at any point in time through the eight years, and we will move children through that group depending on their experience in out-of-home care. This will give us not only a sense of how many children go home with or without an intervention, it will also give us a great amount of data and detail. The nature of our systems at the moment means that this is essentially a manually driven control group. With 300 children in the group, we are working hard to build the supporting systems to make sure that we have accurate data. All of the data will be independently verified, because it is crucial in calculating the payment to Burnside, and then the return to the investors.

Criticisms of the social bonds initiative: 'Cash for kids'?

One criticism that has been presented to us internally from our case workers, and also from places like the Council of Social Service of New South Wales, is the risk of this program being perceived as 'cash for kids'—the idea that payment is made for each successful restoration. This is something that we did have to wrestle with during the planning and negotiation phases. We needed to ensure that there was no opportunity for gaming on either side of the negotiation. With this being a commercial contract, we needed to ensure that Community Services did not cherry pick the most difficult cases to refer to UnitingCare Burnside. We also needed to make sure that restorations were safe, that they were real, and that they were successful.

We have used the contract to make these specifications, so there are very solid criteria about the children that are referred. Firstly, there has to be agreement about each child transferred between FACS and Burnside. Secondly, successful restoration may be paid upon year two: we test the restoration in the following year, and if a child has gone back into out-of-home care during that year, the payment is reversed. That indicates how much pressure is upon Burnside, but also how much pressure is on the data—we need to be sure that we are tracking these children accurately. However, these arrangements have also served as an avowal that this program is absolutely about good outcomes and not, as some people have described, about cash for kids.

Implementing SBBs has been a very exciting opportunity, and so many times I have said to people, 'This is like being part of history'. Looking back, I simply underestimated how hard history can be to make. And yet, it has been exciting; it is something to get passionate about, because there is so much opportunity to make an impact. The chance to mix the part of the work that I love (good outcomes for children) with something new and different in contracting has been brilliant. I would encourage people to think about the opportunities that sit in their spaces, as well as the challenges that may come with them.

Reference

Cowling, Sally and Simone Walker. 2013. 'NSW social benefit and bonds pilot.' NSW Government: Family and Community Services. Slide presentation at the ANZSOG conference 'Delivering under Pressure'. Brisbane, 6–8 August.

15

SITUATING MUTUALS IN THE AUSTRALIAN PUBLIC SECTOR CONTEXT

Les Hems
Ernst & Young

First, here is some contextual information relating to the potential of public service mutuals in Australia. Cooperatives and mutual organisations have a rich history in Australia, but largely go unrecognised. In fact, it was only in 2013 that for the first time a National Business Council for Cooperatives and Mutuals was established, launched in Melbourne at the Royal Automobile Club of Victoria (RACV) Club. This lack of recognition is quite startling when we consider the numbers. There are 1,600 cooperatives and mutuals nationwide, yet it is only recently that there has been a national register (usually it is difficult to capture the work of these organisations across state boundaries). At present eight in 10 Australians are members of cooperatives or mutuals. In fact, there are more members of coops and mutuals in Australia than there are shareholders. Some of these organisations have huge asset bases, whether they are financial or insurance companies, or big agricultural coops. They are a very powerful part of the economy. Nor are they a completely new phenomenon; some of these cooperatives and mutuals have been delivering public services for years.

My own experience of Australian public policy dates back to the end of 2009 and the beginning of 2010. Approaching the 2010 federal election, a productivity report was released on the role of the not-for-profit sector, especially in relation to public service delivery. I was shocked at the scale of the not-for-profit sector here—huge organisations like UnitingCare, Anglicare, the Salvation Army, and so on. This contrasts with the UK, where post-war many comparable organisations were nationalised and pulled into the National Health System (NHS). That did not happen here. The scale of outsourcing to the not-for-profit sector is quite different here to the UK, and I think that raises the issue of what the scope is for 'spinning out' parts of government, when in effect the not-for-profit sector is already providing a lot of that service.

Over the last three years, I have been very impressed by the innovative organisations and hybrid forms that have emerged to deliver public services. During this time, we have seen the failure of a large for-profit public service provider (ABC Learning Centres), which was a private company that delivered a lot of fundamental public services supported by government funding. ABC Learning Centres was taken over by what is called a 'social enterprise'. There was a significant amount of involvement by the leadership of the previous *for-profit* organisation in creating a *not-for-profit* social enterprise solution to a public sector problem. Relatively recently, we have also seen the emergence of social impact bonds (see the chapter by Simone Walker in this book). Social benefit bonds have been piloted in NSW, and many states are looking at payment for results or 'payment by outcome' mechanisms. There is an increasing interest in employee ownership as an alternative to both for-profit and mutual-type organisations.

Research into 'twenty-first-century public services'

On the back of these two developments, I have been working with a number of organisations to investigate the potential role for cooperatives and mutuals in delivering what I call 'twenty-first-century public services'. We are looking not only to a different organisational form for delivering a public service, but specifically to these organisations being innovative and coming up with new methods of delivery. In other words, we are interested in innovation within the mutual and cooperative movement. I have enjoyed the support of the emergent and now launched Business Council for Cooperatives and Mutuals, and also of bankmecu, which is Australia's first customer-owned bank. They are very committed to the notion that although they are engaged in a commercial activity, they must still deliver community value.

I have tried to conduct my research using a co-production methodology and action learning—I work with organisations and individuals who are undertaking the things I am studying, and make sure they are an active part of the research process and that the research is both applied and relevant. Ultimately, I hope to influence both policy and practice—and the research is geared towards this end.

The key theme of my research is: what is the added value or advantage of using a coop or mutual model? In order to explore that cross-cutting theme, I have examined theory and analysed policy, looking specifically at UK, Canadian, French and Italian public policy in support of cooperatives and mutuals. I have been trying to assemble a body of case studies—both from the UK (which, thanks to the excellent resources from the Cabinet Office, I have been able to compile relatively quickly) and from Australia. My aim is to build an evidence base for the purpose of public policy, and also for practice. I will combine these in the form of a green paper, which will hopefully set out the potential for coops and mutuals in delivering public services (Hems et al. 2014). It will be aimed at academics as well as practitioners—those who are already in cooperatives and mutuals or who potentially could be undertaking their activities through a mutual form. There must be a facilitation and an encouragement of this approach, because it is not a good thing to push people in this direction when they are not ready or do not understand it. I hope that a green paper will be a way of raising interest in this option.

Some of my other research interests include:

1. **Incentive optimisation and trying to change the nature of some of the relationships between producers and consumers.** Sometimes intermediaries facilitate the linking of producers and consumers. Obviously cooperatives can either be producer cooperatives that are employee-owned, or they can be consumer cooperatives where the clients group together to purchase services. I want to understand the nature of the incentives for each of those different groups in using a coop/mutual form rather than the traditional government or market solution.

2. **Information asymmetry.** We are on the cusp of change in the public service delivery landscape—for example, under the National Disability Insurance Scheme (NDIS), individuals will have control over the purchasing of services for themselves or for their family member. Information asymmetry is a significant problem. Perhaps a coop/mutual form would actually provide a better vehicle for resolving some of the problems related to this.

3. **Governance.** There are real issues around community ownership and community democracy, and once again cooperatives and mutuals may have a way of addressing these. Communities are a source of capital and resourcing for service delivery. There are opportunities to understand the comparative advantage of alternative forms (Billis and Glennerster 1998; Birchall 2011).

4. **Would a cooperative-designed service look different if it were planned as such from the beginning?** Exploring what public service delivery systems look like if you start out using cooperative and mutual principles, as opposed to government or market-based systems.

5. **How to access funds.** There is a pot of money that can be used to solve problems of access to capital. I want to look at whether things like social enterprise investment funds actually work.

Mutuals in practice

I am very interested in cases and examples of services involving a government monopoly. The Cleveland Fire Service is a great example of how a government monopoly service has recreated itself as a community interest company that is going beyond its core mandate to deliver significant value to the local community. An example from the UK is the City Health Care Partnerships, which provide healthcare in local communities. There are Australian examples as well: an oft-quoted one is the West Belconnen Health Coop in Canberra—a mutual that offers bulk-billing Medicare services to a population that includes a significant proportion of low-income people. This is a people-owned cooperative. The patients who use the General Practice (GP) services become members if they choose to, which effectively makes them part of the ownership structure of that health service provider.

Another example from the UK illustrates further issues around complex services: MyTime Community Interest Company works with people with complex mental health problems, many from the former Yugoslavia. The traditional support was inadequate, so the 'patients' got together as a community and designed their own services to address their needs. They are hoping to get a social impact bond to scale up their activities. There are many more examples of in-home care and vulnerable groups.

Where there is both a market and a government failure, mutuals and cooperatives can step in. I am referring here to many remote and rural towns on the edge of being failing, unsustainable communities. This may be a way for communities to take control and retain community assets: the Fox & Goose in Hebden Bridge, Yorkshire, is a case in point of a community seeking to buy a pub in order to retain that institution (see Fox & Goose Co-operative Pub). There are many communities here in Australia that might benefit from a similar approach.

Issues in the Australian context

I recently completed a feasibility study for social impact bonds in New South Wales, and one of the things I felt we needed to understand was the appetite for such innovations. I would also argue that we must do a similar thing in relation to some of the policy levers that can lead to mutuals, and especially in relation to the notion of mutual and cooperative bodies being involved in public service delivery. I am keen to test how individuals, communities and organisations would respond to a policy lever such as a right to request, a right to provide, or a community right to challenge.

I sense that there is currently a very polarised response by different parties and stakeholders to payment by results. In the lead up to the 2013 Australian federal election, I did a survey of leaders in the not-for-profit sector. There is definitely a fear of the future around payment by results in the social welfare sector. Essentially, there is strong opposition to payment by results as a concept—although I found pockets of support as well. However, when it comes to social impact bonds (which are obviously based on payment by results) a majority of people do actually support it because it is bringing in new types of finance.

It is important to understand the different stakeholders' perspectives, and this is where incentive optimisation comes in. Cooperatives and mutuals might actually be attractive to many stakeholders but we have to make sure we ask them the right questions and that they understand exactly what a public service mutual is.

Are there parts of the Australian public sector that might be interested in exploring these types of mutualism in the public service? One of the obvious ones to look at, being one of the biggest monopolies, is Australia Post. The Royal Mail Service in the UK is going through the process of looking at employee ownership, mutualising sections of the service. There are parts of the Australian public sector that would certainly look at this type of opportunity as very favourable. By the same token, we should also think about challenging some of these very large not-for-profit organisations, such as Mission Australia or UnitingCare, to give their frontline staff, people working in teams in communities, a similar kind of offer—the kind of offer where staff can spin out the delivery of a particular local service, so there is much greater control by the people who are actually doing the job on the ground.

Similarly, I am keen to look at those policy areas that are going through significant change at the moment. The NDIS is one case in point. What would that scheme look like (and perform) if a cooperative or mutuals solution was one of its fundamental components? The same approach could be taken with in-home care, out-of-home care and foster care, affordable housing, independent living and shelter living for the ageing population, schools, environmental issues—there is a whole raft services that I think would be very open to this type of option.

Another critical issue in the Australian context is that we need to come up with our own definition of a public service mutual. There are concerns here, and we should recognise them. *The Mutation of Privatisation* (Whitfield 2012) is a report that describes how this may be privatisation through stealth. Other people would say it is anti-competitive, because it is fundamentally anti-market. There are trade union perspectives—many zero-hour contracts run in many organisations in the UK at the moment, and there are concerns over what mutuals mean in relation to contracts.

And what of the future? If we do jump on this, what would it look like in 20 years? Would we have a better society if we went down this path? These are all complex questions we need to consider.

Enhancing the potential of mutuals—but let's do it properly

To conclude, I think that as a niche idea, cooperatives and mutuals have huge potential to grow in Australia, and to be operating at scale in the future. But we need to learn from the UK experience; we need to think through what this means in relation to federal, state and local government, and where the opportunities are—the low-hanging fruit.

I think a public services mutuals taskforce would be instrumental in starting the conversation. If we do go down that route, there is a raft of expertise already here in Australia, people who are thinking about these things. But I also know from my contact with these practitioners that the cooperatives and mutuals themselves are thinking about this. They are thinking about this more on a shared value proposition; some of the big health insurance companies, for example, want to be playing a much bigger role in delivering social impact. They do not want it left to the state to resolve things like obesity and type 2 diabetes. There are a number of health service and health insurance mutuals that are actively working on this now because they see a role for themselves in addressing these social problems.

If we do take these ideas forward, I would call from a researcher's perspective for this to be done in an experimental way—not a pilot, but rather a scientific experiment where variables and outcomes are measured, so we know whether they work. There is already some very good organisational-level work taking place, but it needs to be measured. There are some great community-level experiments that we can pick up and develop further. For example, we could use the NDIS to conduct a case study in one community to analyse the suitability and effectiveness of using this type of approach.

As I have outlined, there is great potential in this area, but also a lot of work to be done. I am hoping that the community of policy analysts, policymakers and advisors, and politicians, can turn some of this into reality. If it can deliver some of that comparative advantage, there is actually going to be a better way to do good public service delivery.

References

Billis, David and Howard Glennerster. 1998. 'Human services and the voluntary sector: Towards a theory of comparative advantage.' *Journal of Social Policy* 27(1): 79–98.

Birchall, Johnston. 2011. 'The comparative advantage of member-owned businesses.' *Review of Social Economy* 70(3): 263–94.

Fox & Goose Co-operative Pub. 2015. Online: www.foxandgoose.org/ (accessed 21 May 2015).

Hems, Les, Melinda Leth, Erica Olesson, Luke Turner and Dhakshy Sooriyakumaran. 2014. *Green Paper Public Service Mutuals: The Case for a Third-way for Delivering Public Services in Australia.* Business Council of Co-operatives and Mutuals; Australian Public Service Mutual Task Force. Online: bccm.coop/wp/wp-content/uploads/2014/06/PSMs_GreenPaper_FinalV11.pdf (accessed 13 May 2015).

Whitfield, Dexter. 2012. *The Mutation of Privatisation: A Critical Assessment of New Community and Individual Rights*, European Services Strategy Unit, Research Report No. 5, Online: www.european-services-strategy.org.uk/news/2012/the-mutation-of-privatisation-a-critical-asses/ (accessed 13 May 2015).